ANDREW CARNEGIE'S

MENTAL DYNAMITE

ANDREW CARNEGIE'S
MENTAL DYNAMITE

How to Unlock the Awesome Power of You

NAPOLEON HILL

Edited and annotated by James Whittaker

STERLING
New York

STERLING
New York

An Imprint of Sterling Publishing Co., Inc.
1166 Avenue of the Americas
New York, NY 10036

ISBN 978-1-4549-3609-1
ISBN 978-1-4549-3610-7 (e-book)
ISBN 978-1-4549-4224-5 (export edition)

Distributed in Canada by Sterling Publishing Co., Inc.
c/o Canadian Manda Group, 664 Annette Street
Toronto, Ontario M6S 2C8, Canada
Distributed in the United Kingdom by GMC Distribution Services
Castle Place, 166 High Street, Lewes, East Sussex BN7 1XU, England
Distributed in Australia by NewSouth Books
University of New South Wales, Sydney, NSW 2052, Australia

For information about custom editions, special sales, and premium and corporate purchases, please contact Sterling Special Sales at 800-805-5489 or specialsales@sterlingpublishing.com.

Manufactured in the United States of America

2 4 6 8 10 9 7 5 3 1

sterlingpublishing.com

Cover design by Igor Satanovsky
Interior design by Scott Russo

"The finest kind of security is the personal security that is developed from within."

—*Andrew Carnegie*

CONTENTS

NOTE TO READERS

By James Whittaker

I t's a strange feeling to read a manuscript that so few people have seen. It's even stranger to read through a manuscript based on conversations that took place more than a century ago yet strike to the heart of almost every problem we face today, whether in relationships, education, politics, career advancement, homelessness, business management, financial independence, or even democracy.

I've been a student of Napoleon Hill for many years, but there's something special about this book you hold in your hands. I don't recall ever having felt the energy running through my veins quite the way it did while I was perusing what should be regarded as a national treasure.

This book carries with it both the promise of hope and a blueprint for success, offered by one of the world's most successful individuals and prepared by one of the best-selling authors in history.

To illustrate its power properly, we must quickly explore the humble beginnings through which its namesake, Andrew Carnegie, began his life. After spending his first thirteen years in Scotland, Andrew and his family moved to the United States in 1848; they sought steady work, a more comfortable life, and a fresh start. But fortune continued to elude the family after their long voyage, and so that same year, to help put food on the table, young Andrew obtained a job at a textile mill, where he worked twelve hours a day, six days a week.

Although poor in possessions, the boy was rich in intellectual curiosity, which found its release when a local businessman gave him regular access to a library. Carnegie was so grateful for the kindness shown to him that he vowed to pay kindness forward to other poor children if ever he found himself in a position of wealth. It was in these most humble beginnings that his potential first sparked.

Many years later, the unshakable seed of philanthropic obligation still empire, having revolutionized the steel industry in a way that turned ordinary workers into millionaires and created opportunity for countless other industries.

Yet a funny thing happened. Having spent a lifetime acquiring one of the largest personal fortunes in recorded history, Carnegie dedicated his remaining days to giving it away. Not giving it away in the sense of "making it rain" on city streets or providing material possessions for those in need—no. The business legend realized there was something far richer than money, a treasure buried deep within every person fortunate enough to grace the earth: potential.

If society could only find a way to recognize and unlock the potential of every individual on the planet, widespread harmony finally would be achievable. After all, that was Carnegie's aim—*harmony*. Those who live in harmony willingly offer their service to others, continue to learn as much as they can, and work diligently in their own manner to make the world a better place. With a global population working in a spirit of harmony—the ultimate mastermind—standards of living, investment in healthcare, and a general feeling of purpose would all be elevated significantly.

At the time of Carnegie's passing, his fortune was estimated at more than $400 billion, adjusted for inflation. But the steel magnate never sought recognition for his financial wealth. He believed the real measure of someone's success in his or her short stint on earth was represented by how many people that individual had helped. Carnegie believed that wealthy people had an obligation to give back because he recognized, through the all-commanding laws of nature, that we're all—the population, the planet, and the economy—intricately connected. What you do to one, you do to all, and vice versa.

Today, Andrew Carnegie is still listed as one of the top philanthropists in history. His business acumen enabled him to build an enormous fortune, but his generosity helped everyone, from humble workers who wanted to obtain an education to warring countries that sought peace.

Think and Grow Rich has confused many who simply study the title and avidly pursue financial gain at all costs. As Hill so aptly says about Carnegie in this book, "His own attitude toward money was revealed by the fact that he gave away most of his huge fortune before he died." While the Scotsman was busy determining the best avenues for giving away more than 90 percent of the material wealth he had been able to accumulate, he also sought to create and to distribute—as far and wide as possible—a practical philosophy that would show everyday people how to unleash their own brilliance, a philosophy that encapsulated all elements and obstacles of life.

Reader, make no mistake about the power of the book you hold in your hands—it might just be the most life-changing book you've ever read. But even more important, recognize the power of the heart in your chest and the brain in your head, which can be directed toward creating any circumstances you desire.

This book provides a comprehensive blueprint for approaching the challenges of everyday life and creating opportunities for a life of greater prosperity than you ever thought possible. This approach is illustrated through three fundamental principles: self-discipline, learning from defeat, and the Golden Rule applied. This is a book about leadership, first through taking the reins of your own life and second by helping others do the same thing. For those in the midst of trauma, heartbreak, or some other misfortune, this book offers a practical method for staging a comeback grander than you ever imagined.

After each conversation, you will find a detailed analysis from Hill, using real-world examples, of what he learned and how it can be applied. Even though the material is undoubtedly timeless, I've included annotations to help illustrate the key themes and provide more modern examples of these principles in action. These illustrations will provide further evidence that Carnegie's teachings continue to launch every innovation, transform every industry, and spawn the champions we cheer on today.

Although the conversations between Hill and Carnegie took place in 1908, Hill's notes, which are included in this book, were not prepared until 1941. I'm sure you'll be astounded, as I was, that something written so long ago can quickly strike at the heart of the major issues that we face today, especially in the digital age.

On a personal note, I must express my deepest gratitude to Don Green, the executive director of The Napoleon Hill Foundation, for trusting me with this important project. My previous book, *Think and Grow Rich: The Legacy*, was written in partnership with the Foundation to introduce the powerful *Think and Grow Rich* principles to today's generations, inspiring them to self-belief through the journeys of the world's most revered entrepreneurs, thought leaders, and cultural icons.

I've interviewed countless people who credit Hill as the catalyst for their success, and there are hundreds of thousands more around the world who profess a similar debt of gratitude. Of course, Hill was quick to give full credit to his mentor, the great steel magnate Andrew Carnegie, for trusting him to package and share this philosophy with the world.

I am honored to again be of service to The Napoleon Hill Foundation and to you, the reader. Although it was not possible for me to live up to the extremely high standard set by these two great icons while I prepared this book, I hope my contributions will add clarity to these powerful lessons and give you a clear avenue to apply them in your own way in your own life.

However, I must caution you that this book is not a spectacle for you to witness from the sidelines; far from it. This book is an invitation for you to engage with life—to think about what circumstances you most desire, to take action in creating those circumstances, and then to arouse the world by helping others do the same thing.

"Action is the real measure of intelligence," as Napoleon Hill said. To that end, we are excited to offer *The Napoleon Hill Success Journal* as the ultimate companion to this book to help you translate your efforts into results. Those actions extrapolated will become your life, your impact, and your legacy. It doesn't matter what happened in your past—what result you received on a standardized test, what job position you were overlooked for, what relationship deteriorated, or what unforeseen medical trauma stopped you in your tracks. The only thing that matters is what you do *now* and henceforth.

Reader, I hope you're excited! After you read the brief foreword by my dear friend Don Green, I invite you to join me in this fascinating conversation between two of the greats. May their teachings continue to illuminate the potential in all of us.

Onward and upward always,
James Whittaker

FOREWORD

By Don Green

In 1908, a young magazine reporter, Napoleon Hill, was ushered into the study of Andrew Carnegie, steel magnate and philanthropist. Expecting to conduct a brief interview as the basis for a magazine article, young Napoleon instead spent hours listening to Mr. Carnegie explain the principles he believed had led to his success and that of others. Mr. Carnegie invited Napoleon to devote the next twenty years of his life, without pay, to interviewing the great people of America to develop and illustrate the philosophy of success.

Napoleon Hill accepted the challenge and wrote *The Law of Success,* published in 1928, twenty years after the meeting with Mr. Carnegie. The book detailed his findings based on twenty years of interviews with hundreds of successful businesspeople. In 1937, Hill published a condensed version titled *Think and Grow Rich*, which has been sold in virtually every language in the world and remains a prolific best seller.

In 1941, Dr. Hill wrote a series of booklets that he titled *Mental Dynamite*. Each booklet dealt with one of the seventeen principles he had discussed with Mr. Carnegie. Within months of their publication, the United States entered World War II, and the booklets were put on the shelf and largely forgotten. The Napoleon Hill Foundation, founded by Dr. Hill in 1962 to perpetuate the teaching of the philosophy of success, has retrieved these booklets from its archives and selected three of the principles for inclusion in this book.

In Chapter 1, which is dedicated to the principle of self-discipline, Napoleon Hill begins his interview with Andrew Carnegie. Mr. Carnegie explains the importance of self-discipline for controlling the seven positive and seven negative emotions that motivate action. He sets forth the importance of using self-discipline to control and use the strongest emotions: love and sex. Self-discipline also permits one to "close the door" on past problems and negative emotions.

Mr. Carnegie tells young Napoleon how self-discipline can be reinforced by employing a thirteen-point psychological formula that can be used as a daily mantra. He describes it as essential to turning one's definite major purpose into achievement. Then he sets forth the relationship between self-discipline and willpower, describing how essential both are for reaching the goal of success. Mr. Carnegie makes a convincing argument that self-discipline is essential, not merely helpful, to successful application of his achievement formula.

After reporting on his interview with Mr. Carnegie, Dr. Hill details the accomplishments of many people who became successful through the use of self-discipline. They include Charles Dickens, Robert Louis Stevenson, Benjamin Disraeli, Gene Tunney, and Marshall Field, along with many who overcame serious physical problems to achieve success, including Helen Keller, Theodore Roosevelt, Thomas Edison, and Glenn Cunningham. He tells the amazing story of how Alice Marble used self-discipline to defy doctors and become a world tennis champion. He sets forth a creed of how to use self-discipline daily to control the six departments of the mind.

Dr. Hill then offers a detailed explanation of how past difficulties and failures can be overcome by self-discipline and transmutation; this is especially important for those who have experienced disappointment in love. He concludes with an analysis of why many in the United States at the time of writing, shortly after the end of the Great Depression and at the beginning of World War II, were losing their self-discipline and becoming dependent on government handouts.

Chapter 2, focusing on the principle learning from defeat, also begins with Napoleon's interview of Andrew Carnegie in 1908. Mr. Carnegie states that his gift to the world is knowledge that will enable people to be self-determining and learn how to find happiness in their relationships with others. His philosophy of success will permit people, many of whom have become prisoners in their own minds after encountering defeat, to free themselves. He lists forty-five major causes of failure, the most important ones being lack of a definite major purpose and lack of willpower.

Defeat must be viewed as temporary and as a challenge to greater effort. Mr. Carnegie states that people must turn stumbling blocks into stepping-stones.

He gives examples of people who overcame physical disabilities and succeeded, such as Helen Keller, Thomas Edison, and Beethoven. Faced with adversity, they developed their willpower and self-discipline.

Mr. Carnegie explains how verbal and even physical assaults can be defeated by mental and spiritual forces rather than by violence. Defeat can be beneficial in that, like pain, it is an indication that something needs fixing. Sorrow, too, can change one's attitude from negative to positive by leading to a manifestation of willpower in a successful effort to overcome defeat and unhappiness.

Dr. Hill follows these excerpts from his earlier interview with his own analysis of what Mr. Carnegie told him and what he learned in the intervening years about learning from defeat. He lists the habits that lead to failure and defeat and urges readers to take a personal inventory of how they are dealing with overcoming these habits. Having a definite major purpose can eliminate eighteen of the forty-five causes of failure identified by Mr. Carnegie. Using the poetry of Walter Malone and the essays of Ralph Waldo Emerson, Dr. Hill eloquently explains how even the deepest sorrow and the harshest tragedy can lead one to discover strength and character sufficient to overcome them and achieve even greater successes.

Chapter 3, the final chapter of the book, explains the principle of the Golden Rule applied. It too begins with young Napoleon's interview with Andrew Carnegie. Mr. Carnegie explains the many benefits of applying the Golden Rule. Perhaps the least of them is the benefit obtained by the recipient. The person giving to another benefits in many ways. That person, by following the Golden Rule, achieves harmony in the mind, which leads to the development of sound character. Application of the Golden Rule drives out greed and selfishness and leads its adherent to provide needed services.

Mr. Carnegie lists many more benefits to be gained by following the Golden Rule, including the elimination of opposition and the promotion of cooperation that undoubtedly leads to success. He concludes that today not enough people are following the Golden Rule and that this failing could lead to the ruin of the country.

Napoleon Hill follows this recounting of the interview with his own analysis of the Golden Rule. Clearly, he believes it to be among the most important principles of the philosophy of achievement. (He named his first magazine publication, started approximately ten years after his interview with Mr. Carnegie, *Hill's Golden Rule Magazine*.) He describes following the Golden Rule as leading an "impersonal life"—that is, a selfless life.

Dr. Hill states that applying the Golden Rule develops strong character, which produces a surplus of faith that is needed in times of emergency, when willpower and the reasoning faculty are inadequate for human needs. He explains how five of the nine basic motives that drive humankind are furthered by the application of the Golden Rule.

Dr. Hill then provides examples of many people who have benefited themselves and others by applying the Golden Rule, including John D. Rockefeller, Jr., William Penn, Benjamin Franklin, Simón Bolívar, Florence Nightingale, Johnny Appleseed, and Fanny Crosby. He tells of American businesses that have prospered by applying the Golden Rule, including the Coca-Cola Company and McCormick & Company.

Mr. Carnegie commissioned Napoleon Hill to spend twenty years of his life developing the philosophy of achievement so that people could attain material wealth but, more important, so that they could become educated in how to live in harmony with others. A generous man, Mr. Carnegie gave away most of his wealth for the betterment of humankind, contributing to the building of more than three thousand public libraries in the English-speaking world.

However, his greatest gift was the philosophy of achievement, which he had already discovered at the time of his 1908 interview with Napoleon Hill and which Hill refined, developed, and promoted from that day forward until his death in 1970.

In this book you will learn how these three lessons, when diligently applied, can permit one to live a happy, peaceful, and rewarding life.

To your success,
Don Green
Executive Director
The Napoleon Hill Foundation (2000–Present)

PART 1

SELF-DISCIPLINE:
TAKING POSSESSION
OF ONE'S OWN MIND

*Thinking, education, knowledge, native
ability—these are nothing but empty words
unless they are translated into action.*

—Andrew Carnegie

INTRODUCTION TO SELF-DISCIPLINE
By Napoleon Hill

This chapter cannot be assimilated in one or two readings. It covers a subject that overlaps the other principles of this book. The analysis at the end of the chapter describes one of the most important subjects in the entire field of mental phenomena: the principle through which the six departments of the mind may be organized and directed to any desired end.

The chart of the six departments of the mind (included toward the end of our conversation on this lesson) provides a quick reference to the forces that must be brought under self-discipline if one is to become the master of oneself. The principle by which this mastery may be attained is described in detail, but do not be misled by the apparent simplicity of the principle to underrate its astounding influence or the scope of its possibilities, because it is the master key to the entire philosophy of achievement.

With a working knowledge of this principle, one may take full possession of one's mind, a feat that can be accomplished by no other method. Through this principle, every adversity, temporary defeat, worry, and negative emotion, such as anger and fear, can be organized and used for the attainment of one's major purpose in life. This principle explains Andrew Carnegie's statement that "every adversity . . . carries with it the seed of an equivalent advantage." Moreover, it describes how "the seed" may be germinated and developed into a full-blown flower of opportunity.

Do not try to familiarize yourself with this principle until you have carefully read and digested Mr. Carnegie's approach to it. Follow the instructions for the use of this principle to the letter; then observe the astounding change that will come over you. Your imagination will become more alert. Your enthusiasm will become keener. Your initiative will become more active. Your self-reliance will be obviously greater. Your personality will become more magnetic, and you will find people seeking you out who previously paid you no attention. The scope of your vision will be extended. Your problems will melt before you as flakes of snow melt under the rays of the sun. Your hopes and your ambition will be strengthened. You will begin to see the world through a different set of eyes. Your relationships with other people will become more pleasant and harmonious.

These and other promises of even greater proportions will reveal themselves to you if you get from this chapter all that has been presented for you.

Do not read this chapter hurriedly. Think as you read. Test the lesson by your own experiences and observe how accurately it portrays certain truths that you will readily recognize although you may never have understood their full significance. Read with pencil in hand and underscore the lines that impress you most. Come back to these lines often and make the thought behind them your own.

EDITOR'S NOTE:

As we begin, let's quickly reflect on the best way to read books such as this one. Hill's books have sold more than 120 million copies around the world, yet not everyone who reads them feels their power. Why do you think that is? Many people have mentioned to me that not only were these books truly transformational but also that just staring at the cover often made them feel better, whereas others have tried reading them but failed to notice any life changes at all. Why is it that the same words on the same pages turn dreams to reality for some while being retained as fantasy for others?

This dichotomy comes from how the reader, or the listener of audiobooks, approaches it. This is not a novel that you skim through it and then place on a shelf. To get the most out of this book, keep a notepad handy and think about how you can apply these lessons in your own life. Then apply them! As you will see, action is a core theme of this book and of the entire achievement philosophy, just as it should be for you.

Importantly, research shows that you're 42 percent more likely to achieve your goals if you write them down. That's how the true power of this book is unleashed and how your immense potential is ignited.

On the relationship between thought and action, Carnegie notes: "Without control over thoughts there can be no control over deeds." Even the best formula is useless unless it is expressed in *action*.

SELF-DISCIPLINE:
Taking possession of one's own mind

$\triangle$

Perhaps there is no word in the English language that better describes the major requirement for individual achievement than the subject of this chapter. This entire philosophy serves primarily to enable people to develop control over themselves, this being the greatest of all the essentials of success.

In this chapter, Mr. Carnegie has taken great pains to emphasize the necessity of self-discipline, because he learned from his own experience in dealing with thousands of people that no one may hope to achieve noteworthy success without first gaining control over themselves! He learned from his own experience and from his observation of other people that when a person once takes possession of their own mind and begins to rely upon it, that person has achieved a victory of the highest order, one that places them within easy grasp of whatever they set their head and their heart upon.

Self-discipline, then, may be defined as the act of taking possession of one's own mind!

The definition is short and clear, but it is so charged with meaning that to overlook its significance may invalidate this entire philosophy. Fortunately, however, the method by which we may take possession of our own mind is known, and it will be clearly described in this chapter. But mere knowledge of the method will not be of any use until this knowledge is put into action. Self-discipline is something we cannot acquire as we learn the multiplication table, but it can be acquired through persistence, by following the procedure outlined in this chapter. The price of self-discipline, therefore, is eternal vigilance and continuous effort in carrying out these instructions. In no other way can it be acquired, and it has no other bargaining price. We get self-discipline through our own efforts, or we do not acquire it at all.

Without self-discipline, an individual may be likened to a dry leaf that is blown back and forth, round and round, by the stray winds of circumstance, without the slightest chance of coming within sight of anything that even remotely resembles personal success.

People who take possession of their own minds, and use them, may set their own price tag on themselves and make life pay what they ask. Those who fail to do so must take whatever life tosses to them, and we need offer no evidence that this always is barely more than the mere necessities.

I take you now to the private study of Andrew Carnegie, where you will be privileged to sit in while he instructs me, his student, on the subject of self-discipline.

HILL:

Mr. Carnegie, you have designated self-discipline as a principle of individual achievement. Will you describe the part that self-discipline plays in personal achievement and indicate how this principle can be developed and applied in the practical affairs of daily life?

CARNEGIE:

Very well. Let us begin by calling attention to some of the uses of self-discipline. After that, we will discuss the methods by which this important principle may become the possession of anyone who is willing to pay the price.

Self-discipline begins with the mastery of one's thoughts. Without control over thoughts, there can be no control over deeds! Let us say, therefore, that self-discipline inspires one to think first and act afterward. The usual procedure is just the reverse—most people act first and think afterward, if and when they think at all.

Self-discipline gives us complete control over the fourteen major emotions. This enables us to eliminate or subjugate the seven negative emotions and exercise the seven positive emotions in whatever manner we desire. The effect of this control becomes obvious when we recognize that emotion rules the lives of most people and largely rules the world.

Self-discipline must begin, if it begins at all, with a complete mastery of these fourteen emotions.

The seven positive emotions:	The seven negative emotions:
1. Love	1. Fear
2. Sex	2. Jealousy
3. Hope	3. Hatred
4. Faith	4. Revenge
5. Enthusiasm	5. Greed
6. Loyalty	6. Anger
7. Desire	7. Superstition

All these emotions are states of mind, subject to control and direction. The seven negative emotions obviously are deadly if they are not mastered. The seven positive emotions may also be just as destructive if they are not organized, mastered, and guided under complete control. In these fourteen emotions is the "mental dynamite" that may lift us to great heights of achievement or reduce us to the lowest depths of failure, and no amount of education, experience, intelligence, or good intentions can alter or modify this possibility.

EDITOR'S NOTE:

This is a core theme of Carnegie's lessons and of Hill's subsequent teachings: just as we have everything we need to be successful, we also have everything we need to self-destruct. Our minds will act on whatever we feed them, good or bad. It's important to note that human nature, as is emphasized with technology and modern comforts, reverts to doing that which is easy. Without a clear idea of what we want, it's much easier to fall victim to distraction and procrastination, which might be something as simple as binge watching television, gorging on junk food, or mindlessly scrolling through social media. Yet if success is our goal, we must never lose sight of this balance between positive and negative emotions and of how those emotions influence our trajectory.

I've had the honor of speaking on stages around the world, and in every presentation I display a slide that says: "Each day, if you do not make the decision to win, you have automatically made the decision to lose." This sentiment is directly influenced by Hill's lessons suggesting that success comes to those who become success conscious. Understanding this principle is a fundamental requirement for all who wish to be high achievers. Those who aren't success conscious eventually will be forced to concede to poverty, illness, and misery. *Think and Grow Rich* might just as well have been titled *Think and Grow Poor*—the premise is the same.

Your first and most important battle is within.

HILL:

It seems obvious that lack of control of the seven negative emotions may lead one to sure defeat, but it is not clear how one may use the seven positive emotions for the achievement of desirable ends. Will you make this clear, Mr. Carnegie?

CARNEGIE:

Yes, I will show you exactly how the positive emotions may be transmuted into a driving power that can be used in the attainment of any purpose. I can best do this by describing the way one man made effective use of his emotions. That man is Charlie Schwab, and my analysis of his use of emotions is based upon close association with him over a long period of years.

Shortly after he began work with me, he made up his mind to become an indispensable part of my business family, thereby directing to a definite end the emotion of desire. In carrying out his desire, he applied the following principles of achievement:

1. Definiteness of Purpose
2. Mastermind
3. Attractive Personality

4. Applied Faith
5. Going the Extra Mile
6. Organized Endeavor
7. Creative Vision
8. Self-Discipline

Through the principle of self-discipline, he organized the other seven principles and brought them under his control. Reinforcing this self-control, he placed all of his emotional feeling on, and expressed it through, his loyalty to his associates, enthusiasm over his work, hope of successful achievement in connection with his work, and faith in his ability to achieve; and reinforcing all these emotions was the emotion of love for his wife, whom Schwab was seeking to please by his achievements.

The motive that inspired him to organize and use his emotions for the attainment of a definite end, as is obvious, was the twofold motive of a) love and b) desire for financial gain.

> **Necessity is the mistress and guide of nature.**
> **Necessity is the theme and inventress of nature,**
> **her curb and her eternal law.**
> —Leonardo da Vinci

HILL:

I think I understand what you mean, Mr. Carnegie. Will you check me while I describe my understanding of Mr. Schwab's rise to power? First, he decided what he wanted, thereby putting into use the principle of definiteness of purpose. He adopted a plan for getting what he wanted, and he began carrying out his plan by Going the Extra Mile, thereby making use also of the principle of organized endeavor.

By working in harmony with you and his other associates, he made use of the mastermind principle. By his adoption of such a high aim, he showed that he understood and used the principle of creative vision, and also demonstrated his understanding and application of the principles of applied faith. By the pleasing, harmonious way he related himself to you and his other associates, he indicated his understanding and use of the principle of an attractive personality.

By the intelligent manner in which he used all these principles and by sticking persistently to his undertaking until he completed it, he demonstrated his understanding and use of self-discipline, through which he subordinated all his desires to the one sole purpose of making himself an indispensable part of your organization.

Behind this endeavor were the two motives of love for his wife and his desire for financial achievement, through which he harnessed and used all his positive emotions for the attainment of a definite purpose. Now, does that about state the case?

CARNEGIE:

That was the procedure followed, exactly! And you will notice that his chances of success would have been lessened had he failed to use any of the principles mentioned. It was through a carefully planned application of all these principles that he attained success. The application required self-discipline of the highest order. If he had squandered any of his emotional power in any other direction whatsoever, the results would have been different, a fact of which I am reminded by the experience of another man who started out to attain the same relationship in my organization that Charlie Schwab successfully attained.

This man had everything that Charlie had as far as ability was concerned. In addition to this, he had a much better education, having graduated from one of the best-known colleges, where he specialized in industrial chemistry. He made just as effective use of every one of the principles mentioned as Charlie did, with one lone exception, and that was the motive by which he was inspired. His motive was a desire for financial gain not as a means of expressing love for his wife but to feed his own vanity. He had a love for power not as an expression of his pride of achievement but as a means of lording his authority over other people.

Despite this weakness, he climbed steadily until he became an official member of my mastermind group. Then he took a tumble, through which he dashed his hopes and his opportunity to pieces by his arrogance and vanity. He was reduced in rank out of necessity for us to maintain harmony in our mastermind group and wound up finally at the bottom of the ladder, right where he started. His demotion inflicted a wound to his vanity from which he never recovered.

HILL: What was this man's greatest weakness, Mr. Carnegie?

CARNEGIE:

I can answer that in three words: lack of self-discipline! If he had gained mastery over his feelings, he could have succeeded with much less effort than Charlie Schwab put into his job, because he had more education and possessed every other attribute of success that Schwab possessed.

He failed to control and direct his positive emotions. When he saw himself slipping, he began to give way to many of the negative emotions, particularly to jealously, fear, and hatred. He was jealous of those who had succeeded—he hated them because they had excelled him, and he feared everyone, particularly himself. No one is strong enough to succeed with such an array of enemies as this working against him.

HILL:

I judge from what you have said that personal power is something that must be used with discretion or it may turn out to be a curse instead of a blessing. Is that correct?

CARNEGIE:

Yes. I have always made it a part of my business philosophy to caution my associates against the dangers of indiscreet use of personal power, especially those who through promotions have but recently come into the possession of increased power. Newly acquired power is something like newly acquired riches; it needs watching closely lest a person become the victim of their own power. Here is where self-discipline gives a good account of itself. When people have their own mind under complete control, they make the mind serve them in a manner that does not antagonize other people.

HILL:

If I understand you correctly, Mr. Carnegie, self-discipline calls for a complete mastery of the seven negative emotions and a controlled guidance of the seven positive emotions. In other words, people must stand with their feet on the necks of the seven negative emotions while they organize and direct to a definite end the seven positive emotions. Is that the idea?

CARNEGIE:

Yes, but self-discipline calls for mastery over traits of character other than the emotions. It calls for a strict budgeting and use of time. It calls for mastery of the inborn trait of procrastination. If someone aims for a high station in life, they have no time to spend on nonessential activities other than those they need for recreation.

EDITOR'S NOTE:

In this passage, Carnegie introduces the importance of managing our time, specifically of ensuring that we have sufficient urgency—a clearly defined deadline—for whatever we wish to accomplish. When this urgency is strapped to motive and packaged with mastery of the fourteen emotions, we are far less likely to fall victim to distraction and procrastination and far more likely to achieve our goals.

Let's consider a simplified example at a university. We know that most students complete their assignments right before the due date, which might be six weeks (or more) away. However, if the professor said there was an assignment worth 60 percent of their grade that was due in forty-eight hours, do you think many students would wait before they made it their primary focus? Absolutely not.

For every goal you have, create a fixed deadline with clear milestones to track your progress along the way. Even the Pomodoro Technique, a powerful tool for time management, relies on the urgency created by having a timer with a visible countdown placed on your workstation.

Without this urgency, it's easy to finish the day and have nothing to show for it. Do you think your favorite entrepreneurs, athletes, and business leaders, the ones obsessed with breaking records and changing the world for the better, have time to waste?

HILL:

Will you name the traits of character that most often stand in the way of self-discipline?

CARNEGIE:

Let us assume for the present that the major enemies of self-discipline are the seven negative emotions. These are the obstacles to which we must give attention first if we wish to be sure of success. Self-discipline begins with the formation of constructive habits—especially the habits connected with food, drink, sex, and the use of one's so-called extra time. Generally speaking, when we get these habits under control, they help to regulate all our other habits.

Consider, for example, what definiteness of purpose does to fix our habits. When we begin to apply the principle of Going the Extra Mile, we make a long step forward in the establishment of constructive habits because in doing more than we are paid for, we are forced to budget our time to better advantage.

Consider, then, what happens when we become obsessed with a strong motive that we begin to express through the principle of organized endeavor in conjunction with the principle of creative vision. By the time we get control of these principles, we have already gone a long distance toward the adoption of habits that, of themselves, constitute the finest sort of self-discipline. Do you see how this works?

HILL:

Yes, I do, and I can see, too, that everything we do centers around the primary motive behind our definite major purpose. Motive really is the starting point of all achievement, is it not?

CARNEGIE:

Yes, that is right, but you should take care to say that this motive must be *obsessional*. That is, it must be so strong that it impels people to subordinate all their thoughts and efforts to its attainment. Too often, people don't distinguish between motive and a mere wish. Wishing will not bring success. If it did, everyone would be successful, because all people have wishes. They wish for everything from the earth to the moon, but wishes and daydreams amount to nothing until they are fanned into a hot flame of desire based upon a definite motive, and this must become the dominating influence of their mind; it must be given obsessional proportions sufficient to cause action.

Those motives that serve as a driving force behind one's chosen major purpose should be underscored and emphasized so they will not be over-looked. They should be included, also, in the written description of one's definite major purpose. A definite purpose without an obsessional motive behind it is as useless as a locomotive without any steam in the boiler. Motive is the thing that gives power, action, and persistence to one's plans.

Without a sense of urgency, desire loses its value.
—Jim Rohn

HILL: That reminds me to ask you, Mr. Carnegie, what is your motive in spending all this time coaching me to organize this achievement philosophy? You have more material riches than you need. You have recognition as the leading industrialist of the world. Your entire life has been a stupendous success, and as far as I can see there is nothing you desire that you do not already possess.

CARNEGIE:

Now, that is where you are wrong. I do not have everything I wish. It is true that I have more material riches than I need, as is evidenced by the fact that I am giving my money away as rapidly as I can do so safely. But there is something I want more than all else, and it is an obsessional desire to provide the people of America with a safe and dependable philosophy by which they may acquire riches in their highest form, riches that will enable people to relate themselves to one another so that they may find peace of mind, happiness, and joy in the responsibilities of life.

My obsessional desire grew out of my experiences with people, through which I have learned of the great need for such a philosophy. It is the exception rather than the rule when I find a person who is trying to benefit themselves without damaging others. On every hand, I see people unwisely trying to get something for nothing, although I know well enough that all they will get is grief and disappointment.

My motive in helping to organize a dependable philosophy of individual achievement is the same as that which prompts some people to erect great monuments of stone to mark the spot where their earthly remains will finally rest. Monuments of stone crumble with time and go back to dust, but there is a type of monument that can be made eternal, and it will last as long as civilization itself. It is the monument a person may build in the hearts of others, through some form of constructive service that benefits humankind as a whole.

It is such a monument that I hope to build, through your cooperation, and may I suggest that in helping me to build it you may let it serve also as your own monument?

HILL:

I see your point, Mr. Carnegie. Was that your motive at the outset of your career?

CARNEGIE:

No, it was not. In the beginning, I was motivated by a desire for self-expression and the desire for financial influence with which to make that expression widespread in its influence. But in carrying out my original motive, I happily hit upon a bigger and a nobler motive—the motive of making *people* instead of making money. I caught the vision of that greater motive as the result of having discovered, in the process of making money, the great need for better people. If civilization is to evolve to still higher standards of living or hold even the gains it has made, we must be taught higher standards of human relationship than those that now prevail.

And, above all, people must learn that there are riches vastly greater than any represented by material things. The need for this wider vision is sufficient to challenge even the greatest of people. It was this challenge to which I responded when my obsessional motive became that of giving the people a sound philosophy of individual achievement.

EDITOR'S NOTE:

Carnegie's effectiveness as a businessperson is surpassed only by that of his philanthropic efforts. As Don Green, executive director of The Napoleon Hill Foundation, noted in the Foreword, the steel magnate's commitment to helping civilization unlock its potential is still evident around the world today. There is a misconception that money is the root of all evil, when in fact having more resources at our disposal not only provides us with freedom to structure our days however we like and the ability to contribute to the causes we care about most but also allows us to fund innovation that improves our standard of living and enhances the quality of life for people everywhere.

Carnegie was driven by a purpose far greater than himself, one that he hoped would ignite a flame of ambition around the world and give people the greatest gift: the ability to help *themselves*. More than a hundred years after his passing, we see how Carnegie's example is met by today's leading figures, such as Warren Buffett, Bill Gates, and Li Ka-shing, who, after achieving their business objectives, turned their hands to philanthropy. This philanthropic focus, primarily on education and healthcare, aims to create peace, cure disease, and raise the standard of living for people everywhere.

In addition to offering great financial generosity, Carnegie provided his achievement philosophy—as refined and circulated by Hill in books such as this one—in hopes that it would teach people, above all else, to be self-sufficient. The more resources you have at your disposal, the more you're able to help others. That leads us to another fundamental theme in this book: the best way to help others is to help *yourself* first.

HILL:

From all you have said, I deduce that self-discipline is largely a matter of the adoption of constructive habits. Is that the idea?

CARNEGIE:

That is precisely the idea! What a person is and what a person accomplishes—both in failure and success—is the result of that person's habits. Fortunately, habits are self-formed. They are under the control of the individual. The most important of these are the habits of *thought*. One comes, finally, to resemble, in one's deeds, the nature of one's thought habits. Gaining control over these thought habits goes a long way toward the attainment of self-discipline.

Definite motives are the beginning of thought habits. It is not difficult for someone to keep their mind on the thing that serves as their greatest motive, especially if the motive becomes obsessional. Self-discipline without definiteness of motive is impossible. Moreover, it would be without value. I have seen fakirs in India who had such perfect self-discipline that they could sit all day long on the sharp points of nails driven through a board, but their discipline was useless because there was no constructive motive behind it.

HILL:

If I understand you correctly, Mr. Carnegie, self-discipline, in the sense that it is designated as one of the major principles of individual achievement, has reference to complete mastery of both our thought habits and our physical habits. Is that your idea?

CARNEGIE:

Yes, that is correct. Self-discipline means exactly what the word implies: complete discipline over self! It calls for a balancing of the emotions of the heart and the reasoning faculty of the head. That is, we must learn to respond to both our reason and our feelings according to the nature of each circumstance calling for our decisions. Sometimes it will be necessary to set aside emotions entirely and allow our head to rule. In matters of physical relationships, this ability becomes highly important.

HILL:

Would it not be safer if a person controlled their life with their reasoning faculty, leaving the emotions out of their decisions and plans?

CARNEGIE:

No, that would be very unwise even if it were possible, because the emotions provide the driving power, the action force, that enables us to put our "head" decisions into operation. The remedy is control and discipline of the emotions, not elimination of them.

Moreover, it is very difficult, if not impossible, to eliminate the great emotional nature of human beings. Our emotions are like a river in that their power can be dammed up and released in whatever proportions and whatever directions one desires, but they cannot be eliminated. Through self-discipline, we can organize our emotions and release them in a highly concentrated form as a means of attaining the object of our plans and purposes.

The two most powerful emotions are love and sex. These emotions are inborn, the handiwork of nature, the instruments through which the Creator provided for both the perpetuation of the human race and the social integration by which civilization evolves from a lower to a higher order of human relationship.

One would hardly wish to destroy so great a gift as the emotions even if this were possible, because they represent humankind's greatest power. If you destroyed hope and faith, what would you have left that would be of use? If you removed enthusiasm, loyalty, and the desire for achievement, you would still have left the faculty of reason (the "head power"), but what good would it be? There would be nothing left for the head to direct!

Now, let me call your attention to an astounding truth: the emotions of hope, faith, enthusiasm, loyalty, and desire are nothing but specialized applications of the inborn emotions of love and sex diverted, or transmuted, into different purposes! In fact, every human emotion outside of love and sex has its roots in these two natural, inborn traits. If these two natural elements were destroyed, that person would become as docile as an animal that has been de-sexed. The reasoning faculty would remain, but what could be done with it?

HILL:

Self-discipline, then, is the tool with which we may harness and direct our inborn emotions in whatever direction we choose?

CARNEGIE:

That is correct. And now I wish to call your attention to another astounding truth: creative vision is the result of self-discipline through which the emotions of love and sex are transmuted into some specialized plan or purpose. No great leader, in any form of human endeavor, has ever attained leadership without mastery and direction of these two great inborn emotions!

The great artists, musicians, writers, speakers, lawyers, doctors, architects, inventors, scientists, industrialists, and salespeople, and the outstanding people in all walks of life, attain their leadership by harnessing and directing their natural emotions of love and sex as a driving force behind their endeavors. In most instances, the diversion of these emotions into specialized endeavor is done unconsciously, as the result of a burning desire for achievement. In some instances, the transmutation is deliberate.

HILL:

Then it is no disgrace for one to be born with great capacity for the emotions of love and sex?

CARNEGIE:

No, the "disgrace" comes from the *abuse* of these natural gifts! The abuse is the result of ignorance, the lack of training as to the nature and potentialities of these great emotions.

> *Practices zealously pursued become habits.*
> —Latin maxim

HILL:

From what you have said, Mr. Carnegie, I get the impression that the most important application of self-discipline is that through which we take possession of our love and sex emotions and transform them into whatever form of endeavor we desire—is that true?

CARNEGIE:

You have caught the idea precisely. And I may add that when we acquire discipline over these two emotions, we will find it easy to discipline ourselves in all other directions, because those emotions are reflected, either consciously or unconsciously, in practically everything we do.

Failure to gain control over the emotions of love and sex generally means failure to gain control over other traits. Take the case of Charles Dickens, for example. Early in life, he met with a great disappointment in love. Instead of allowing his unrequited love emotions to destroy him, he transmuted that great driving force into a novel called *David Copperfield*, which brought him fame and fortune and led him to create other literary works that made him a master in his field.

Abraham Lincoln was a mediocre lawyer who had failed dismally at everything he had undertaken until the deep wells of his emotion were opened wide by his great sorrow over the death of Ann Rutledge, the only woman he ever truly loved. He converted his sorrow into a public service that made him one of America's immortals. It is regrettable that none of his biographers caught the significance of or made explanatory references to the tragedy that marked the turning point in the life of the great statesman.

Napoleon Bonaparte's creative genius as a military leader was largely an expression of his mastermind alliance with his first wife. Observe, with profound significance, the tragedy that overtook this man after his head overruled his heart and he put his first wife aside in furtherance of the ambitions of his head.

In your research, as you organize the achievement philosophy, carefully observe that whenever a couple in love pools their emotions in a spirit of harmony for the attainment of a definite end, they become almost invincible against all forms of discouragement and temporary defeat.

It is through this harmonious alliance that we come into possession of the greatest spiritual power! Perhaps the Creator willed it so, but be that as it may, the fact remains that the world has record of no great men or women whose lives had not been definitely influenced through the emotions of love and sex!

Let it be clearly understood that in speaking of sex, I have reference to that inborn creative emotion that gives humankind our creative ability and not merely to the physical expression of that power. It is the wrong use and the burlesque connotations of this great emotion that have sometimes degraded it to the lowest levels.

HILL:

So the emotion of sex may be either our greatest asset or our greatest liability, according to our understanding and application of the emotion?

CARNEGIE:

Exactly right. And now I wish to call your attention to another significant fact: the emotion of sex, without the modifying effect of the emotion of love, as it is expressed in "illicit" sex relationships, is our most dangerous influence. When these two great emotions are expressed jointly, they become a creative power that savors of a spiritual nature.

HILL:

Then I take, from your remarks, that the emotion of sex without the modifying influence of the emotion of love is purely a biological force that may be disastrous if it is not controlled?

CARNEGIE:

You have the idea exactly! But let me tell you something about the method by which this emotion should be controlled. The safety valve consists in the principle of transmutation, through which this great driving power may be converted and placed behind one's definite major purpose. When used in this manner, it becomes a priceless asset even without the modifying influence of the emotion of love.

The emotion of sex will not be denied some form of expression. It resembles a river in that it can be dammed up and its powers diverted into whatever forms of action one desires, but it cannot be shut off from expression without great damage. Like the waters of a river that have been dammed, if it is not released under controlled conditions it will break out, by the sheer force of its own inherent power, in ways that are destructive.

Self-discipline, through which these great powers are guided into safe channels of human endeavor, is the only sensible solution to the problem they present.

HILL:

If love and sex are the predominant emotions where one should exercise self-discipline, will you now analyze their influence in the practical affairs of daily life? How do these emotions play in the essential factors of human relationships, in all walks of life?

CARNEGIE:

Any truly practical philosophy of individual achievement must enable people to surmount the practical problems of daily life—and I mean *all* the problems!

EDITOR'S NOTE:

What never ceases to amaze me about Carnegie and Hill is how well they understand and present solutions to problems that would be faced by people decades later. When Hill was commissioned to prepare a practical blueprint of achievement for people of all backgrounds, it was important that it serve as counsel for *every* problem with which the individual was faced. Yet more than ever, people are looking for answers and often find short-term salvation in the lure of extravagant material possessions.

Inevitably, these attempts at materialistic solace offer only fleeting happiness. People then find themselves dealing with the same problems that plagued them earlier. Carnegie succinctly notes here that any worthy philosophy of individual achievement must allow people to navigate the thousands of forks in the road they're presented with each day.

One of my favorite Hill quotes is "Having a definite plan for your life greatly simplifies the process of making the hundreds of daily decisions that affect ultimate success." First, through books like this and *Think and Grow Rich*, learn all you can about the habits of extraordinary achievers. Then, with an idea clearly in mind about what you want most, prepare a detailed plan to achieve it—let *The Napoleon Hill Success Journal* guide you. If you've mastered those two steps, there's not a single problem that can arise in daily life that you won't have an astute answer to.

CARNEGIE:

As we have already seen, all human activity is based upon motive. It was not by chance that the motives of love and sex were placed at the head of the list of the basic motives. That is precisely where they belong, because these two motives inspire more action than all other motives combined.

The greatest literature, poetry, art, drama, and music have their roots in love. In Shakespeare's works, you will observe that both the tragedies and the comedies are highly colored with the motives of love and sex. Remove these motives from the Shakespearean plays and you would have nothing left but commonplace dialogue, no better than that of an ordinary playwright. You see, therefore, that these creative emotions can serve the highest purpose in literature.

Accomplished orators, in whatever field of endeavor they may be engaged, give color and magnetic force to their words by transmuting the emotions of love and sex into enthusiasm and thus impart feeling through the spoken word. I have heard orations that, although they were masterpieces in both their theme and their perfect English, failed to impart feeling because the orator marshaled thoughts from the head instead of the heart. They put no feeling into their words because they either lacked emotional capacity or were ignorant as to its use.

> *History will be kind to me, for I intend to write it.*
> —Winston Churchill

In ordinary conversation, everyone imparts, through the spoken word, the exact coloring of their own feelings, or their lack of feelings, and it is by this means that experienced observers arrive at the actual state of mind of the speaker. As we all know, words often are used not to convey one's thoughts but to conceal them! Therefore, the experienced analyst judges people not by their words but by the feeling or the lack of feeling they unconsciously impart with their words.

In view of this, consider how important it is to understand and to deliberately use the power of *emotion* in speech and in writing, because no one ever speaks a word or writes a line without consciously or unconsciously betraying the presence of their feelings or the lack of feelings no matter what the construction of their words may be intended to convey.

HILL:

If I understand you correctly, Mr. Carnegie, our words are colored by the nature of emotions, whether the emotions are positive or negative.

CARNEGIE:

Yes, that is true, but the negative emotions, such as fear, jealousy, and anger, can be controlled and transmuted into a constructive driving force. It is through this sort of self-discipline that the negative emotions may be shorn of their dangers and made to serve useful ends. Sometimes fear and anger will inspire actions in which we would not otherwise engage, but all actions growing out of negative emotions should have the modifying influence of the head so they may be guided to constructive ends.

HILL:

Should one submit both the negative and the positive emotions to the modifying influence of the reasoning faculty, or the "head," as you express it, before expressing the emotions in action?

CARNEGIE:

Yes, that is one of the major purposes of the reasoning faculty. No one should ever, at any time, act on their emotions without first modifying their impulses of thought by submitting them to their reasoning faculty. This is the major function of self-discipline. Self-discipline consists of a proper balancing of the powers of the head and the heart.

HILL:

Now that brings up a subject about which I have thought very little. It never occurred to me that both the head and the heart needed a master, but I can see from what you say that they have a potential master in the faculty of willpower.

CARNEGIE:

Yes. Ego, acting through will, sits as a presiding judge over both reason and emotions, but do not lose sight of the fact that this judge acts only for the person who has trained their ego to act, through self-discipline. Without self-discipline, the ego minds its own business. This leaves the head and the heart to fight out their battles as they please, but where one dominates alone, the other is badly hurt.

HILL:

So the human brain has within it a complete form of government of its own, judging from all you have said?

CARNEGIE:

That is a good way of stating the matter. The government consists of many departments which, when they are coordinated and properly guided through self-discipline, enable an individual to negotiate a path through life that encounters little opposition from others.

These departments consist of:

- The faculty of imagination, wherein one may create ideas, plans, and methods of attaining desired ends;

- The faculty of reason, wherein one may weigh, estimate, and properly evaluate the products of the imagination;

- The conscience, wherein one may test the moral justice of one's thoughts, plans, and purposes;

- The faculty of the emotions, wherein exists the driving force that sets one's thoughts, plans, and purposes into action;

- The memory, which serves as the keeper of records of all experiences; and

- The ego (expressed through willpower), over and above all the others, which sits as a Supreme Court with the power to reverse, modify, change, or eliminate the entire work of all the other departments of the mind.

Doubtless, Shakespeare had in mind this intricate system of self-government when he wrote those profoundly significant words of admonition:

> *This above all: to thine own self be true,*
> *And it must follow, as the night the day,*
> *Thou canst not then be false to any man.*
> — Hamlet

The great dramatist must have recognized that the person who has their six-department self-government in proper working order, with all departments functioning naturally and properly, will be wise enough not to be false to anyone.

From these observations, it becomes quite clear that self-discipline is the procedure by which one coordinates the six departments of their own government in such a manner that none of these departments gets out of control.

HILL:

Which of these departments of self-government should one watch more closely, Mr. Carnegie?

CARNEGIE:

Without doubt, the department of the emotions, because this is the action department, and casual observation of people forces one to the conclusion that actions arising from the emotions, without the modifying influence of the head, generally result in disaster. Yes, emotion without reason is our greatest enemy!

HILL:

Would you care to modify that statement, Mr. Carnegie?

CARNEGIE:

Not in the slightest. Instead, I wish to emphasize the statement by calling attention to the fact that in almost every instance in which one submits their emotional desires to examination by their head, they are compelled to modify them in one way or another. The things we desire most will always bear the closest scrutiny by our heads, and the person who has acquired self-discipline knows this to be true. Hardly a day passes in our lives when we don't have the experience of "feeling" like doing something that our head tells us not to do, if it has a chance to tell us.

EDITOR'S NOTE:

Reflect on the strength in Carnegie's words related to acting on emotion. Hill asked Carnegie whether he wished to modify his staunch belief that emotion without reason is our greatest enemy, yet Carnegie refused and in fact doubled down. Clearly, Carnegie had observed countless people whose lack of control over their emotions had led to the destruction of both their careers and their personal lives.

Let's think about a modern example. Many people have been reprimanded or fired after impulsively sending emotional emails or venting on social media before taking a moment to consider what might happen. A proper modifying influence, such as a quick walk outside for some fresh air or seeking the counsel of a respected colleague, would prevent an action that, once released, would cause irreparable harm to an individual's reputation with the people in question. How many careers would have been saved if the right self-discipline had been applied?

Disastrous actions stemming from unkempt emotions quickly create distrust and are one of the surest means by which to sabotage one's own progress. After all, we're free to make any choice we like, but we're not free from the *consequences* of those choices.

With successful alignment of head and heart, it's not that you don't feel like doing something—it's that you make the right choice as it relates to getting you to where you want to go.

HILL:

Then harmony is something that should begin at home, in one's own mind. Should it not?

CARNEGIE:

The mastermind principle cannot operate without perfect harmony between the individuals constituting the mastermind group. We cannot become a harmonious unit of a mastermind group unless and until we attain harmony among the six departments of our own mind.

HILL:

I can see from your explanations that harmony within one's own mind is a condition precedent to the successful application of the entire philosophy of individual achievement.

CARNEGIE:

You have the right idea. And remember that internal harmony is produced through self-discipline and in no other manner. Once you understand this truth, you will realize my object in emphasizing the importance of mastery over self.

HILL:

Haven't you left out the importance of willpower?

CARNEGIE:

No, there has been no omission. Willpower belongs to the human ego. That is how it comes by the power to set aside the acts of all the other departments of the mind. When you speak of willpower, you are speaking of the prerogative power of the ego, consisting, as it does, of an alliance with the soul, or of some power greater than that which is inherent in any of the other five departments of the mind.

The ego is the court of last resort. Its decisions are final, and we need no proof that they are binding on all other departments of the mind. What power lies beyond the ego or what may be the exact nature of the source of its power are questions I deem to be beyond the scope and the purpose of the philosophy of individual achievement.

All we know of this hidden power is that it exists, and we may draw upon it only by an understanding and application of the principles described throughout this philosophy. Is this not enough? Let us first make intelligent use of the known principles of approach to this hidden power before we begin to inquire into its source and nature, since such an inquiry may result in confusion, and it is sure to result in individual controversies.

HILL:

In sum and substance, then, your advice is that we should learn more about the nature and the usage of the six departments of our own minds before concerning ourselves as to the source from which the mind gets its power?

CARNEGIE:

That's my advice exactly! I am not concerned with any plan to provide more power than is available through this philosophy until we learn how to use the power we have to better advantage. You must remember that by some combination of the principles of this philosophy, the leaders of the American way of life have given the world the highest standard of living yet known to civilization.

With the application of this philosophy, they have developed a great industrial empire, a system of banking that is unparalleled, a system of life insurance that provides economic security to millions of people, a system of transportation and communication that is without equal, a system of advertising and merchandising that is the envy of the world, and a system of education far ahead of any that has been provided by any other country.

Although none of these institutions are perfect, they are still evolving and are being refined and improved almost daily. Therefore, let us keep on with these improvements, assuming, as I believe we may safely do, that if we do our part, the power above and behind all this human activity will reveal to us greater sources of individual power when we are ready to use them intelligently and for the good of humanity.

> *Create the highest, grandest vision possible for your life,*
> *because you become what you believe.*
> —Oprah Winfrey

HILL:

I think your rebuke is quite justified, Mr. Carnegie, and I agree with you that we should make better use of the "talents" with which we have been entrusted before demanding more or greater powers.

CARNEGIE:

And you might well have added that self-discipline is the medium by which a better use of our powers may be attained. The one thing that every living person needs, perhaps more than anything else, is greater discipline over self.

We need self-discipline, first of all, over the six departments of the mind. But this is not enough. We need discipline over the physical appetite, and sex, and speech, and personal adornment, and reading, and we especially need the strictest of discipline in the use of our time. If the time that most people wasted in idle gossip were more wisely used, through an adequate time budget, they would procure all the luxuries of life they could ever need.

We need discipline over all our relationships with others. So, you see, there is no end to the need for self-discipline, and the tragedy of this need lies in the fact that self-discipline is within easy reach of everyone, and no one has to consult another in order to make use of it.

HILL:

Why, Mr. Carnegie, has this prerogative been so generally neglected?

CARNEGIE:

The philosophers back through the ages have been asking that same question. The common admonition of every great philosopher has been "Know thyself" because it is obvious to the philosopher that all we need is to know the nature of the power wrapped up in our own minds. With understanding and application of this power, we can get *everything* we need or desire. All we must do is take possession of our own mind, bring it under self-discipline, and lo! It will serve us as an Aladdin's lamp with which we may acquire our every wish.

But to answer your question more directly, I would say that this prerogative has been overlooked because no one has ever provided the world with a practical philosophy that has incorporated all the essentials of a well-managed life. It was because of my recognition of the need of such a philosophy that I commissioned you to begin its organization.

The philosophers of the past, from Aristotle and Plato on down to the moderns, have concerned themselves too much with the abstract principles of life and too little with the practical, concrete rules of human relationship by which we may negotiate our way through life successfully.

It has been no one's responsibility to provide such a philosophy, and apparently no one has cared to undertake its organization, mainly, I suppose, because of the stupendous amount of unprofitable effort that must be spent in research, investigation, and study. All I can promise you, as an inducement to begin the organization of the philosophy of individual achievement, is twenty years of profitless labor, but I am encouraged by the hope that you will carry on until you complete the job, inspired by the motive of pride of achievement, plus the material compensations that will come to you after you finish the job.

As to why no other person has ever undertaken to organize such a philosophy, I do not know. Your guess is as good as mine! That is a question I cannot answer except by calling your attention to the fact that when civilization needs the volunteers to broaden its horizons, somehow those people always make their appearance. Thus humanity has risen from the very dawn of civilization, and thus will it continue to rise. Behind it all lies some great plan and purpose that we who volunteer to make this a better world need not necessarily understand. We shall have to be contented by the reward of self-satisfaction that is the major source of compensation for all who render useful service.

EDITOR'S NOTE:

It's here that we get a real insight into why the philosophy of achievement is so relevant today. These principles worked for everyone Hill interviewed in *Think and Grow Rich*, released in 1937, just as they worked for everyone in *Think and Grow Rich: The Legacy*, released eighty years later, and for the hundreds of other people referenced in titles published by The Napoleon Hill Foundation.

Success does not discriminate, and no one is born with a gold medal around his or her neck. Success comes to all those who do what needs to be done. Rest assured, dear reader: these principles will work for you, too.

HILL:

Is it not true, Mr. Carnegie, that those who render outstanding service on behalf of humanity thereby demonstrate self-discipline of a high order?

CARNEGIE:

Yes, that is true, and the very fact that the rendering of such service tends to develop self-discipline is sufficient compensation for the service they render, because there is no greater asset than that of self-control. If we have control over ourselves, we may have control over practically anything else we desire.

HILL:

Isn't it true, Mr. Carnegie, that those who acquire great power through strict self-discipline seldom use it to the detriment of others?

CARNEGIE:

Yes; when people are truly self-disciplined, they do not desire to wield their power to the disadvantage of other people. History shows us that all those who violated this rule soon lost their power.

For example, the founders of our nation attained power through self-discipline. Study the record of George Washington, Thomas Jefferson, and others of their type and era, and you will find evidence of self-discipline of the highest order. These individuals were distinguished because of their demands for liberty for all humanity.

HILL:

Mr. Carnegie, I have observed that most people allow their spirit to be broken by the unavoidable disappointments and failures of life, especially those arising from the loss of material things and the loss of friends. In what way may self-discipline be of help to such people?

CARNEGIE:

Self-discipline is the *only* solution for such problems. The discipline should begin with the recognition that there are only two kinds of problems: those we can solve and those we cannot. The problems that can be solved should be liquidated by the most practical means available, and the problems that cannot be solved should be cast out of the mind and forgotten.

Self-discipline, which means mastery over all the emotions, enables us to close the door between ourselves and the unpleasant experiences of the past. The door should be closed tightly and locked securely so that there is no possibility of its being opened again. The door should also be closed against the problems that have no solution. Those who lack self-discipline not only leave the door open between themselves and unpleasant memories and unsolvable problems, but they also stand in the doorway and look backward into the past instead of closing the door and looking only forward into the future.

This door-closing expedient is necessary and important. It calls for the support of our ego, but that support is available only if we have the other departments of our mind under the control of our ego.

HILL:

The first step, then, in closing the door behind unpleasant memories and unsolvable problems is that of gaining control of one's own mind?

CARNEGIE:

That's the idea. We cannot easily close the mental door on past experiences and be sure of keeping it closed until we gain control of our own mind. Remember, too, that unless we form the habit of closing the door between ourselves and the past, we will not be able to open the door of opportunity that stands just ahead of us.

Opportunity for self-promotion, for the attainment of happiness, and for the accumulation of material riches stands tightly closed against those whose minds are occupied with past mistakes and failures or other discouraging thoughts. Successful people are stouthearted people! They have to be. They not only lock behind them the doors of the past, they throw away the key.

EDITOR'S NOTE:

Whoa! How powerful is that? Just as success comes to those who are success conscious, opportunity comes to those who focus on a prosperous future rather than dwell on the misfortunes of the past. This can be especially difficult for those who have experienced a serious medical trauma or physical adversity, and there are three friends of mine who I feel personify this focus greatly:

- Janine Shepherd was a cross-country skier who had qualified for the Winter Olympics in Calgary, Canada. Just a few months out from the games, while on a bicycle training ride through Australia's Blue Mountains, Shepherd was hit by a speeding truck. She was airlifted to the hospital, where her parents were told that she would not live. After ten days in a coma, "Janine the Machine" woke up but was forced to spend six months in the spinal injury ward with countless surgeries and the daunting reality that not only had her athletic hopes evaporated but her physical body had been damaged beyond repair and was unrecognizable.

- Today, the woman who made a career out of defying the odds is a multiple best-selling author who travels the world as a walking paraplegic sharing her inspirational story with leading companies— including Amazon, Google, and Cisco—and with nonprofit associations and schools to remind people that we are not our bodies but the defiant human spirit. I'll never forget the one lesson she shared with me, which sums up her attitude perfectly: "I just don't listen when someone tells me I can't do something."

- Because of a rare birth defect, Jessica Cox was born without arms. Rather than dwelling on her misfortune, Cox resourcefully found a solution—she had two feet and would use them as a substitute. Spurred on by every challenge, she learned how to drive a car, type quickly and accurately on a keyboard, scuba dive, and change contact lenses, and at age fourteen she even earned a black belt in taekwondo.

In the midst of her many other noteworthy achievements, Cox learned to fly, and she was recognized by Guinness World Records as the world's first armless pilot. Today, she teaches individuals, companies, and associations how to live the impossible.

- At the age of seventeen, Jim Stovall failed a routine physical for his high school football team. Three doctors sat him down and explained that he would soon go totally and permanently blind and that there was nothing they could do to prevent it. True to prophecy, Stovall's world began to literally fade to black, but Stovall recognized that if he had this affliction, he would just have to find its compensating benefit.

    A few years later, Stovall realized that there was no way for the millions of blind and visually impaired people around the world to enjoy television programming, and so he went to work to rectify the situation. Today, the Narrative Television Network operates in more than a dozen countries and has provided enormous value to those who previously had felt ostracized. Stovall is also the author of thirty best-selling books despite never having written a book before going blind.

The journeys of Janine Shepherd, Jessica Cox, Jim Stovall, and countless others around the world remind us that we must face the future courageously irrespective of what happened in the past, having faith that there's plenty more life for us to live.

Dwelling on the business partner who wronged you, the former spouse who robbed you of your dignity, or the circumstance that you never could have foreseen is the very thing that prevents you from being happy in the present. Channel the energy into constructive means and find the gift in every adversity. Purposeful action is the best remedy.

HILL:

I like that expression concerning the "closing of doors." But doesn't this door-closing habit make one hard and unemotional?

CARNEGIE:

Perhaps it does make one firm, but I wouldn't say it makes one hard. Firmness is a quality one must have in order to become self-disciplined. Please remember that self-discipline is no mere gesture through which we slap ourselves gently on the wrist and say, "Now, be good!" Self-discipline is a definite mental attitude that searches deeply into our very soul, discovers the deadwood of our being, and throws it out boldly.

It permits no lurking memories of sad experiences, and it wastes no time worrying over unsolvable problems. It closes the door tightly against fear and opens the door widely to hope and faith. It closes the door tightly against jealousy and opens the door widely to love. It closes the door just as definitely against hatred, revenge, greed, anger, and superstition and stands guard behind the door to make sure that it is not opened by anyone for any cause.

There can be no compromise on this door-closing business. We either place our willpower behind the door leading to experiences we wish to forget and close the door tightly or we do not acquire self-discipline. This is one of the major services that self-discipline performs.

> *Most folks are about as happy as they make up their minds to be.*
> —Abraham Lincoln

HILL:

But what of those people who have their hearts broken by disappointments in love? What are they to do about this door-closing habit that you say is so essential?

CARNEGIE:

Disappointment over love is not unlike disappointments over other things.

These wounds may be more easily healed by redirecting one's affections in a new field. Here, then, the remedy is to close the door tightly and begin to find a new love interest.

HILL:

But this remedy is more easily prescribed than it is applied, is it not?

CARNEGIE:

No door-closing job is easy! If it were, there would be no need to close the door. The trouble with most people is that they leave the door either slightly ajar or wide open, thereby compromising with the things that should be closed out of their lives. One cannot afford to temporize with memories that are unpleasant. They destroy the power of creative vision, undermine initiative, weaken the imagination, upset the faculty of reason, and confuse all the departments of the mind. Self-discipline permits no such interference no matter what the course may be.

HILL:

From what you have said, self-discipline enables us to master everything that gets in our way or causes us any sort of discomfort?

CARNEGIE:

Yes, it does just that. It tolerates no interference with the orderly functioning of the mind. Like an ocean minesweeper, it clears our path of all detrimental obstacles and leaves us a wide-open path into the future. It causes us to look forward, not backward. It will not tolerate discouragement or worry. It either removes the cause of these or closes the door so tightly behind them that they cannot come through.

On the other hand, self-discipline just as adamantly refuses to allow the door to be closed between us and the seven positive emotions. The door to these is always left wide open, and if they do not enter, voluntarily self-discipline goes out and brings them in and puts them to work.

HILL:

In other words, self-discipline feeds and nourishes the positive emotions but keeps the doors closed against the negative emotions. Is that the idea?

CARNEGIE:

Yes, but it does more than encourage the positive emotions. It keeps them in their place and forces them to share their influence with the faculty of reason, thereby keeping them under control. Take the emotion of enthusiasm, for example. No one has ever been known to achieve anything truly great without enthusiasm, yet unbridled enthusiasm may, and often does, get people into trouble. So it has to be kept under control and guided to definite ends.

The same thing is true of the other positive emotions, especially the emotions of love and sex. These two, being the most powerful of the group, need the closest watching. When they get out from under control, they may wreck one permanently. Hope, faith, and loyalty are the only emotions that seldom give one any reason to hold them in check. But even these must be modified at times by the faculty of reason; otherwise they would be misplaced and abused.

HILL:

I am beginning to think that self-discipline is an asset that can be enjoyed only by strong people.

CARNEGIE:

That is right! And why not? What would one expect of weak minds? The purpose of self-discipline is to make minds strong. What do you think the philosophy of individual achievement is intended for except to make strong minds? That is its major function. Its purpose is to help people take possession of their own minds and use them for every needful end.

No one has possession of their own mind until they develop self-discipline enough to enable them to *organize* their mind and keep it clear of disintegrating influences.

HILL:

Do you think most people will care to pay the price necessary to gain self-discipline, Mr. Carnegie?

CARNEGIE:

Of course not! But those who succeed will have to pay the price. They will become leaders in their chosen fields of endeavor; that will be their reward for having paid the price. Remember, once and forever, that there is no such thing as something for nothing. Everything worth having has a price tag upon it, and those who get it must pay that price or they do not get it. They may get something else, but never something for nothing.

HILL:

That is the equivalent, I presume, of your saying that the benefits of the philosophy of individual achievement may not be enjoyed by those who are not willing to acquire self-discipline?

CARNEGIE:

You have stated the case perfectly. In view of what I have just stated about the impossibility of getting something for nothing, you would hardly expect people to appropriate the benefits of such a complete philosophy without earning those benefits.

You must remember that when we master this philosophy and apply it appropriately, we have achieved the object of our highest hopes and aims. This is a promise that cannot be assured from any other source or for any other cause. Therefore, it seems to me that no price would be too great for any individual to pay for such assurance.

But the price we must pay for the benefits of this philosophy is infinitesimal in comparison with the benefits it promises. Moreover, the price is within the reach of any person of average intelligence, sound body, and sound mind. It consists of a persistent determination to appropriate and use the philosophy! Surely there is nothing formidable about this. I would say that the greatest portion of the price one will have to pay for the benefits of this philosophy will be the effort needed to develop self-discipline, and that is almost entirely a matter of willpower, plus an appropriate motive of sufficient magnitude to ensure continuous effort.

The whole thing is within the choice of the individual.

HILL:

I am glad to hear you say this, Mr. Carnegie, and you have my assurance that I share your views fully. My questions do not connote doubt on my part. I asked them only to make certain that you could defend your views, because the time will come when I shall have to substitute for you and answer these same questions for those who seek self-determination through the use of the philosophy. There are many "Doubting Thomases" in the world, and I must be prepared to convince them that the rules of individual achievement are known and that the rules will work for all who will practice them.

CARNEGIE:

I like that way of putting it, because you are right in saying the rules will work for all who will practice them. No philosophy will work by itself, as if it were a sugar-coated pill whose effects can be gained simply by swallowing it and going to sleep. But with intelligent application, you may be sure this philosophy will work.

And why wouldn't it? It is not a mere set of abstract rules; it represents, or will represent when it is completed, the life experiences of more than five hundred successful people who have built huge successes upon it. If a rule is sound, it will work time and time again, and it will serve one person as well as any other of equal ability to apply it.

HILL:

Now I wish to ask you a question concerning something that has given me much cause for thought. Why is it, Mr. Carnegie, that the most successful people—the ones who have attained influence as well as fortunes—do not achieve their success until they are well along in years?

CARNEGIE:

There are two very good reasons for this. First, because there has been no definite philosophy of individual achievement available in the past, people have been forced to learn by trial and error, and that takes time. Second, as people attain maturity in years, they sometimes acquire wisdom as well as age, and when they do, you may be sure they have submitted themselves to a strict self-discipline.

HILL:

What is the greatest purpose that self-discipline can be made to serve, Mr. Carnegie?

CARNEGIE:

Without hesitation, I would say that its greatest potential benefit consists of its use in support of one's willpower! The ego, in which we may assume is the seat of willpower, is the Supreme Court of the mind, with the power to set aside the work of all other departments of the mind. If that source of power is protected and supported through strict self-discipline, its potentialities are stupendous in both their scope and their power.

We are never really defeated until our own willpower accepts the verdict of defeat!

I have known people to fail in business and lose every material thing they possessed when well beyond the middle age period of life, yet they made a comeback and recouped their losses. What they did not lose was their self-discipline, through which they had developed indomitable willpower.

HILL:

Then do you subscribe to the axiom "Our only limitations are those we set up in our own minds"?

CARNEGIE:

Yes, I do! And I can tell you something else about the power of the mind. It will establish its own limitations if the individual does not take possession of it and direct it to definite ends, through self-discipline. The mind is unlimited in its power only to the extent that unlimited demands are made upon it.

In many ways, the mind is like a fertile garden spot that, if cultivated, can be made to yield any desired crop, but if neglected, it voluntarily raises a fine crop of weeds! Understand this characteristic of the mind and you will know why it is necessary to control it through self-discipline.

> **The finest kind of security is the personal security**
> **that is developed from within.**
> —Andrew Carnegie

HILL:

By way of summarizing the more important potentialities of self-discipline, will you briefly describe the features of this principle to which one should give first attention?

CARNEGIE:

Well, categorically speaking, I would say that when we get our mind under control through self-discipline, our control over everything else that concerns us will become automatic. Surely beginners should start by forming strict habits of self-discipline over the six departments of their own mind. This will require patience, persistence, and a definite motive to inspire continuous application of these qualities.

The procedure is not complicated. It should begin with the adoption of a definite major purpose, backed by an adequate motive for the achievement of that purpose. This beginning will, of necessity, call for self-discipline.

EDITOR'S NOTE:

Here Carnegie mentions a fundamental reason people fail to attain their goals. Research shows that by the second week of February, approximately 80 percent of people who set their goals for the new year have abandoned those goals. This means that out of the minority of people who actually set goals in the first place, only one in five is still working on achieving them just six weeks after they were set!

Undoubtedly inspired by Carnegie's emphasis on motive, Hill writes elsewhere that "drifting is the primary cause of failure." This tells us that the goals that are most likely to be achieved are those which stem from a definite major purpose, reinforced with adequate motive for *why* one wants to achieve it. This makes it far easier for the goals to be emotionally charged, which, as we have read, is important for inspiring the consistent and purposeful action required for them to become reality.

Remember, the stronger the motive, the more ardent the action.

CARNEGIE:

In addition, I would recommend autosuggestion as a means of making one's self alert and aware of the need for self-discipline. This can constitute a daily repetition of a psychological formula, as follows:

1. I recognize that my mind consists of a system of government made up of the six departments of imagination, conscience, reasoning faculty, emotional faculty, memory, and finally willpower, which resides in the ego and serves as the Supreme Court over all the other departments.

2. I will cultivate my imagination by using it persistently.

3. I will keep on good terms with my conscience by consulting it when in doubt but never overriding it.

4. I will develop my faculty of reason by submitting all my plans, purposes, and opinions to it for strict analysis before action.

5. I will encourage the seven positive emotions, but I will modify these at all times by submitting them to my faculty of reason before expressing them.

6. Because I recognize the danger of the seven negative emotions, I will gain such control over them that I will give no form of expression to them except that which I can transmute into some form of constructive action.

7. I will respect the Supreme Court of my mind—willpower— by throwing myself on its side and giving it complete control over all the other departments of my mind, no matter how much effort this requires.

8. I will keep my memory keen and alert by taking care to impress it clearly with all that I desire to recall promptly.

9. As a means of developing these six departments of my mind, I will adopt a definite major purpose and devote some form of effort to its attainment daily, no matter how little.

10. I recognize that my mind has no limitations except those which I establish in it or permit others to establish. Therefore, I will close the door tightly against every negative influence that enters my mind and every unpleasant experience I have had in the past, and I will keep that door closed regardless of the effort required.

11. Recognizing the power of habit, I will develop complete self-discipline by forming daily habits that harmonize with the nature of my definite major purpose, realizing that my subconscious mind will take over these habits and automatically carry them out.

12. For the faithful performance of this commitment, I will keep my mind open for the guidance of Infinite Intelligence, realizing that my own plans may require modification from time to time.

13. The commitment shall constitute my daily prayer!

It would be impossible for one to follow this commitment daily, in a spirit of faith, without getting desirable results! The picture of the commitment will be taken over sooner or later by the subconscious mind and acted upon automatically.

The commitment should be carried out in a spirit of humility of the heart. It should be carried out privately, without the knowledge (and the consequent possibility of interference) of others. This should constitute a compact that a person makes with themselves and their Creator.

The commitment will do many things that will change one's mental attitude. It will:

- Make one discipline-conscious;

- Help to kill off discouragements of every nature;

- Develop self-reliance and definiteness of decision in the daily affairs of one's life;

- Enable one to master procrastination;

- Bring pleasing changes in one's personality, which will become almost immediately noticeable by the changed attitude of those with whom one associates daily;

- Attract opportunities for self-advancement in ways too numerous to be mentioned; and

- Cause one to be eternally on guard against weaknesses to which one has previously yielded without resistance.

In brief, it will constitute self-discipline in its highest and most beneficial form—self-discipline that will reflect itself in *all* one does and all one thinks!

EDITOR'S NOTE:

Autosuggestion is a process that is simple to prepare but difficult to maintain unless you're fully committed. We've learned already that success with this process requires that you harness the energy currently used in complaining about your circumstances and redirect it to constructively create the circumstances you most desire. The process of autosuggestion is a wonderful way to test your resolve.

In an inspirational keynote (available online), critically acclaimed author, speaker, and pastor Dr. Eric Thomas, known as the Hip Hop Preacher, asks the audience a simple question: *"How bad do you want it?"* He shares a story to illustrate the importance of creating the perfect time rather than waiting for it. In the story, Thomas says, "When you want to succeed as bad as you want to breathe, then you will be successful."

Today we see more and more people opining on the benefits of starting the day with some type of adversity, no matter how insignificant, to give themselves the feeling of accomplishment. Whether your first task of the day involves repeating a daily mantra, taking a cold shower, meditating, journaling, or making the bed, your attitude toward that first task will determine your effectiveness that day.

If you're not ready for success, step aside for the person who is.

HILL:

Mr. Carnegie, haven't you overlooked the most important of all the departments of the mind, the subconscious department?

CARNEGIE:

No, I have not overlooked the subconscious, but it is not under the control of the individual. I have mentioned only the departments of the mind that are subject to self-discipline. The subconscious mind is the connecting link between our conscious mind and Infinite Intelligence, and no one can discipline or control it. It works in its own way, its major function being that of appropriating and acting upon the dominating thoughts of the conscious mind.

You should know, however, that self-discipline enables one clearly and definitely to impress one's conscious mind with any desired purpose, thereby preparing the way for that purpose to be taken over and acted upon by the subconscious mind without delay.

HILL:

What, if anything, will speed up the action of the subconscious mind?

CARNEGIE:

Intensity of plan and purpose! When one is motivated by a burning desire for the achievement of a definite purpose, one's subconscious mind often acts on that desire *immediately*. The action usually takes the form of a plan for the attainment of the purpose, which it passes over to the conscious mind through what is generally known as a "hunch."

That is, the plan is flashed into the mind without any aid from the imagination or the reasoning faculty, and its origin may be recognized by the feeling of enthusiasm that accompanies it. In this manner, the work of the subconscious mind is easily recognizable.

HILL:

From what you have said, I conclude that the major purpose of the psychological formula you have described is that of conditioning the mind to receive and act upon one's aims, plans, and purposes. Is that the idea?

CARNEGIE:

Precisely. The formula aids one in clearing the mind of useless impediments and negative influences, and it encourages the presence of positive influences.

HILL:

Does intensity of the emotions always speed up the action of the subconscious mind, Mr. Carnegie?

CARNEGIE:

No, the subconscious mind takes its own good time for action, but there are times when it acts immediately after receiving an impulse of desire. For example, in the time of emergency, such as a near collision between two automobiles, the subconscious mind has been known to carry a driver safely through hazards that the driver would not, and perhaps could not, negotiate by relying upon their conscious mind. I have known of several such circumstances.

It is a well-known fact that a person who faces a great danger, such as being in a house that is on fire, often develops what appear to be superhuman powers of both physical strength and mental strategy in extricating themselves from the dangers of the hazard. In such cases, the subconscious mind takes over and gives orders, even going to the extent of taking complete charge of both the mind and the body.

One characteristic of the subconscious mind is that it does not take orders from the head. It acts only on the orders of the emotions. You see, therefore, why it is essential for us to develop and control our positive emotions: because the subconscious mind will carry out the orders of the negative emotions just as quickly as it will act on the positive emotions. It makes no attempt to distinguish between these.

HILL:

Then that is why people who are surrounded with mental and physical evidence of poverty so often become the victims of poverty, is it not?

CARNEGIE:

Yes, you have the right idea. The subconscious mind acts upon the dominating influences of one's emotions. That is, it acts on those emotions which are the strongest—those that occupy the mind the greater portion of the time.

HILL:

May we say, then, that we literally think ourselves into poverty if we permit our minds to dwell upon poverty?

CARNEGIE:

That is precisely what happens. And you should add that the mind that is not organized and directed toward a definite end through a strict system of self-discipline leaves itself open to the infiltration of the influence of its environment.

The mind is everything.
What you think, you become.
—Buddha

HILL:

But the mind that is kept occupied with a definite major purpose based upon opulence and abundance has a tendency to attract the ways and means by which plenty may be acquired. Is that the idea?

CARNEGIE:

Yes, but a mind so charged with definiteness of purpose has more, much more, than a mere tendency to attract the object of that purpose. It goes the full distance and actually attracts that object. Show me the sort of mental food any mind feeds upon daily, and I will tell you accurately what the owner of that mind may expect to receive from life.

HILL:

Have you in mind any thought in connection with this principle that you would like to emphasize as the climax of the discussion?

CARNEGIE:

Yes, I have! And it is so important that it might well serve as the climax of this entire philosophy. I have been waiting for you to ask a question that would bring out the thought I have in mind, but you have not done so. Please understand that I am not criticizing you for the oversight, since it is natural that the thought I have in mind should occur only to one who is mature and experienced in the ways of humanity.

Now, I will tell you what I have in mind. I have drawn a clear picture of the six departments of the mind, and the functions of each department have been plainly described. However, there is one department that transcends all the others by such stupendous proportions that it is deserving of special emphasis. I refer to the ego, the seat of willpower.

The Six Departments of the Mind

To show how self-discipline can be maintained, numbered in the order of their relative importance.

SUBCONSCIOUS MIND:
The connecting link between the mind and Infinite Intelligence.

(1) **EGO:** Seat of willpower. The Supreme Court over all the other departments of the mind; its seat of power is in the subconscious mind.

(2) **FACULTY OF THE EMOTIONS:** Seat of the action power of the mind.

(3) **FACULTY OF REASON:** Seat of judgment and opinions.

(4) **FACULTY OF IMAGINATION:** Origin of ideas and plans.

(5) **CONSCIENCE:** The moral guide of the mind.

(6) **MEMORY:** Keeper of the records of mind.

By comparison, I might say that willpower is to the other departments of the mind as the United States Supreme Court is to the other two departments of the American form of government, but this comparison would hardly be sufficient to give one a full conception of the part willpower plays in human affairs.

Physics teachers have a trick question with which they have a great deal of fun as they try it out on beginner students. The question is: "What happens when an immovable body comes into contact with an irresistible force?"

The person experienced in the field of physics knows, of course, that there is no such reality as an immovable body or an irresistible force. But that is in the realm of physical laws. In metaphysics, there is an irresistible force, and it is known as *willpower*.

Because willpower is irresistible, one may truthfully say that the only limitation anyone has is what they set up in their own mind by the limitation of the use of their willpower.

This power is so great that it has been known, countless times, to stay the hand of death! It has performed feats of human achievement that, for want of a better explanation, have been called "miracles."

When the emotions are backed by an indomitable will, the subconscious mind has been known to hand over information never before known to humanity. It was by this power that Thomas Edison perfected some of his most outstanding inventions. Without a doubt, it was this power that enabled George Washington to wrest the victory from superior forces that gave this nation its liberty.

Willpower is the instrument with which we may close the door against any experience or circumstance we wish to put behind us forever. With this same instrument, we may open the door of opportunity in any direction we choose. If the first door we try is difficult to open, we will try another and another, until at long last we will find one that will yield to this irresistible force. Thus, the Supreme Court of the human mind may also become the military power with which the dictates of the court may be carried out.

Become a master of self and you may become the master of every other thing needed to adjust yourself to life in your own way. If you allow this thought to escape your attention, you will miss the better portion of this philosophy. But you will not miss it. I shall see to it that you do not, because you will need willpower, more than anything else, to carry you through the long years of research you must put into the organization of the philosophy.

Your own willpower will open doors to you that would otherwise be closed against you. It will do the same for anyone who relies upon it.

It has always seemed to me that the whole power of the universe is available to the person who has an indomitable will. It has served me where money was useless. It has served me when everything else failed me. In all my experience, it has never let me down when I relied upon it implicitly, although in my case, as in the life of every person, there have been times when I did not make the fullest use of this power.

There are no insurmountable difficulties for those who understand their own willpower. They find a way around them, albeit the way may not be what they would wish it to be.

Early in my career, I had an experience that I shall never forget. I wanted to purchase a certain piece of property, which required an outlay of several million dollars. I had no such amount of money available. At first, I tried to negotiate a loan through several banks, asking each bank to supply a portion of the money, but all I secured was refusals.

A meeting of the board of directors of the company from which I desired to purchase the property was scheduled for the following morning. On my way to that meeting, I carried with me a determined feeling that I would get the property, money or no money, and in that spirit I entered the meeting. Before I reached the place of the meeting, I had formulated the plan whereby I knew I would acquire the property without paying a single penny of the purchase price. My plan was to issue bonds for the entire amount, with a liberal amount added as a bonus over and above the purchase price, as an inducement for the owners to sell.

Without saying a word about my having been refused the loan of the money by the banks, I placed my offer of the bonds before the owners, and they accepted it without question. In fact, they expressed great joy because of my offer of the bonus.

When I told the bankers what I had done, one of them exclaimed, "Impossible!" Nothing is impossible when someone with a determined will goes to bat. In the years that followed, I had many other occasions to purchase property without money.

It always seems impossible until it's done.
—Nelson Mandela

HILL:
Then the starting point of the approach to willpower is definiteness of purpose?

CARNEGIE:
Definiteness of purpose is the starting point to *everything* that humanity achieves. Willpower is the thing that keeps us going until we accomplish what we set out to do.

HILL:

One might say that indomitable willpower plus resolute purpose equals achievement?

CARNEGIE:

That's the story in one brief sentence, and if you should ask what gives one resolute purpose, I would say *motive*.

HILL:

Then let us put it this way: motive plus resolute purpose plus the power of indomitable will equals achievement.

CARNEGIE:

That is still better, and I may add that in that single sentence you have described the entire philosophy of individual achievement.

HILL:

What sustains willpower, Mr. Carnegie, when it begins to slow down because of opposition and the pressure of circumstances?

CARNEGIE:

Motive! Plus a burning desire for its realization. If our motive is deeply seated and our desire for its attainment is strong, there is a natural inflow of willpower. If we are under complete self-discipline, we have the ability to summon willpower whenever we need it. This is one of the major benefits of self-discipline.

HILL:

Does willpower disintegrate through disuse, the same as other powers that one does not use?

CARNEGIE:

Yes, the powers of the mind develop through use, the same as the physical powers of the body. This is a fundamental law that extends throughout all nature: the Law of Growth Through Use. Nature discourages idleness in all its forms. Every living thing must continue to grow through struggle and action. The moment action stops, death begins, whether one is studying vegetable matter or the higher orders of life.

HILL:

And that is why you have stressed the importance of action throughout our discussions, is it not?

CARNEGIE:

Exactly! I have tried to make it very clear that no principle of this philosophy is of value until it is expressed in action! Out of action, growth and strength are born. If you want an impressive example of what happens when people stop using their minds, take a look at anyone who has retired and quit work. The mind is like a piece of machinery in that it soon rusts when it is taken out of use.

EDITOR'S NOTE:

Carnegie concludes the first conversation by emphasizing the importance of getting out of our comfort zone because despite any discomfort or apprehension we may have at the time of leaving it, outside that zone is where all growth occurs. We are made strong by our struggles, but more than ever—with the advent of big-screen televisions and never-ending social media news feeds—we choose to watch the show roll on in front of us rather than actively participate.

Do you recall the passage in "Note to Readers" in which I reminded you that this book is an invitation to engage with life? I'm hoping that now you're feeling the excitement of opportunity and already have a detailed list of actions to take.

Often, we resist opportunities to get out of our comfort zone, but forging the habit of accepting those opportunities has led to my establishing the relationships and opportunities that have provided literally every success I am grateful to enjoy today. You are safe in your comfort zone, but nothing grows there.

Challenge yourself to attend events, meet positive people, and expand your mind in pursuit of creating a far greater life than you ever thought possible— for you, your family, and your community.

ANALYSIS: SELF-DISCIPLINE
By Napoleon Hill

E arlier, I presented a perspective of the six departments of the mind over which self-discipline can be maintained. The departments have been numbered in what I consider the order of their relative importance, although it is difficult to say which is absolutely the most important of these departments. All are necessary.

Mr. Carnegie has emphasized the seat of willpower so convincingly that I have been left no other choice than to give it first place. As he so clearly states, "Willpower controls all the other departments," and he has very appropriately called it the Supreme Court of the mind.

It seems to me that the faculty of emotions is next in importance since it is a well-known fact that "the world is ruled by its emotions."

The faculty of reason surely takes third place in importance since it is the modifying influence through which emotional action may be prepared for safe use. The well-balanced mind represents a compromise between the faculties of emotion and of reason.

The faculty of imagination comes in fourth since it is the department that creates ideas, plans, and ways and means of attaining desirable ends.

The other two departments, conscience and memory, are necessary adjuncts of the mind, and though both are important, they surely belong at the end of the list.

The subconscious mind has been given the top position because it is the superpower on which the mind may draw for cooperation. It has not been included as a part of the government agencies of the mind because it acts independently, and it is not subject to any form of discipline other than that of suggestion. It acts in its own way and voluntarily, although, as Mr. Carnegie has stated, its action can be speeded up by intensifying the emotions and applying willpower in a highly concentrated form.

The relationship between the subconscious mind and the six departments of the conscious mind is similar in many respects to that of the farmer and the laws of nature through which crops are produced. The farmer has certain duties to perform, such as preparing the soil, planting it at the right season of the year, and so forth, after which the farmer's work is finished. From there, nature takes over, germinates the seed, grows it to maturity, and yields a crop.

The conscious mind may be compared to the farmer in that it prepares the way by formulating plans and purposes, under the direction of willpower. If its work is done properly and a clear picture of what it wants is created (the picture being the seed of the purpose it desires to achieve), the subconscious takes over the picture and presents to the conscious mind practical ways and means of attaining its object.

Unlike the laws of nature that germinate seed and produce a crop within a definite, predetermined length of time, the subconscious takes whatever time it pleases, with the exceptions stated.

Mr. Carnegie's emphasis on willpower indicates his belief that highly concentrated effort of this power produces definite results, but he does not claim that the results always come from the action of the subconscious mind. On this point, no one seems to have definite information. However, there is plenty of evidence to support Mr. Carnegie's claims about willpower, regardless of what the source of that power may be.

EDITOR'S NOTE:

We're continuing to see the importance of concentration and intensity for producing the best results irrespective of the field of endeavor. You might have been blessed with a highly intelligent brain, a prestigious education, an athletic body, or a powerful social network, but if you're unsure of the result you want, your assets are superfluous, and ultimately you will be outdone by those with more direction, resourcefulness, and resilience.

For example, you might have a superyacht with the most expensive furnishings, but if you don't know your destination—or, worse, how to actually use the vessel at your disposal—you'll be destined to sit at the dock. With each day that the yacht serves no purpose, more and more barnacles attach to the hull, which slowly but surely begins to corrode. Eventually, under extreme duress, your superyacht will sink.

Having the self-discipline to create a definite major purpose allows the six departments of the mind—a metaphysical mastermind in itself—to spin their rotors in a common purpose. This is the importance of willpower in undertaking the highly concentrated effort mentioned by Carnegie and Hill as a strategy to produce definite results.

Think about what results you want, what work is required to get those results, and how you're going to prove your commitment to your goal each day. Let your dreams be big ones, fueled by concentrated intensity and reinforced with consistency. It's not a sexy formula, but it's certainly the most potent.

Most people want to overcomplicate the success formula, which leads to blaming others, inaction, or the hunt for a magic bullet. Unfortunately, social media has only exacerbated this phenomenon. Is it any wonder, then, that in the United States alone more than $73 billion is spent on lottery tickets each year? This figure is five times the amount that is spent on books, which have a strong chance of transforming your life in some capacity, but how many lottery tickets do you need to buy before you see a return on investment? With a 1 in 300 million chance of hitting the jackpot, you may *never* see a return on investment.

As Carnegie and Hill have outlined, self-discipline is evident in consistency: in putting in the work, in persisting in the face of adversity, and in focusing on the actions taken each day rather than on the results attained.

We all know that we are never permanently defeated until we accept defeat in our own mind, which means that we are not defeated until we ease up on our application of willpower!

In sales, for example, it is well known that the persistent salesperson generally heads the list in sales results. In advertising, the same rule applies: the most successful advertisers carry on, with persistence, repeating their efforts from month to month with unabating regularity, and professional advertising experts have convincing evidence that this is the only policy that will produce satisfactory results.

The pioneers who settled in America when this country was only a vast wilderness demonstrated what can be done when willpower is applied with persistence! Later in the history of the country, after the pioneers had established a semblance of a democratic society, George Washington and his little army of underfed, half-clothed, underequipped soldiers proved once more that willpower applied with persistence is unbeatable.

Then came the founders of American industry and commerce who, with indomitable willpower and persistence, gave this country a standard of living that the world had never seen before. Let us examine the records of a few of the leaders who, by their willpower and persistence, have made stupendous contributions to the national wealth of the United States, to say nothing of having accumulated adequate rewards for themselves.

Andrew Carnegie himself ranks high on the list.

He came to America as a steerage passenger when he was very young and began working as a laborer. He had only a few friends, none of whom were influential, and very little education, but he *did* have an enormous capacity for willpower and perseverance.

By working at menial labor during the day and studying at night, he learned telegraphy, finally working his way up to a position as a private telegraph operator for a division superintendent of the Pennsylvania Railway Company. In this position, he made such effective use of some of the principles of this philosophy that he attracted the attention of the high-ranking officials of the railroad.

At this point, he had precisely the same advantages that hundreds of other telegraph operators who worked for the Pennsylvania Railroad Company enjoyed, but no more. But he did have something that the other operators apparently did not have, or, if they did have it, they failed to make use of it. It was the will to win coupled with the persistence to carry on until he did win.

As far as I can learn from the records of his life and from the close personal working alliance that I had with him over a long period of years, his outstanding qualities were persistence and willpower, plus a strict self-discipline through which these qualities were controlled and directed to a definite end. Beyond this, he had no outstanding qualities that were not possessed by the majority of people engaged in the same sort of work that he performed.

By exercising his willpower, Carnegie adopted a definite major purpose and clung tenaciously to that purpose until it made him a great industrial leader, not to mention a great personal fortune. Out of his willpower, properly self-disciplined and directed to a definite end, came the great United States Steel Corporation, which revolutionized the steel industry and provided (and still provides) employment for a huge army of skilled and unskilled workers, not to mention the wealth he added to the nation, a sum so huge that it is beyond estimate.

> *Set aside one hour out of every twenty-four*
> *to be still and listen for the small,*
> *still voicethat speaks from within.*
> —Andrew Carnegie

But that is not the whole story of this immigrant boy. His willpower goes marching on, making its influence or good felt in every part of the US and in many foreign countries, although he has passed on to his final reward.

The material fortune he amassed was given back to the people in the form of educational facilities, some of it through gifts to public libraries, but "the greater portion of it," to use his own words, was offered through his achievement philosophy, which is now available to people in all walks of life in this and other countries.

Thus, the influence of this one man is beyond estimate! The principles of individual achievement through which he amassed his personal fortune are now available to all who desire this knowledge. Thanks to his foresight, this philosophy includes the experience of more than five hundred other distinguished leaders of industry and commerce, and it is destined to render useful service as long as civilization lasts.

EDITOR'S NOTE:

Hill mentions that the achievement philosophy is available to all those who *desire* it. Fans of Hill will recognize this as a foundational theme in all his work, such as *Think and Grow Rich*, where it is listed as the very first principle, with Hill noting: "The starting point of all achievement is desire."

The philosophy's earlier wording is much more powerful than it appears at first glance. The achievement philosophy commissioned by Carnegie and carried out by Hill is now readily available in the more than 120 million copies in public circulation and to this day is referenced by industry leaders, cultural icons, and professional athletes who continue to transform the world.

But if people know what to do, why is it that success continues to elude so many? The reason lies in a lack of desire. Therefore, the first role of any leader hoping to develop others should be to get them excited about the infinite possibilities for the future and then comprehensively define what success looks like to them.

Since Mr. Carnegie recognized that his achievements were the result of his application of willpower and persistence, it is little wonder that he emphasized the importance of these qualities. These *self-acquired* qualities are just as effective in other forms of application as they are in the leadership of industry, as we are reminded when we consider the achievements of individuals such as Helen Keller.

Shortly after birth, Helen Keller became deaf, dumb, and blind—afflictions that left her no hope other than that which she provided by taking possession of her mind. Through willpower and persistence, she bridged her afflictions so effectively that she learned to speak, and by her sense of touch she learned to connect her mind with much more of the outside world than the average person with two good eyes ever sees.

With that same willpower, she:

- Acquired peace of mind far beyond the average;
- Acquired the hope necessary to sustain her in a life of darkness; and
- Educated herself sufficiently to enable her to perceive the nature of the world about her as well as or better than the average person with all faculties intact.

If we need evidence that self-discipline justifies all the time devoted to acquiring it, we have that evidence in Helen Keller's remarkable achievements. Yet her triumph over seemingly insurmountable obstacles is only slightly more dramatic than that of Thomas A. Edison.

Beginning his career at a very early age, after having been sent home from school after only three months with a message from his teachers to the effect that he had an "addled" mind and could not therefore be taught, Edison took charge of that "addled" mind and developed it into one of the great minds of the world. Those who knew him intimately are my authority for the belief that Edison's chief asset was his indomitable willpower.

He demonstrated time and again the truth of Mr. Carnegie's statement that willpower is irresistible. After having moved from place to place as a "tramp" telegraph operator, the great Edison took charge of his mind in earnest and began working on the invention that was destined to give him world recognition: the first successful incandescent electric lamp.

Most schoolchildren know the story of this invention, but hardly anyone has caught the full significance of the real power that carried the inventor triumphantly through more than ten thousand failures before the lamp was perfected. Here we find willpower and persistence allied in their highest form, but the possibilities of these qualities do not become apparent until we stop to consider that the average person becomes discouraged and quits anything they undertake after one or two failures, while a very great number do not wait for failure to overtake them but quit because of *anticipation* of failure. Others are so lacking in the understanding of willpower that they never quit—because they never begin!

EDITOR'S NOTE:

Hill touches on one of the fundamental problems with our antiquated educational system. We teach math, science, history, and more, all of which have their time and place for practical use. However, in an era when children are increasingly coddled to protect them from the world, perhaps the best lesson that school can teach any child is to enjoy the pursuit of increasing challenge in whatever field he or she chooses. In this manner, failure moves from possibility to probability, and this will enable the child to learn from the situation, reevaluate the course of action, and then advance, stronger and more resilient than ever before.

Exposure to failure toughens the spirit, strengthens the resolve, and helps us determine exactly what we want. When we're hungry for a solution, our chances of succeeding—in business and in life—are far greater because we recognize that every challenge has a solution. Better yet, through the pursuit of increasing challenge, we're ably equipped to find that solution.

In speaking of his failures in connection with his experiments with the incandescent lamp, Edison said that he went at the job with a determination to complete it, even if it required the remainder of his life. There is no such word as "impossible" in the vocabulary of such a person.

When Edison's friends referred to him as a "genius," he always smiled indulgently, then replied, "Genius is one percent inspiration, ninety-nine percent perspiration."

And this was no mere gesture of modesty on his part. He meant every word of it.

When Mr. Carnegie said that willpower is an irresistible force, he undoubtedly meant that it was irresistible when properly organized and directed to a definite end in a spirit of faith. Obviously, this definition emphasizes three principles of this philosophy as the seat of its stupendous power. Here, then, are the three principles that belong on the "must" list of all who aim for outstanding achievements.

Evidence of this "genius" definition can be found by studying the record of any person who achieves noteworthy success. Try as we might, we cannot escape the conclusion that the level of one's success is directly proportionate to the degree to which one organizes and intelligently applies these three principles:

1. Definiteness of purpose

2. Applied faith

3. Self-discipline over willpower

Mastery over these principles can be attained in one way and one way only, and that is by constantly *applying* the principles! Willpower responds only to motive persistently pursued. It becomes strong in precisely the same way that a muscle becomes strong: through systematic use. The same law that develops a strong muscle also develops strong willpower.

> **Mastery demands all of a person.**
> —Albert Einstein

Early in its history, Chicago was wiped out by a fire. A group of merchants stood looking over the ruins of what a few hours earlier had been their retail stores in the Loop section of the city. One by one, they shook their heads in discouragement before turning and walking away. Their hopes were gone, and they'd made up their minds to leave Chicago for a fresh start elsewhere.

One man did not turn away. He looked straight at the smoldering embers of his store, pointed his finger in that direction, and exclaimed, "On that very spot, I will build the world's greatest store!" His name was Marshall Field, and though he has long since passed, the physical evidence of his willpower remains on that very spot today. It is said that the spirit of the great merchant still manifests itself in the personality of every person who works in the renowned Field store.

During the American Civil War, a humble leader stood before an army of soldiers that had just been badly defeated. He had reason to be discouraged: the war was going against him, and he was acutely aware of the seemingly insurmountable difficulties that stood ahead. When one of his officers mentioned the bleak outlook, General Grant lifted his weary head skyward, closed his eyes, clenched his fists, and exclaimed, "I propose to fight it out along this line if it takes all summer!"

That one decision, backed by an indomitable will, determined the victory that preserved the union of the states.

One school of thought says, "Right makes might!" while another says, "Might makes right!" But I say, "Willpower makes might!" whether right or wrong, and I have the history of civilization to back me. Study extraordinary achievers wherever you find them and you will find evidence that willpower, organized and persistently applied, is the dominating factor of their success.

You will also find that successful people submit themselves to a stricter system of self-discipline, by far, than any that is forced upon them by circumstances outside of their control. They work when others are playing or sleeping, and they go the extra mile, and if need be, another, and still another, never stopping until they have contributed the utmost service of which they are capable.

Follow in their footsteps for a single day and you'll see that they need no taskmaster to drive them on:

- They may appreciate commendation, but they do not require it to sustain them.

- They listen to condemnation, but they do not fear it.

- They fail, like others, but failure only spurs them on to greater action.

- They encounter obstacles, as does everyone, but these they convert into stepping-stones on which they climb higher toward their chosen goal.

- They experience discouragements, just as others do, but they close the door tightly behind unpleasant experiences and transmute their disappointments into renewed energy with which they struggle ahead.

- When death strikes in their families, they bury the dead but not their indomitable wills.

- They seek the counsel of others, extract from it that which they can use, and reject the rest, although the whole world may criticize them for their judgment.

- They know they cannot control all the circumstances that affect their lives, but they do control their own state of mind by keeping it free from negative influences.

- They recognize their own emotions as a source of great power that must be organized and guided through self-discipline, but they place this power behind their efforts, not in front of them.

- They are tested by their own negative emotions, as are all people, but they keep the upper hand by making dutiful servants of these disastrous states of mind.

Let us remember that self-discipline enables us to do two important things, both of which are essential for outstanding achievement. First, we may completely control the negative emotions by transmuting their power into constructive effort. And second, we may stimulate the positive emotions and direct them to any desired end. Thus, by controlling both negative and positive emotions, we leave the faculty of reason—and that of imagination—free to function.

Control over the emotions is attained gradually by the development of good habits. Such habits should be formed in connection with the small, unimportant details of daily life. One by one, the six departments of the mind can be brought under complete self-discipline, but the start should be made by forming habits of control over the emotions since most people are victims of their emotions all through life. They are the servants, not the masters, of their emotions because they have never established definite, systematic habits of control.

All those who have decided to control the six departments of their own minds through a strict system of self-discipline should adopt and follow a definite plan designed to keep this purpose ever before them and at the same time develop daily habits of self-discipline. One student of this philosophy wrote a creed which he followed so successfully that I am presenting it here for the benefit of others who may wish to use it.

The creed was written, signed, and repeated out loud twice daily—once upon rising in the morning and again upon retiring at night. This gave the student the benefit of the principle of autosuggestion through which the creed's purpose was conveyed clearly to his subconscious mind, where it was acted upon automatically.

The creed was as follows:

MY DAILY CREED

Willpower:

Recognizing that willpower is the Supreme Court over all other departments of my mind, I will exercise it daily when I need the urge to action for any purpose, and I will form habits designed to bring willpower into action at least once daily.

Emotions:

Realizing that my emotions are both positive and negative, I will form daily habits that encourage the development of the positive emotions and aid me in converting the negative emotions into some form of useful effort.

Reason:

Recognizing that both the positive and negative emotions may be dangerous if they are not controlled and guided to desirable ends, I will submit all desires, aims, and purposes to my faculty of reason, and I will be guided by it in giving expression to these.

Imagination:

Recognizing the need for sound plans and ideas if I am to attain my desires, I will develop my imagination by calling upon it daily for help in the formation of all my plans.

Conscience:

Realizing that emotions often err in their overenthusiasm, and that the faculty of reason often is without the warmth of feeling necessary to enable me to mix justice and mercy with my judgments, I will encourage my conscience to guide me as to what is right and what is wrong, but I will never set aside the verdicts it may render.

Memory:

Realizing the value of an alert memory, I will encourage mine to become alert by taking care to impress it clearly with all thoughts I wish to recall promptly, and by associating those thoughts with related subjects that I call to mind frequently.

Subconscious:

Recognizing the influence of my subconscious mind over my willpower, I will take care to submit to it clear and definite pictures of my constructive desires, beginning always with definiteness of purpose and backed by a burning desire for its attainment.

(SIGNED) _____

Discipline is gained, little by little, through the formation of habits that we can control. Habits begin in the mind; therefore, a daily repetition of this creed will make one habit conscious in connection with the habits needed to develop and control the six departments of the mind.

Merely repeating the names of these departments has an important effect. It makes one conscious that these departments exist; that they are important; that they can be controlled by the formation of habits; and that the nature of one's habits determines one's success or failure in the matter of self-discipline.

When we recognize that our success and failure throughout our entire lives is largely a matter of control over our emotions, it is a fortunate day indeed! Yet before we can recognize this truth, we must recognize the existence and the nature of our emotions, an action many people *never* indulge in during their entire lifetime.

Peace begins with a smile.

—Mother Teresa

Anyone who recognizes the benefits of repeating the daily creed will see, almost from the day they began repeating the creed, that we have emotions—some that need encouraging by use and others that need control by diverting their power to constructive ends. All those who repeat this creed daily will find that it almost certainly forms habits that harmonize with the commitments it contains, both consciously and unconsciously.

Military strategists note that "an enemy recognized is an enemy half defeated." This also applies to the enemies that operate within one's own mind and to those existing outside the mind, and it especially applies to the enemies of negative emotion. Once these enemies are recognized, we begin almost automatically to set up habits to counteract them—habits that divert their power into constructive effort.

The same reasoning applies to the benefits of the mind, because "a benefit recognized is a benefit utilized." The seven positive emotions are beneficial, but only if they are organized and controlled through strict self-discipline. If they are not so controlled, they may be just as dangerous as any of the seven negative emotions. Let's look at the emotions again.

The Seven Positive Emotions:	The Seven Negative Emotions:
1. Love	1. Fear
2. Sex	2. Jealousy
3. Hope	3. Hatred
4. Faith	4. Revenge
5. Enthusiasm	5. Greed
6. Loyalty	6. Anger
7. Desire	7. Superstition

For example, faith becomes helpful only when it is expressed through organized action toward constructive ends. Faith without action is useless—

it devolves into mere daydreaming and wishing. When definiteness of purpose is persistently followed, self-discipline stimulates faith.

A person should embark on a life of discipline by establishing habits that stimulate the use of willpower, because it is in the human ego—the seat of willpower—that all desires originate. It's where desire and faith pair, and if you stimulate one, you stimulate the other. Wherever strong desire is found, faith may be found at precisely the same intensity as that person's desire. Control and direct one through organized habits and you control and direct the other automatically. And this control is self-discipline in its highest form!

Great leaders in all walks of life have their desire and their faith so perfectly organized and controlled that they can call them into action anytime, anywhere. They will its attainment and quickly find themselves in possession of the faith necessary to acquire it, irrespective of the object in question, whether it be health, medical discovery, material possession, technological innovation, or any other definite end.

FINDING TODAY

By Agnes Martin

I've closed the door on yesterday
Its sorrows and mistakes;
And locked within its gloomy walls
Past failures and heartaches.

And now I throw the key away
To seek another room,
And furnish it with hope and smiles,
And every spring-time bloom.

No thought shall enter this abode
That has a hint of pain,
And every malice and distrust
Shall never therein reign.

I've locked the door on yesterday
And thrown the key away.
Tomorrow has no fears for me
Since I have found today.

Alice Marble is an example of someone who applied self-discipline and other principles of this philosophy and ended up becoming a world champion tennis player. Her remarkable story began in San Francisco, when, at the age of seventeen, Marble took the first step toward the self-discipline that was destined to bring her world fame by adopting as her definite major purpose the determination to become a world champion tennis player.

Self-discipline was not handed to her on a silver platter. Before she attained it, she was forced to test her mettle in ways that would have defeated the average person. At the outset of her career, Marble attracted the attention of Eleanor Tennant, the famous tennis coach, who came out to Golden Gate Park to watch her play.

It was a great day for the would-be world champion.

When the game was over, she ran anxiously to Tennant, hoping to receive her approval and hearty applause, but the famous coach gazed at her for a few moments in utter silence before deciding to throw a hurdle in her way that would reveal, definitively, whether the young aspirant had what it took to achieve her goal.

"So, you wish to become a world champion?" Tennant queried. "That's a mighty big order, but a most admirable ambition. Do you realize the hard work ahead of you? Are you prepared for the heartaches and disappointments that your ambition will involve? Are you willing to sacrifice every joy that young girls generally prize so highly at your age in order to give yourself the self-discipline that a world championship demands?"

"Yes!" Alice exclaimed. "I am willing to give up everything that is necessary, and I shall do so willingly."

Tennant noticed an indescribable quality in the young woman's resolute words and sparkling eyes and consented to become her coach.

"Remember, Alice," Tennant admonished, "that you can make the grade if you care enough. Ambitions can be made realities if diligently pursued with work, patience, and determination, but self-discipline must be your watchword."

During the four months that followed, Marble learned the true meaning of self-discipline. At times, she complained that her coach treated her like a piece of machinery rather than a human being, but she fed off Tennant's confidence. When Alice thought she had played a good game, her coach only shook her head and said, "Not good enough yet."

Finally, the day arrived when Tennant, skilled psychologist that she was, decided to put her student strictly on her own. As coach and student parted, Tennant said, "Alice, forget that you ever had a lesson. You are naturally an athlete and a tennis player. Play naturally and you will become great. Your only stumbling block will be mental and physical laziness. A tennis champion is one who wins when she is not playing her best. Winning is easy when the going is smooth. When the going is tough, you must be a great fighter to win."

Then came Alice's big opportunity: she was selected in an elite squad to be sent to Europe. Before its departure, the team was wined and dined, first in New York, then again on the boat, and again after arriving in Paris. Here is where the young star's self-discipline had its first real test—a test that so many would-be stars do not survive, since one's first success often plays havoc with one's self-discipline. At long last, she had been recognized, and her reaction to that recognition would reveal whether she was champion material.

Marble played her first match on center court at Roland Garros, against Madame Henrotin. The American knew this tournament would define her, so she prepared diligently to have herself in an optimal state both physically and mentally before putting everything she had into the match.
During the match, the exertion became too much, and Marble collapsed.

When she awoke, Marble found herself a patient at the American Hospital in Paris. This appeared to be a glimpse of the price her distinguished coach had told her she might have to pay for a championship. Mental agony and physical pain combined in what seemed to be a conspiracy to test her mettle.

Shortly after, the doctor informed her that she had pleurisy and would never play tennis again.

What a good excuse to quit! Many would have grabbed it freely, but Marble's desires outweighed whatever opinions she would hear along the way, no matter how qualified. The doctor could make any diagnosis he wished, but she would play tennis again. Despite being in a crippled state, Marble found her dream was stronger than ever—a decision born of self-discipline. Marble had been preparing in her mind for such an emergency for months, and she was ready to meet it without quitting.

Confined to a wheelchair, Marble returned to the US. A familiar face met her at the dock in New York, and soon Marble and Tennant were on their way to California.

"Her cheerfulness en route to California," said Marble of her mentor, "made me realize that she was sharing my misery and expecting me to regain my health!"

Leading doctors in Paris, New York, Los Angeles, and San Francisco all had the same story to tell. "You will be a semi-invalid, and you will never play tennis again," they solemnly warned Marble.

After six months of receiving hopeless counsel, Marble took her case in her own hands. She began in earnest to do something for herself that no doctor could do, something that no medicine could accomplish. Calling in Tennant, she unburdened herself of her decision in no uncertain terms. Marble proclaimed that she was through with doctors and their opinions that would have her confined to a sickbed for the rest of her life.

The decision pleased Tennant. It was this decision for which she had been waiting, but she knew well enough that it was a decision that had to come from Alice herself. Here again, self-discipline came to the rescue. The hopelessness was supplanted by a "will to win," which worked a miracle.

Marble instructed Tennant to pack her clothes and get ready to leave the hospital at once. It was 9:00 P.M., but that made no difference—she was leaving immediately. The doctors could learn about her decision in due time, but the decision was final, and no one could change it.

Let's pause our story to quickly reflect upon self-discipline. Alice Marble had come to the turning point of her career: she could accept the defeat predicted by medical experts, or she could activate her willpower and demand that it restore her to health. Everything depended on this battle in her own mind. Marble had pledged to make whatever sacrifices were necessary to become a world champion. That was her motive for putting up a fight.

Leaving the hospital that eventful night, Marble said, "From now on, I will whip this health problem by myself. Poor health is a rich person's luxury and I can't afford it, for I have a job to do and I'm going to do it. I figure that there are two me's—the strong and the weak. From now on you will see the strong me, because I shall leave the weak me here in the hospital."

As she walked to the waiting vehicle, her knees shook but her mind was firm. The decision was made, of her own volition, and she would defend it with everything she had. Marble knew right then what Carnegie and other great achievers knew: that self-discipline gives one the courage to make life-changing decisions and provides the willpower to carry them out. Her body remained the same, but her mind was more determined than ever.

Arriving home, Marble diligently laid out a plan to become world champion, one that required her to start at the humblest of beginnings. Her plan called for a walk each day, beginning with a block or two and increasing daily until she would walk at least three miles. After that, she would add jumping rope to strengthen her legs. To keep herself in the right mental attitude, she would sing each day.

Step by step, Marble would send over to her subconscious mind a clear picture of the athlete who had a very clear destiny. Importantly, she never allowed the idea to leave her mind. With every bound, she reviewed her major purpose. With every skip, she reinforced that purpose. As the days passed, her body grew stronger, slowly but surely.

Then Marble made some revisions. Having gained temporary victory over her body, she began working on a systematic plan for extending the control over her mental faculties too. She asked Tennant's permission to take over the management of their home, which meant she had to supervise the maid's work, order and plan meals, make appointments, type letters, pay bills, and more. Being so busy with constructive work left no time for brooding, giving Marble the opportunity to close the door tightly between herself and her past disappointments.

A few months later, a curious Marble arranged an appointment with a doctor, who, delighted by his patient's progress, cleared her to play tennis again.

Later that year, after only four months of preparation, Alice Marble won the national championship. In 1939, she was ranked number one in the world. Reflecting on the roller-coaster journey, she said, "If you care, and if you have an objective in life and are willing to work, there are no obstacles that cannot be hurdled."

There is the element to be developed: definiteness of purpose, backed by a motive! Without this, no one may hope to gain self-discipline. With it, self-discipline is easily attainable.

We must also credit another important principle that helped along this extraordinary journey: the power of the mastermind. It was Marble's long-term bond with her coach, Eleanor Tennant, that gave her the courage she needed to take possession of her own mind. Battles like the one the tennis duo faced are even more difficult when faced alone.

After her recovery, Marble said, "My illness was a blessing in disguise because I am now better equipped to meet life and its daily obstacles; better equipped, perhaps, than one who has not had to battle for health and has not experienced the retarding of objectives."

Yes, it is helpful for us to be tested from time to time! It seems that nature has so planned things that no one is ever allowed to triumph in connection with their major purpose in life without undergoing some form of severe test of their resolve. Most people who achieve outstanding success are compelled to undergo many such tests, but each test brings one out stronger and more courageous if one accepts the tests with the right mental attitude.

> *Only through experience of trial and suffering can the soul be strengthened, ambition inspired, and success achieved.*
>
> —Helen Keller

"It is apparent," said Marble, "that any success which I have been fortunate enough to enjoy has come largely as the result of two factors: first, the will to win; and second, the support of my efforts contributed by my friend, coach, and companion, Eleanor Tennant. By far the most valuable contribution that she has made to my life has not been in the mechanical art of playing tennis, though that is important, but in the creation and encouragement in me of the will to win."

In the last three words you have the secret of her success!

Alice Marble won because she had the *will to win*. That will grew as a result of her self-discipline, her mastery over her emotions, her definiteness of purpose, and her determination to take possession of her own mind and become her own master.

"There is really very little difference between the champion and the also-ran," Marble explained. "The difference usually appears in the pinches, when the extra ounce of energy, the minutest difference in relentless determination spells victory or defeat. There is really very little mechanical difference in the tennis efficiency of the leading twenty players. That is true in other walks of life as well as in tennis. I could name hundreds of my fellow contestants who had an abundance of ability, the best of training, alert minds, but lacked the little spark—the champion's heart—when the showdown came. They were lacking only in the indomitable will to win."

Ability, experience, and education are of little value if you fail to discipline yourself with the will to win. This is the turning point that determines, more than all else, what you get from life.

EDITOR'S NOTE:

This DNA is replicated in every champion, former and future, in every endeavor.

To illustrate this lesson, let's step back to 1953, when two mountaineers began to climb Mount Everest, the tallest peak on earth. Never before had Everest been summitted. Treacherous geography, freezing temperatures, and extreme altitude all added immeasurable complexity while excitement about the endeavor reached fever pitch in the climbing community.

Seven weeks into their grueling expedition, the courageous pair—New Zealander Edmund Hillary and Nepali-Indian Tenzing Norgay—made it to the top in an athletic feat that would be etched in history for its bravery, skill, and seeming impossibility.

After such an extraordinary achievement, to what would the revered mountaineers credit their success? Surely preparation, physical prowess, and maybe even a dash of dumb luck? Wrong. They attributed it to mental fortitude: the will to win. "It is not the mountain we conquer," Sir Edmund Hillary stated, "but ourselves."

Boxing icon Muhammad Ali shared a similar viewpoint. "Champions aren't made in gyms," Ali said. "Champions are made from something they have deep inside them—a desire, a dream, a vision. They have to have the skill, and the will. But the will must be stronger than the skill."

On the omnipresence of willpower that forges destructive habits just as often as productive habits, big-wave pioneer surfer Laird Hamilton warns, "Make sure your worst enemy is not living between your own two ears."

Accordingly, Serena Williams notes, "I don't like to lose—at anything. Yet I've grown most, not from victories, but setbacks. If winning is God's reward, then losing is how he teaches us."

Cometh the hour, cometh the champion.

Careful scrutiny of all great leaders reveals that every one of them was inspired by the will to win. In addition, before they arrived, they were repeatedly tested by some sort of obstacle that tried their mettle.

Benjamin Disraeli, who many believe to be the greatest prime minister in the history of the United Kingdom, attained that high station through the sheer power of his will to win. He began his career as an author, but he was not highly successful in this field. He published a dozen books, but none of them made any great impression on the public. Failing as an author, he accepted his defeat as a challenge and entered politics with his mind definitely set upon becoming prime minister.

In 1837, he became the member of Parliament from Maidstone, but his first speech in Parliament is universally regarded as having been an outright failure. Again he accepted defeat as a challenge to make an even greater effort and to pursue higher ambitions. Fighting with never a thought of giving up, he became the leader of the House of Commons by 1858, later becoming the chancellor of exchequer, and by 1868 the prime minister and the most powerful man in the British Empire.

Here Disraeli met with overwhelming opposition that resulted in his resignation. Yet far from accepting his temporary failure as permanent defeat, the determined statesman staged a comeback and was elected prime minister a second time. During this second term, he became a great builder of the vast British Empire, extending its influence in many directions. However, perhaps Disraeli's greatest achievement was the building of the Suez Canal, a feat that was destined to give the British Empire unprecedented economic advantages.

The keynote of his career was *self-discipline*. Summarizing his achievements in one short sentence, Disraeli said, "The secret of success is constancy to purpose."

Theodore Roosevelt is another example of what can happen when one is motivated by the will to win. During his early youth, Roosevelt was seriously handicapped by chronic asthma and weak eyes. His friends despaired of his ever regaining his health, but Roosevelt did not share their view. He went West, joined a group of hard-hitting outdoor workers, and placed himself under a definite system of self-discipline through which he built a strong body. The doctors said he couldn't do it, but he said he could, and he did!

In the battle to regain his health, Roosevelt acquired such perfect discipline over his mind that he returned to the East Coast, entered politics, and strove forward until his will to win made him the president of the United States. Those who knew him best have said that his outstanding quality was a will that refused to accept defeat as anything more than a stepping-stone.

Beyond this, Roosevelt had no ability, education, or experience superior to that of those around him, of whom the public heard nothing.

While he was president, some army officials complained about an order he had given the army to keep physically fit. To show that he knew what he was talking about, Roosevelt rode horseback a hundred miles over rough roads in Virginia. He kept Washington, DC, constantly amused by his habit of exhausting the Secret Service personnel who were assigned to follow him for protection when he went hiking. On one occasion, the president even outdistanced the Secret Service so greatly that he lost them completely in Rock Creek Park.

Behind all this physical action was an active mind that was determined not to be handicapped by physical weakness, and that mental activity reflected itself throughout Roosevelt's administration. When the mind says, "Go forward," the physical body responds to the command, thereby proving that Andrew Carnegie was right when he said that "our only limitations are those we set up in our own minds."

Personal power is wrapped up in the will to win! The will to win is acquired only through self-discipline—it is the result of intentionally formed habits that control the six departments of the mind. Every habit plays a part in self-discipline no matter how insignificant the habit or what the cause of its adoption. Remember, too, that habits are more easily formed if they are based on alluring motives and backed by definiteness of purpose.

Nobody can hurt me without my permission.
—Mahatma Gandhi

From the day of his birth, Robert Louis Stevenson was a delicate youth. His health prevented him from working steadily at his studies until he was seventeen years old. At twenty-three, his health became so poor that his physicians sent him away in hopes that he would get better.

In France, Stevenson met the woman with whom he fell in love. Stevenson's love for her was so great that he began to write, and although his physical body was scarcely strong enough to enable him to carry on, he managed to enrich the whole world with his writings, now universally accepted as masterpieces. His motivating force was love. That same motive has given wings to thoughts of many others who have, like Robert Louis Stevenson, made the world richer for having lived. Without this motive, Stevenson doubtless would have died without making his contribution of the love and letters that have inspired so many. Stevenson transmuted his love for the woman of his choice into literary works that have made him immortal.

In this manner, he expressed his self-discipline in actions that made the whole world richer, which reminds us that there can be no self-discipline without some form of appropriate action. Mere hoping and wishing does not, and cannot, give one self-discipline. Self-discipline begins with a motive, backed by definiteness of purpose, expressed through definite habits that place the six departments of the mind under control.

In a similar manner, Charles Dickens converted a love tragedy into literary works that have enriched the world. Instead of going down under the blow of disappointment from his first love, he focused on writing as an intensely creative outlet. This purposeful action closed the door behind an experience that many would have used as an excuse for permanent defeat. Through his self-discipline, Dickens converted his greatest sorrow into his greatest asset.

There is one unbeatable rule for the mastery of sorrow and disappointment, and that is that emotional upheavals must be transmuted through definitely planned work. It is a rule that has no equal! But it requires self-discipline of the highest order. Along the way, all sorrows and disappointments can be made to serve rather than destroy.

EDITOR'S NOTE:

Napoleon Hill fans will recall one of his most renowned quotes, inspired by his tutelage under Carnegie: "Every adversity, every failure, every heartache, carries with it the seed of an equal or greater benefit." Understanding that has catapulted some of the most successful people who ever lived to success.

We all know people who after a marriage breakdown, business hardship, or other personal misfortune go through life with an ever-growing chip on their shoulders. However, the action of complaining about how they were wronged is what stymies the opportunity for a much greater good to enter their life at a later date, one that would finally allow them to close the door on the past. The same energy used to complain about the past and what they don't have could be redirected toward creating favorable circumstances in the present.

That energy is what propelled Barbara Corcoran, after her boyfriend and business partner left her for her secretary, to strengthen her resolve and build a real estate empire. Today, she is one of the world's most recognizable entrepreneurs, having sold The Corcoran Group for $66 million, appeared as the host of the hit television show *Shark Tank*, and partnered with dozens of start-ups that are disrupting industries all over the world.

We all face adversity, but make no mistake—the way an individual responds to adversity when it inevitably strikes is what separates an ordinary person from an extraordinary achiever.

The rule of being able to convert emotional pain into useful action also applies to the habits of intemperance through which so many defeat themselves. Alcoholism, for example, which has assumed the proportions of a national tragedy in the US, can be mastered only by self-discipline backed by sheer willpower. Medicinal cures are likely to be useless unless they are accompanied by a will to master the evil. The idea that people can drown their sorrows in alcohol is tragically disappointing. We must educate society until everyone understands that sorrows can be drowned only by transmuting them into some form of useful action.

When people become busy with work they like to do, in such a way that they devote all their time to that work, they form habits that leave no place for thoughts of discouragement.

Those who are thoroughly self-disciplined never run away from anything they fear. Instead, they drop the object of their fear into the open, transmute their fear into faith, and not only subdue or annihilate the object of their fear but gain great mental strength in the process. Every time we use our willpower, we add something to its strength.

Become familiar, by all means, with that word "transmutation"! It is the key that unlocks the door to the solution of almost all of life's problems. To master any fear, disappointment, or worry, transmute it into some form of intense activity that keeps your mind so busily occupied that it forms new thoughts and habits associated with self-confidence, faith, hope, and courage.

It is futile to attempt to run away from disagreeable experiences, no matter where we go. It is still more futile to try to drown them with intoxicants, since that only weakens willpower without eliminating the thing we are trying to drown! The attempt to drown troubles with liquor or drugs is as foolish as trying to put out a fire by throwing gasoline on it and just as dangerous.

Willpower, expressed in action, is the only known cure for fear and worry. Willpower supplants defeatism with courage. There has never been a great athlete who did not owe their achievements to their own will to win.

> *Yesterday I was clever, so I wanted to change the world. Today*
> *I am wise, so I am changing myself.*
> —Rumi

Boxer Gene Tunney wrested the world heavyweight title from legendary champion Jack Dempsey through sheer application of his will to win and not by his superior physical strength. It is generally conceded that Dempsey was, far and away, the strongest "mauler," but Tunney had him bettered in the use of mindpower. One year later, they met for a rematch, from which Tunney again emerged victorious. After the bout, Dempsey raised Tunney's arm and said, "You were best. You fought a smart fight, kid."

Alice Marble's story of triumph over physical illness in her rise to tennis stardom is replete with evidence demonstrating that the secret of her success was her will to win. She emphasizes this fact in every detail of her story. Study it and you will observe the precise moment when the turning point in her career was experienced: it was of course when she reached a decision, in her own mind, to leave the hospital and take ownership of her destiny.

There are hundreds of thousands of true champions in all walks of life who, like those mentioned here, have crowned themselves with victory via their will to win. They attained their championship by first recognizing their weaknesses and then, by the power of their will to win, transmuting those weaknesses into strength. There is no defeat for those who acquire the art of converting their weaknesses into strength, and there is plenty of evidence that such conversions can be made whether the weakness is mental or physical. It is a matter of *self-discipline*.

No problem is too great for willpower when that power has been brought under control through self-discipline and has been directed to a definite end.

If we can gain control over our strongest emotions through our own will-power, think what we might do in directing our lesser emotions. When we have gained control over these emotions and have learned how to transmute these great driving forces into organized effort in connection with our chosen occupation, we will have no difficulty in likewise converting our negative emotions into useful service.

Some who read this chapter will be able to go back into their memories and recall experiences of unrequited love. Only those who have passed through such an experience will be impressed by our statement that this is the sort of test that reaches deeply into the human soul and brings one face-to-face with that "other self" which one seldom meets under the ordinary experiences of life.

Sometimes one survives the test through sheer willpower and comes out from under it a bigger, nobler, and stronger person, but this calls for self-discipline that is not required under any other life circumstances.

Failures in business, the loss of money, the loss of a position that one values highly, make heavy demands upon one's reserves of willpower, but these are slight indeed in comparison with the demands made through the loss of a great love. But the compensation for such a loss consists in the spiritual forces that are tapped and made available provided one has prepared oneself through self-discipline to transmute wounded emotions into some form of useful service. The transmutation takes place through willpower, and nothing else.

Mentally and physically, through the tragedies of life or otherwise, people who have loved deeply may become separated, but the spiritual oneness created by their alliance can never be broken. The Creator arranged it so! For what purpose? It is neither our privilege nor our right to know. But it is both our right and our duty to transmute the spiritual power of such an alliance into useful activity that if we use it can lift us to great heights of understanding and wisdom.

Therefore, in the adversity of unsatisfied love, we may find the seed of an equivalent advantage that we would not otherwise discover. However, the advantage is only potential until self-discipline gives us the willpower to make the advantage real. There is but one safe remedy for a disrupted or unsatisfied love, and that is *transmutation* of this emotion into other constructive action.

We all have problems over which we have no control, and exercising control over our mental reactions to our problems is difficult. We cannot control other people's actions toward us, but we can control our mental reactions to those actions.

We cannot eliminate our feelings whether they are positive or negative, but we can harness these feelings and transmute them into some form of intense action of a beneficial nature.

We cannot always avoid defeat, and sometimes we cannot avoid temporary failure, but we can so organize the feeling growing out of such experiences that it may be transmuted into an equivalent advantage.

Understand this truth and you will have a working knowledge of what Andrew Carnegie meant when he said, "Every adversity carries with it the seed of an equivalent advantage." In that statement, he expressed one of the most profound of all truths, but it is of little benefit to any except those who have so thoroughly disciplined themselves that they can place their emotions under the direction of willpower.

Life is so filled with tragedy and disappointments that no one may be truly happy without acquiring a working knowledge of this emotional energy transmutation principle. It is the master key to all great achievements. With it, one may both open the doors to opportunity and lock the doors that shut out worry, despair, discouragement, fear, and all other unpleasantness.

Do not leave this chapter until you have appropriated this master key and made it your own property. With this key in your possession, the six departments of your mind will be at your service when you need them.

With its help, every stray thought that makes its way to your mind may be harnessed and put to work. Every worry can be converted into a priceless asset. Envy, greed, anger, and superstition can be transmuted to yield dividends. Enemies can be made to serve as benefactors who serve profitably without being on your payroll.

And remember, although we have repeated this thought in various ways, embracing definiteness of purpose persistently backed by work is the best method of transmuting emotions. There is no known substitute for work. There is no blessing that equals work. There is no remedy for worry and discouragement that equals it. But if work is to be a blessing, it must be useful effort applied in a positive mental attitude.

There is but one thing that can take the place of work, and that is failure. One might say, conversely, that nothing can take the place of failure except work. The two make poor bedfellows. Where one exists, the other cannot. We discovered, during the Great Depression, that there is one thing that is worse than being forced to work: it is being forced *not* to work. Work is the very foundation of self-discipline provided it is performed in the spirit of a sincere desire to be useful.

Work is the beginning of all material riches. It is the only thing a penniless individual has to give in return for money. The very fact that the whole universe is so planned and maintained that every living thing is forced to work or perish is profoundly significant. It is the medium of major importance through which we may go the extra mile in all forms of self-promotion. It is the only medium with which to drown sorrows and disappointments without damaging ourselves.

Work confers its greatest blessings upon those who perform it willingly. Its super blessings go only to those who perform it in a spirit of enthusiasm by

Going the Extra Mile. Work is a drudge or a pleasure according to the motive that inspires it. I have heard experienced people say that the greatest of all pleasures is that which one experiences in a labor of love, where one engages in labor based upon the pride of achievement, or in serving one's friends and loved ones.

> *No one can give orders intelligently until they learn how to take orders gracefully and to carry them out efficiently.*
> —Andrew Carnegie

No labor of this sort is ever performed without compensation. If the compensation does not come in a material form, it comes in personal satisfaction that cannot be measured in material terms. It might otherwise come in strengthened character, greater self-discipline, or a better understanding of one's associates.

If I seem to be overstressing the importance of work, be assured it is because I recognize that a lack of willingness to work is one of the greatest evils of the times in which we live. The people of the US have been cursed by some strange influence that has caused millions of men and women to demand something for nothing.

This influence has had the effect of spreading the spirit of defeatism. It is destroying the spirit of personal initiative that made this the richest and freest country of the world. It has caused great numbers of people to supplant the traditional American spirit of self-determination with a willingness to accept public charity—nay, to *demand* public charity! The sign is an unhealthy one.

EDITOR'S NOTE:

This passage reminds me of the roller-coaster journey the renowned educator Dr. Dennis Kimbro was on before releasing *Think and Grow Rich: A Black Choice*. Kimbro was feeling the pressure on all fronts: he lacked inspiration for the manuscript, felt he'd failed as a provider for his young family, and battled to stay positive under the pressure.

One day, Kimbro broke down beneath the unrelenting burden. With nowhere else to turn, he forwent professional courtesy and unloaded to financial titan Arthur George Gaston halfway through their interview. Gaston opined in no uncertain terms that the acceptable person who will rise to the ranks of champion in any field "must first be tested in the furnace of adversity." Even more pointedly, he told Kimbro that if he wasn't ready for success, he should step aside for the person who was.

Gaston's direct advice struck Kimbro like a bolt of lightning. Reframing his seemingly dire situation, the thirty-nine-year-old returned to his home in Atlanta, where his stalling manuscript served as an outlet for his renewed enthusiasm. Upon completing it, Kimbro posted the manuscript to The Napoleon Hill Foundation, which at the time was headquartered in Chicago, confident that this time his efforts would be enough but nonetheless nervous in anticipation.

Soon afterward, Kimbro was flown to Chicago to attend a board meeting with the Foundation. As he walked in, he noticed that everyone seated around the table held a copy of his book in front of him or her.

Acclaimed insurance magnate W. Clement Stone stood, walked over, and asked, "Young man, what have you learned about success and achievement?"

"Well, at the counter of success, there are no bargains," Kimbro responded. "You must pay the price in advance, and in full."

In his darkest moments, Dr. Dennis Kimbro had been shown the light that would accompany him to success for the rest of his life.

A willingness to accept something for nothing, not to mention the outright demand for it, is just the opposite of self-discipline. Those who have their own mind under control are not only willing to give something of value for everything they receive, but they demand this privilege for themselves and give more than is required of them.

Those who accept something for nothing are at the mercy of everyone who wishes to exploit them. Personal freedom and independence belong only to those who, by their own efforts, have developed their mind to where it serves their needs, with or without the consent of others. There is no dependable form of individual independence except that which a person acquires through their own willpower.

If you fail to share the thought I am here emphasizing, I suggest that you take a trip to the nearest shelter and observe those who, because of circumstances over which they have no control, are forced to accept public charity. Study the faces of those unfortunates, observe their lack of enthusiasm, notice the spirit of hopelessness in which they move, and then you will understand why I say that the greatest of all blessings is that which belongs to the person who has the privilege of converting their own mindpower into whatever material and spiritual values they desire.

Asylums and shelters are institutions of mercy. A civilized world makes their maintenance necessary, but we have never yet seen a person who would prefer this sort of mercy to the freedom that most people provide for themselves through the exercise of their personal initiative. And we suspect that there are few people who would not prefer living their own lives in the humblest log hut to accepting public charity, even if doing so enabled them to live in the finest mansion.

Freedom, independence, and economic security are the results of personal initiative based on self-discipline. In no other way may these universal desires of humankind be attained. When self-discipline is slackened, personal freedom goes with it in proportion.

Occasionally, someone complains that in presenting this philosophy I have overemphasized the application of the philosophy as a means of procuring the *material* needs of life. Some have complained that I should have stressed the spiritual values of the philosophy more forcefully. My only reply is to cite for my critics the fact that spiritual values and poverty make poor bedfellows. Spiritual values belong to people who have attained personal freedom through self-discipline—not to those who, for any reason, are forced to accept charity.

I suspect that if you consulted people who are out of a job and have no source of income and tried to interest them in spiritual values, they would tell you quickly enough that their greatest concern is acquiring a source of income through which they may become independent.

In summary, let us remember that the greatest benefit of self-discipline is that which we may obtain by transmuting emotions (both negative and positive) into whatever ends we wish to attain. Remember, too, that all mind power is useful if it is brought under strict self-discipline and directed to definite ends. Turn your attention to this subject of transmutation and master it. You may then become the master of many circumstances over which you would otherwise have no control.

Do not expect to become a master at transmutation the first time you try—the emotions cannot be managed until they have been conquered. Conquering is a matter of habit. Keep on trying and never yield an inch of ground once you have gained it.

> *Thinking, education, knowledge, native ability—*
> *these are nothing but empty words unless*
> *they are translated into action.*
> —Napoleon Hill

The starting point is definiteness of purpose, backed by adequate motive. You can manage any of your emotions if your motive for doing so is strong enough. Without a definite purpose supported by a strong motive, you will make no headway in gaining control over your emotions.

And do not forget that a purpose without action will avail you nothing. The greatest of all methods of gaining control over our emotions is that of enthusiastic endeavor in connection with work into which we may throw our heart and soul.

Self-discipline is the master key to taking the action that converts your motive and purpose into success.

PART 2

LEARNING FROM DEFEAT: EVERY ADVERSITY CARRIES WITH IT THE SEED OF AN EQUIVALENT BENEFIT

The power with which we think is mental dynamite, and it can be organized and used constructively for the attainment of definite ends. If it is not organized and used through controlled habits, it may become a mental explosive that will blast one's hopes of achievement and lead to inevitable failure.

—Andrew Carnegie

LEARNING FROM DEFEAT:
Every adversity carries with it the seed of an equivalent benefit

△

Two important facts stand out boldly:

- The circumstances of life are such that everyone inevitably is overtaken by defeat, in many different ways, at one time or another; and
- Every adversity carries with it the seed of an equivalent benefit!

Search where you will, but you cannot find a single exception to either of these circumstances either in your own experience or that of others. The burden of this chapter, therefore, is to describe *how* defeat may be made to yield "the seed of an equivalent benefit," to explain how to convert it into a stepping-stone to greater achievement, and to contend that it is not necessary to accept defeat as a ready excuse for failure.

This chapter begins in the private study of Andrew Carnegie. Sit and learn what the great steel master thought of defeat.

HILL:

Mr. Carnegie, you have stated before in our interview that there are no limitations to mental capacity except those that we set up in our own mind, and you have explained this by saying that defeat can be converted into a priceless asset if one takes the right attitude toward it. Will you now explain what the right attitude is?

CARNEGIE:

First, let me say that the right attitude toward defeat is refusing to accept it as anything more than temporary, and this is an attitude that we can best maintain by developing willpower such that we look upon defeat as a challenge to test our resilience. That challenge should be accepted as a signal, deliberately hoisted, to inform us that our plans need mending.

Defeat should be looked upon in precisely the same manner as the unpleasant experience of physical pain. Physical pain is nature's way of informing us that something needs attention and correction. Pain, therefore, may be a blessing and not a curse!

The same is true of the mental anguish we experience when overtaken by defeat. The feeling, as unpleasant as it may be, is nevertheless beneficial in that it serves as a signal to stop us from going in the wrong direction.

HILL:

I see your logic, but defeat sometimes is so definite and severe that it has the effect of destroying our initiative and self-reliance. What is to be done in such a circumstance?

CARNEGIE:

Here is where the principle of self-discipline comes to our rescue. Well-disciplined people allow nothing to destroy their self-belief and permit nothing to stop them from rearranging their plans and moving ahead when they are defeated. You see, they change their plans if they need changing, but they don't change their purpose.

HILL:

Defeat, I assume, should be accepted as a sort of mental tonic that can serve as a means of stimulating our willpower. Is that the idea?

CARNEGIE:

You've stated it correctly. Every negative emotion can be transmuted into a constructive power and used for the attainment of desirable ends. Self-discipline enables us to change unpleasant emotions into a driving power, and every time this is done, it helps to develop our willpower.

You must remember, also, that the subconscious mind accepts and acts upon our "mental attitude." If defeat is accepted as permanent instead of being regarded as a mere stimulant to taking greater action, the subconscious mind acts accordingly and makes it permanent. Now do you see how important it is that we form the habit of searching for the good there is to be found in *every* form of defeat? This procedure becomes the finest sort of training of willpower and serves at the same time to bring the subconscious mind into action on one's behalf.

> **No matter how often defeated,**
> **you are born to victory.**
> —Ralph Waldo Emerson

HILL:

Yes, of course! You mean that the subconscious mind carries out our mental attitude to its logical conclusion regardless of the nature of the circumstance that brings it into action?

CARNEGIE:

Yes, but you have hardly stated the matter fully. The subconscious mind responds always to the dominating thoughts in our mind. Moreover, it gets into the habit of acting quickly on the thoughts that are repeated most often. For example, if we fall into the habit of accepting defeat as negative, the subconscious mind makes the same mistake and forms similar habits.

Our mental attitude toward defeat eventually becomes a habit, and this is one habit that must be controlled if we are to make defeat an asset instead of a liability. You have no doubt seen people who, by their immediate reactions, seem to automatically accept defeat and who thus become confirmed pessimists.

HILL:

Yes, I see what you mean. The "seed of an equivalent benefit" that is to be found in every adversity consists of the opportunity we have to use the experience to develop our willpower by accepting it as a mental stimulant to undertake greater action. Is that your idea, Mr. Carnegie?

CARNEGIE:

That states the idea in part, but you omitted saying that by accepting defeat with a positive mental attitude we thereby influence the subconscious mind to form the habit of doing the same thing. In time, this habit becomes permanent, after which the subconscious mind will be reluctant to accept any experience with anything other than a positive attitude.

In other words, the subconscious mind can be trained to convert all negative experiences into an inspirational urge to greater effort. Now, that is the point I wish to emphasize.

EDITOR'S NOTE:

Former US Navy SEAL commander Jocko Willink used a simple response to help reframe the mindset of those under his command. Whenever one of them would vent to him about an injury, adversity, or a challenging circumstance, Willink would respond, "Good!"

"When things are going bad," Willink explained on his podcast, "there's always going to be some good that comes from it." One tiny word helped reveal the absolute truth that every problem is simply an opportunity to figure out a solution, which is where real growth occurs. The more solutions you have at your disposal, the more likely you are to achieve mission success, whether on the battlefield or in the boardroom.

"If you can say the word 'good,' it means you're still alive," offered Willink about his management style. "It means you're still breathing. And if you're still breathing, then you've still got some fight left in you."

When faced with your next problem, do not give in to frustration. Instead, consider it an inspirational indication that it's time to increase your effort.

HILL:

Apparently there is no escape from the law that fastens habits upon one. If I understand you correctly, Mr. Carnegie, failure can become a habit.

CARNEGIE:

Not only can failure become a habit, but the same thing applies to poverty, worry, and pessimism of every nature. Any state of mind, whether positive or negative, becomes a habit the moment it begins to dominate the mind.

HILL:

I never thought of poverty as being a habit.

CARNEGIE:

Well, you must think again, because it is a habit! When anyone accepts the condition of poverty, that state of mind becomes a habit, and poor that person is and remains.

HILL:

What do you mean by "accepting poverty"? How do we signify acceptance of a condition as undesirable as poverty in a country like ours, where there is an abundance of riches of every nature?

CARNEGIE:

We accept poverty by neglecting to create a plan to acquire wealth. Our act may be, as it usually is, entirely negative, consisting of nothing but the lack of a definite purpose. We may not be conscious of this acceptance, but the result is the same. The subconscious mind acts on our dominating mental attitude.

> *Failure is so important. We speak about success all the time,*
> *but it is the ability to resist failure or use failure*
> *that often leads to greater success.*
> *I've met people who don't want to try for fear of failing.*
> —J. K. Rowling

HILL:

And accordingly, success is a habit?

CARNEGIE:

Now you are getting the idea! Of course success is a habit. It is a habit that we form by adopting a definite major aim, laying out a plan for the attainment of that aim, and working the plan for all we are worth. Beyond that, the subconscious mind comes to our rescue and helps by inspiring us with ideas through which the object of our aims may be acquired.

HILL:

It is true, then, that those who are born in an environment of poverty, where they see nothing but poverty, hear nothing talked of but poverty, and associate daily with those who have accepted poverty, have "two strikes" on them to begin with?

CARNEGIE:

That's precisely right, but do not assume that there is nothing one can do about such a circumstance! For it is a well-established fact that most of the successful people of America began under just such a condition as you have described.

HILL:

Well, what is one going to do to master a condition that brings most children into the world in an environment of poverty in a country like ours, where there is plenty for everyone? Is there not a responsibility resting upon someone to help correct such a condition? Are helpless children to be left to their own fates merely because they were born into the wrong environment?

CARNEGIE:

Now you are getting at the very heart of what I had in mind when I gave you the job of organizing this achievement philosophy, and I am happy to see you becoming fired with enthusiasm in connection with this vital subject. What I propose to do about poverty I am doing right now by preparing you to help people master poverty.

As I have already told you, I am giving away the money I have accumulated, but this is not the solution of any part of the problem you mention. What the people need is not a gift of money but a gift of knowledge with which they may become self-determining, including not only the accumulation of money but the more important matter of learning how to find happiness in their relationships with others.

America is the most desirable country that civilization has ever created, but there is plenty of work yet to be done before it becomes the paradise that it may become. Paradise and poverty do not mix! People's souls cannot grow while their stomachs are empty. The march of human progress cannot move rapidly when a majority of the people suffer with inferiority complexes growing out of the fear of poverty.

And I may as well call your attention, here and now, to the fact that there can be no enduring happiness for the few who have wealth as long as a majority of their neighbors have less than the minimum necessities of life.

Now, do not falsely conclude that I am advocating any system whereby we will all turn socialistic and divide up our possessions with our neighbors. That would not change the condition of poverty, because you must remember that poverty is a state of mind, a habit! Gifts of material things will never save anyone from poverty. The place to begin changing poverty is in the individual's mind, and the way to begin is by inspiring the individual to use their mind: to become creative and to render useful service in return for what they desire.

That is one sort of gift that cannot damage anyone, and it is precisely the sort of gift that I am preparing you to take to the American people.

HILL:

Then you believe that we cannot get the most out of material wealth unless we earn it ourselves. Is that your idea, Mr. Carnegie?

CARNEGIE:

That's it exactly! The highest aim of human beings is a state of mind known as happiness. I have never heard of anyone finding enduring happiness except by some form of personal action of benefit to others. You see, the business of accumulating wealth, if it is carried out in the right spirit, not only provides the necessities and luxuries our nature requires but also inspires happiness in our activities. It is a part of the inherent nature of humankind to wish to build and create and indulge in personal expression, to own material wealth beyond the actual necessities of life, and to attain happiness in proportion to the extent of service performed.

HILL:

You are leading me into pretty deep water, Mr. Carnegie, but I can see your viewpoint. You mean that the possession and ownership of material things cannot, of themselves, give one happiness, but the usage of these things can. Is that your belief?

CARNEGIE:

Not merely my belief but the existing fact! I ought to know, because I have been on both sides of the fence. I began in poverty and worked my way into wealth. Therefore, I speak from experience when I say that real riches consist not in material things but in the use one gives to material things. That is why I am divesting myself of most of my material wealth. But mind you, I am not giving it away to individuals, I am placing it where it may inspire individuals to help *themselves*.

HILL:

It is your idea, then, to provide the people of America with a practical philosophy that will help them to acquire riches in the same way you acquired them, through self-effort?

CARNEGIE:

That is the only safe way for anyone to acquire anything!

It is my aim to provide the American people with a philosophy that will make them success conscious. This is the only possible way, as far as I know, in which the poverty consciousness you mentioned can be mastered.

It certainly cannot be eliminated through any system that gifts material things. That sort of system would only soften the people and make them more dependent.

What this country needs is a philosophy similar to that of the pioneers who settled the country—a philosophy of self-determination that gives every individual both an incentive to acquire wealth themselves and a practical means of accomplishing this end.

HILL:

Do you mean that you do not believe in charity, Mr. Carnegie?

CARNEGIE:

Surely I believe in charity, but do not overlook the fact that the soundest of all forms of charity is that which helps people to help themselves. That form of help begins by aiding people to organize their own mind. Every normal mind has within it the seed of both success and failure. My idea of charity is a system that will encourage the growth of success and discourage the growth of failure.

I believe in giving personal gifts of material things only when individuals are unable, through physical or mental disability, to help themselves. But we often make mistakes in this sort of charity by recognizing physical disability through gifts while ignoring the possibilities of encouraging those who are physically disabled to begin using their minds. I know many people whose physical afflictions are sufficient to justify them in expecting charity, but they refuse such help because they have found ways of earning a living through the use of their minds. In this way, they escape the humility of accepting help from others.

The only easy day was yesterday.
—US Navy SEALs

HILL:

But you do believe in the maintenance of poorhouses for the indigent and aged who are unable to support themselves?

CARNEGIE:

No—emphatically, I do not! The very word "poorhouse" carries connotations that lead to the development of inferiority complexes.

But I do believe in a system of compensation for the aged and the indigent provided it allows the individual to live their own life in an environment of their own choosing.

The proper way to handle such cases is by a carefully supervised system of weekly or monthly allowance that permits the individual to maintain their own home environment. I do not think the system should end with the mere donation of money. It should provide for some form of mental activity if the individual is mentally fit, be it nothing more than reading. The greatest of all curses is that which deprives a person of "mental food" and consigns them to eternal idleness. I never hear of people "retiring" from active life that I do not feel sorry for, because I know those people were not created to remain idle as long as they have a mind with which to think. I know, too, that no idle person is happy.

HILL:

Then you do not believe in the prison system that deprives people of liberty without providing them with adequate opportunity to use their minds and bodies constructively?

CARNEGIE:

No, I do not! Such a system is brutal, because some people have criminal tendencies and cannot be trusted. Every prison should provide ample activity for both the body and the mind. Prisoners cannot be reformed by punishment or by idleness. Reformation can come only through properly guided activity, by force if necessary, which results in the development of the right sort of habits.

The curse of our prison system is the fact that it is generally conducted as a form of "punishment" and not as a system of restoration! If you restore someone to normalcy, you do it by changing the habits of their thinking. And that applies to those who are out of prison the same as to those who are in.

There are millions of people in an imaginary prison who have been charged with no crime. They are prisoners in their own minds, consigned there by their own self-imposed limitations, through the acceptance of poverty and the acceptance of temporary defeat. It is this sort of prisoner that I hope to release through the achievement philosophy.

HILL:

I never thought of free folks as being prisoners, but I can see from your analysis that many are.

CARNEGIE:

Yes, and the worst part of the story is that millions of these unfortunates are little children who were born to such imprisonment—children who did not ask to be brought into the world but find themselves here, in a prison as strong and as deadly as any that is built of iron bars and stone walls. These little prisoners must be rescued! The rescue must begin by awakening them to the realization of the power of their own minds.

> *Let's go invent tomorrow rather than worrying about*
> *what happened yesterday.*
> —Steve Jobs

HILL:

Where and how is this awakening to take place, Mr. Carnegie?

CARNEGIE:

It should begin in the home and be carried on also as a part of the public school system. But nothing along this line will happen until someone comes forth with a practical plan that has public support.

HILL:

And you think there is a nationwide need for some supplementary form of training through which schoolchildren may be taught the fundamentals of individual achievement based on personal initiative?

CARNEGIE:

That is one of America's greatest needs. Remember what I tell you: if such a system is not introduced, the time will come, and very soon, when this country will cease to be the nation of pioneers it has been in the past. People will become indifferent to opportunity; they will cease to act on their own initiative; they will become easy victims of even the slightest form of defeat.

HILL:

You believe, then, that thrift and the spirit of self-determination are qualities that should be taught in the public schools?

CARNEGIE:

Yes, and in the home as well. But the trouble with most homes is that the parents are as much in need of this sort of training as the children. As a matter of fact, parents are the worst offenders in the matter of influencing children to accept poverty, because it is but natural that children accept whatever conditions their parents accept.

HILL:

Then you believe that self-discipline should begin in the home and that it should be demonstrated by the parents in the forms of thrift, ambition, and self-reliance?

CARNEGIE:

Yes, the home is the first place where a child gets an impression of life, and it is here that the child often acquires habits of failure that endure throughout life. Trace the record of any successful person and you will find that somewhere, probably during early childhood, they came under the influence of some success-conscious person, perhaps a family member or close relative.

Those who acquire a success consciousness seldom allow it to be stifled through defeat. You might say that success consciousness gives one a sort of immunity against all forms of defeat.

HILL:

Now, Mr. Carnegie, you must have learned from your wide and varied experience with people what the major causes of failure are?

CARNEGIE:

Yes, I was coming to that in a few minutes because it is essential that a practical philosophy of individual achievement include the causes of both success and failure. You may be surprised to learn that there are more than twice as many major causes of failure as there are causes of success.

HILL:

Will you name these causes in the order of their importance?

CARNEGIE:

No, that would be impractical, but I will name some of them and place at the head of the list the most common of all causes of failure:

1. The habit of drifting through life without a definite major purpose. This is one of the key causes of failure in that it leads to other causes of failure.

2. Unfavorable physical hereditary foundation at birth. Incidentally, this is the only cause of failure that is not subject to elimination, and even this can be bridged, through the principle of the mastermind.

3. The habit of meddlesome curiosity concerning other people's affairs, through which time and energy are wasted.

4. Inadequate preparation for the work in which one engages, especially inadequate schooling.

5. Lack of self-discipline, generally manifesting itself through excesses in eating, alcohol, and sex.

6. Indifference toward opportunities for self-advancement.

7. Lack of ambition to aim above mediocrity.

8. Ill health, often caused by wrong thinking, improper diet, and insufficient exercise.

9. Unfavorable environmental influences during early childhood.

10. Lack of persistence in carrying through to a finish that which one starts (due, in the main, to a lack of a definite purpose and self-discipline).

11. The habit of maintaining a negative mental attitude in connection with life generally.

12. Lack of control over the emotions through intentional and beneficial habits.

13. The desire to gain something for nothing, usually expressed through gambling and more offensive habits of dishonesty.

14. Indecision and indefiniteness.

15. One or more of the seven basic fears: poverty, criticism, ill health, loss of love, old age, loss of liberty, and death.

16. Wrong selection of a mate in marriage.

17. An excess of caution in business and professional relationships.

18. Leaving too much to chance.

19. Wrong choice of business and professional associates.

20. Wrong choice of vocation or total failure to make a choice.

21. Lack of concentrated effort, leading to dissipation of one's time and energies.

22. The habit of indiscriminate spending, without a budget control over income and expenditures.

23. Failure to budget and use time properly.

24. Lack of controlled enthusiasm.

25. Intolerance—a closed mind based particularly on ignorance or prejudice in connection with religion, politics, and economics.

26. Failure to cooperate with others in a spirit of harmony.

27. A craving for power or wealth not earned or based on merit.

28. Lack of a spirit of loyalty where loyalty is due.

29. Uncontrolled egotism and vanity.

30. Exaggerated selfishness.

31. The habit of forming opinions and building plans without basing them on known facts.

32. Lack of vision and imagination.
33. Failure to make a mastermind alliance with those whose experience, education, and native ability are needed.
34. Failure to recognize the existence of, and the means of adapting one's self to, the forces of Infinite Intelligence.
35. Profanity of speech, reflecting, as it does, evidence of an unclean and undisciplined mind and of an inadequate vocabulary.
36. Speaking before thinking. Talking too much.
37. Covetousness, revenge, and greed.
38. The habit of procrastination, often based on plain laziness but generally the result of the lack of a definite major purpose.
39. Speaking slanderously of other people, with or without cause.
40. Ignorance of the nature and purpose of the power of thought and lack of knowledge of the principles of operation of the mind.
41. Lack of personal initiative due, in the main, to the lack of a definite major purpose.
42. Lack of self-reliance due, also, to absence of an obsessional motive founded on a definite major purpose.
43. Lack of faith in one's self, in the future, in one's fellow humans, in God.
44. Lack of an attractive personality.
45. Failure to develop willpower through voluntary, controlled habits of thought.

These are not all the causes of failure, but they represent the major portion of them. All these causes, except number two, can be either eliminated or brought under control through application of the principle of definiteness of a major purpose and mastery of willpower. You might say, therefore, that the first and last of these causes of failure control all the others except one.

EDITOR'S NOTE:

I am constantly blown away by how efficiently Carnegie and Hill can cut to the heart of matters with a simple list. Read through all those items and I'm sure you'll be able to think of people in your life who have embodied one or more of those causes, which led to some type of failure. Perhaps you can reflect on times in your life where you were not receiving the results you wanted, whether personally or professionally, and deliver an exact diagnosis of what happened.

The best part? The solution to each weakness is generally its opposite—that's what makes this list so powerful. The road to achievement may be simple, as the list shows us, but it is not easy. The application of consistent willpower aimed at a definite end is what enables us to reach our goals by granting us the spirit to rise when adversity inevitably strikes.

HILL:

Do you mean that if the first and the last of these forty-five causes of failure were mastered, one would be well on the road toward success?

CARNEGIE:

Yes. If someone is working toward the attainment of a definite major purpose and has their willpower so organized that it is directing the forces of their mind, I would say that person is well within the sight of success.

HILL:

But these two principles alone are not sufficient to save one from defeat, are they, Mr. Carnegie?

CARNEGIE:

No, but they are sufficient to enable one to stage a comeback and go ahead with plans. As I have stated, self-discipline means that an individual will not accept any circumstance of defeat as being more than a temporary experience that serves as an impetus to greater effort.

The most certain way to succeed is always
to try just one more time.
—Thomas Edison

HILL:

Suppose the defeat is of such a nature that it seriously impairs a person's use of their physical body—for example, the loss of legs or hands or a stroke that limits someone's use of their physical body or deprives them of it entirely. Wouldn't that be a serious handicap?

CARNEGIE:

To be sure, it would handicap, but it need not necessarily be accepted as permanent defeat. Some of the most successful people the world has ever known attained their greatest success after having been physically afflicted. Here again, let me remind you that the mastermind principle is sufficient to provide one with every sort of knowledge that is available to humankind, and it can be used to take the place of all physical effort.

HILL:

Yes, of course! Then if people fail to apply the mastermind principle, they may be defeated because of their own neglect, since there is a remedy available to them?

CARNEGIE:

You have understood the idea correctly. The mastermind principle can be used as a substitute for everything, excepting only the use of the brain. As long as people can think, they can use this principle. And it sometimes happens that people do not discover the possibilities of their own minds until they are deprived of the use of some important function of their bodies. In such cases, it may generally be said that their physical handicap becomes a blessing in disguise.

I know a blind man who is one of the most successful music teachers in the US, if not the entire world. Before he was overtaken by this affliction, he earned only a modest living as the member of an orchestra. His affliction had the effect of introducing him to a wider field of opportunity with a much greater financial income.

Helen Keller used her affliction to make her one of America's great women.

HILL:

Adversity was their blessing in disguise?

CARNEGIE:

Yes, and it so happens that at times the disguise is not so very great. If physical handicap has the effect of causing people to arm themselves with greater willpower, it may be, and usually is, a blessing that is obvious. It all depends upon the attitude people take toward their physical handicap. If they are truly self-disciplined, they will convert it into an asset in one way or another.

EDITOR'S NOTE:

Several years ago, I interviewed military veteran Todd Love, whose ability to convert adversity into a blessing was extraordinary. During active duty in Afghanistan, with an M4 carbine in his right hand and a metal detector in his left, twenty-year-old Love led his fellow Marines into an empty compound to clear it of threats. Todd stepped on an improvised explosive device (IED), and the blast launched him fifteen feet backward. The IED was made of low-metallic copper, which had prevented his metal detector from picking it up.

Love's first memory after the incident was waking up in a hospital in Germany two days later. In a lot of pain, he figured that he must have stood on an IED, but because he was heavily medicated, he didn't realize the extent of his injuries.

Several days later, after being transported to the United States for more treatment, Love said, "I started getting curious and went to grab my leg, but it simply wasn't there. All I felt was the hospital bed." He realized shortly afterward that both his legs had been blown off in the explosion.

One of his hands was wrapped in bandages, and it was so badly destroyed that the doctors recommended amputation at the elbow. Love concurred with medical opinion, and after the amputation he was left with only one full limb. His body had been literally torn apart.

Wouldn't it have been completely understandable for Love to hate the world and spend the rest of his life in self-pity? It absolutely would, but Love won't ever let that be the case. The self-described adrenaline junkie has become a skydiving fanatic and has even completed the Spartan Race, a grueling obstacle course, on five separate occasions. A simple Internet image search for "Todd Love" presents a mosaic of inspiration and courage.

Love describes the incident as a "blessing." He explained to me, "It made me fall in love with life again. Even though I have these obstacles to face, I started properly noticing all the people who I really love and care about. That's what life is about. Everyone is going through something in their life right now. For me, my injuries are obvious, but we all have different obstacles in life that we deal with. The important thing is that we stay positive and focus on what we can control."

Although his body was damaged, Love could maintain a perspective that encompassed more than his circumstances. As Carnegie reminded us earlier: "It sometimes happens that people do not discover the possibilities of their own minds until they are deprived of the use of some essential portion of their physical bodies. In such cases, it may be generally said that their physical handicap becomes a blessing in disguise."

Regardless of what narrative we tell ourselves, there is never a valid excuse for permanent defeat.

HILL:

Isn't it true, though, Mr. Carnegie, that most people who suffer from serious physical handicaps accept their affliction in a negative manner, using it as an excuse for failure instead of as a challenge to take possession of their own minds?

CARNEGIE:

Unfortunately, yes, that is true. But the quitter will find an excuse for failure no matter what the condition of their body may be. And I would guess that there are more able-bodied quitters than there are people who quit because of physical affliction.

In a country such as ours, where opportunity for self-advancement is abundant in every field of useful service, there can be no satisfactory apology for complete failure except that which may result from injury to the mind. Helen Keller has proved that the loss of two of the most important of the five senses need not condemn one to failure. Through the use of her willpower, she has very definitely bridged both of her physical impairments. With the aid of the mastermind principle, she is rendering useful service by teaching the whole world the needed lesson that the mind need not remain imprisoned even though the physical body be greatly impaired. Beethoven made a similar demonstration after losing his hearing.

Sometimes the loss of physical qualities only tends to strengthen one's mental qualities, and I have yet to know of the first person who attained great success without having met and mastered great difficulties in the form of temporary defeat. Every time someone rises from defeat, they become mentally and spiritually stronger. Thus, in time, one may actually find one's true inner self through temporary defeat.

If Great Britain had not been defeated by the colonies in the American Revolution, she might not have benefited by the friendly cooperation of the United States in World War II.
—Napoleon Hill

HILL:

Provided they take the right mental attitude toward defeat?

CARNEGIE:

Of course! That is understood. Nothing can help the person who quits the moment they are defeated. Conversely, nothing can stop the person who accepts defeat as a challenge to exert greater effort. The will to live and to win despite defeat brings to one's aid a strange and unknown force that has baffled science throughout the ages.

That sort of will reaches out, through all sorts of unfavorable circumstances, and brings to one's aid a mysterious, unseen ally that seems not to recognize circumstances as stumbling blocks but converts them into stepping-stones. Every observing person has noticed this, but so far no one has ever isolated its cause.

HILL:

Would it be beneficial to a person to have never met with any sort of defeat, or would this be detrimental?

CARNEGIE:

My guess is that the human ego could not stand the inflation it would be subjected to in the person who never failed at anything. I have often thought that defeat may be a closely related associate of the Law of Compensation, of which Emerson wrote: "It helps to keep men mentally balanced in that it proves to man that, after all, he is only man!"

On the other hand, it appears also that defeat may be a wisely arranged plan for testing people. I draw this conclusion from the fact that great leaders seem always to have been forced to undergo more than the average number of personal defeats. In the industrial world, where I am best acquainted with reactions to personal experiences of defeat, I have observed that no one ever remains long as a leader unless they develop the self-discipline necessary to translate defeat into a challenge to greater effort.

It is my theory that every time people refuse to accept defeat as anything more than temporary, they acquire a proportionate amount of greater control over their willpower. Therefore, one may, in time, actually develop an indomitable will through the stimulating effect of defeat. Then, too, one cannot escape the fact that mastery of defeat develops greater capacity for faith, that state of mind which removes all limitations from the mind.

HILL:

Then you believe that we cannot use the power of faith until we rise above the habit of accepting defeat as permanent failure?

CARNEGIE:

Yes, that is my belief. Faith is a state of mind wherein people appear to have been so guided in their thoughts that unattained ends are clearly revealed to them, although they may have no material evidence to support this belief. Obviously, as long as their mind is limited by the acceptance of defeat as permanent, their mind is not open to the influence of faith.

You might say, therefore, that self-discipline in connection with our attitude toward defeat is an essential part of the preparation necessary for the application of faith.

Faith enables us to believe in unattained ends even though we have been temporarily defeated in our efforts to achieve those ends.

HILL:

Defeat, then, should be accepted as a sort of preliminary training that we need in order to make practical application of faith. Is that your idea?

CARNEGIE:

Yes, that is one way of stating it, but many people become confused by mistaking confidence for faith. Confidence is a state of mind where we believe in something because of material evidence or a reasonable hypothesis of facts concerning its reality. Faith is a state of mind in which we believe in something without having the slightest form of material evidence of its present reality. Confidence is the product of the faculty of reason. Faith overrides the faculty of reason, pushes aside all material evidence, and enables us to believe in the unattained and the unseen.

Faith probably operates through the subconscious section of the mind, which, according to the most acceptable theory, is the connecting link between the finite mind and Infinite Intelligence. If this theory is correct, then faith is the revealed light of Infinite Intelligence shining brightly in the conscious mind.

> *They tried to bury us.*
> *They didn't know we were seeds.*
> —Greek proverb

HILL:

I think I see what you mean. For example, when Edison created the first talking machine [phonograph], he had no material evidence of the practicability of such a machine, since no one had ever perfected one, but he conceived an idea that was so clear to him that he had faith in its existence as a workable theory and faith in his own ability to produce the machine. Is that correct?

CARNEGIE:

No, I would state it this way. There was revealed to him, through his capacity for applied faith, the existing theory of the talking machine, and he had confidence in his own ability to perfect the physical apparatus necessary to give that theory a practical application. His invention was, therefore, a combination of self-reliance or confidence and faith. His confidence in himself was based upon his known ability and experience in the creation of mechanical appliances. Obviously, his faith was not the result of confidence in his own ability, based on his experience, because he had never had the experience of building a talking machine.

When people believe in known or provable material facts, or what they assume to be existing facts, no faith is required for the belief because they are being guided by their reason. But when people believe in the unknown, the unproved, and what may be unprovable—for the time being at least— their belief becomes faith. The distinction between confidence and faith is difficult to explain, but it is important that one understand this difference.

Mr. Edison's invention of the incandescent electric lamp was produced through a combination of confidence and faith. He had confidence in his ability to produce light by applying electric energy to a wire and heating it because he had evidence, in the experience of others before him, that this could be done.

But he found that confidence alone was not enough to give him a perfected lamp. Something was needed that would enable him to control the heat of the wire so that the wire would give light without burning out. He had no evidence that the needed factor of control existed, but he had *faith* that it did, and that faith carried him through many thousands of temporary defeats until he found it. Nothing but faith could have sustained anyone through that many defeats.

You might say, therefore, that the incandescent electric lamp was conceived through Edison's confidence and perfected through his faith.

Now is the difference between confidence and faith clear to you?

HILL:
Yes, Mr. Carnegie, quite clear. Confidence is the child of reason, based on material evidence. Faith is the revealed light of Infinite Intelligence, working without material evidence.

CARNEGIE:
Well, let us be conservative and say that faith is revealed light working without material evidence. We cannot prove that it is the projected light of Infinite Intelligence, though we may have faith that it is. We can come no nearer to establishing the true source of the power of faith than we can to proving the real source of electricity, but we can make practical use of both forces, so let us not try to split hairs with definitions.

As a matter of fact, we do not know what life is or where it originates, but we can make sensible use of life by adapting ourselves to the known laws of nature. We can have faith in the infinite power that creates life.

HILL:
From your analysis of defeat, I get the impression that you believe there are benefits in all forms of defeat.

CARNEGIE:
Yes, I not only believe this, but it is true. The benefits consist in the mental attitude one takes toward defeat. A negative attitude may convert defeat into permanent failure and make it, therefore, a detriment. A positive mental attitude toward defeat converts defeat into a beneficial means of self-discipline through which one gains greater control over one's willpower.

Thus, it is easy to understand under what conditions defeat may become either a help or a hindrance. The choice is entirely one of individual preference, because it is under the control of the individual. I cannot always control the sources of defeat, but I can control my attitude toward defeat when it catches up with me. Is this clear to you?

HILL:

Quite clear! I understand from your analysis of defeat that one should voluntarily develop the habit of accepting it as nothing more than a challenge to try again.

CARNEGIE:

Yes, but you did not emphasize that word "habit" sufficiently. That is the all-important thing. Defeatism, with which so many are cursed, is the result of the habit of accepting defeat as final. One should reverse this habit by substituting its opposite. One's attitude toward a single experience of defeat is not important, but it is one's *repeated* attitude toward this experience that counts, because repetition makes habit.

EDITOR'S NOTE:

"Repetition makes habit." I love how succinct that phrase is. Take a moment to think back on how you spent your day, or if you're reading this in the morning, reflect on yesterday. Make a list of three actions you took that brought you closer to your goals and three actions that pushed you away from your goals. On the positive side, it could be attending a yoga session and reading a book such as this one; on the negative side, it could be eating junk food and watching two hours of television.

Now review some of the most famous quotes on habit, some going back thousands of years:

"A journey of a thousand miles begins with a single step." Chinese proverb

"How you do anything is how you do everything." Buddhist proverb

"Excellence is not a single act, but a habit." often attributed to Aristotle

"Rome wasn't built in a day." French proverb

"Look after the pennies and the pounds will look after themselves." Lord Chesterfield

"An ounce of prevention is worth a pound of cure." Benjamin Franklin

"Successful people aren't born that way. They become successful by establishing the habit of doing things unsuccessful people don't like to do." William Makepeace Thackeray

"Progress, of the best kind, is comparatively slow. Great results cannot be achieved at once; and we must be satisfied to advance in life as we walk, step by step." Samuel Smiles

"There is no other road to genius than through voluntary self-effort." Napoleon Hill

"The quality of a person's life is in direct proportion to their commitment to excellence, regardless of their chosen field of endeavor." Vince Lombardi

"Get busy living or get busy dying." Andy Dufresne (*The Shawshank Redemption*)

"Symphonies begin with one note; fires with one flame; gardens with one flower; and masterpieces with one stroke." Matshona Dhliwayo

I'm sure you can think of a few more. These quotes highlight the fact that success is nothing more than the accumulation of small wins, just as failure is the accumulation of incremental—and in most cases seemingly inconsequential—losses. The decision to live with intent not only empowers us to gain clarity on what tasks we must do but also gives us the mental nudge to complete those tasks before turning in each day.

Repetition makes habit, and a carefully plotted daily structure facilitates that repetition. If you haven't done so already, use *The Napoleon Hill Success Journal* to stay focused and accountable. It's been created with one aim in mind: to ensure your long-term success.

CARNEGIE:

If Edison had not understood that all defeat is temporary and need not be accepted as anything more, he would not have gone ahead, through thousands of defeats, until he found the unknown principle he needed to make the incandescent electric lamp a practical success.

You see, therefore, that his attitude toward defeat meant just the difference between success and failure. He merely used each defeat as a brick in the wall of faith, and when that wall became high enough to lift him above the limitations of knowledge that stood in his way, he looked over the wall, saw the answer to his problem, appropriated it, and delivered!

The world has very convincing evidence that we need not stop merely because we are overtaken by defeat. We call this quality *resourcefulness*. The resourceful person is never permanently defeated.

I do not recall ever having undertaken a major operation in the steel industry in which I did not meet with defeat in one form or another. At the very outset of my career in the steel industry, the price of steel was around $130 per ton, and many of the ablest people in the business said the price could not be lowered materially.

I did not accept that belief.

I had faith in the possibility of steel at $20 a ton. I speak of my state of mind as faith because I had no evidence that steel could be produced that cheaply. Driven by faith, I went to work to lower the price of steel, and I hardly need tell you that before I accomplished my purpose I met with scores of defeats. If I had accepted defeat as permanent, the price of steel probably would still be around $130 a ton.

HILL:

What do you consider to be the greatest benefit we may receive from defeat, Mr. Carnegie?

CARNEGIE:

Well, there are so many lessons we may learn through defeat that it is difficult to say which may be of the greatest value, but I can answer your question in another way by saying that the greatest potential benefit we may receive from this experience consists in the fact that it may serve to strengthen our willpower. It makes us resourceful.

I say *potential* benefit because most people allow defeat to weaken, rather than strengthen, their willpower. Defeat becomes a benefit only through self-discipline sufficient to enable us to convert the experience into a challenge to move forward with a renewed and a greater effort.

HILL:
Do you believe that this question of our attitude toward defeat is the major determining factor in our success or failure?

CARNEGIE:
Well, I would hardly go so far as to call it a major factor, but it certainly is one of the commonest causes of failure. Every time we accept defeat as final, we weaken our faculty of will and discourage it from serving us. If we allow it to set in, this attitude will eventually entirely destroy the practical use of the will.

HILL:
Then you believe one should take some appropriate action in connection with every defeat even when defeat is of such a nature that one's losses from it cannot be wholly recovered. Is that your idea?

CARNEGIE:
Yes, that's it! There is no form of defeat that may not yield some benefit, even if it is nothing more than an opportunity to prove that we have willpower to refuse to acknowledge defeat as permanent failure. This not only strengthens our willpower but also develops our self-reliance. If we form the habit of accepting defeat meekly, it is but a question of time until we will have no self-confidence, and that sort of weakness is fatal to individual achievement.

HILL:

Doesn't age have something to do with our attitude toward defeat? For example, is it not true that an elderly person is more apt to accept defeat as permanent than is a young person who has not been worn down by repeated defeats?

CARNEGIE:

In some cases, perhaps, that is true. But it need not be and it should not be true, because with age comes wisdom. The average person who succeeds financially seldom begins to hit their real stride in the accumulation of material things until they are well past forty.

Now, when I say that wisdom comes with age, I mean, of course, that it comes to those who become conscious of the true nature of their mind and form the habit of refusing to accept defeat as permanent.

> *Wrinkles should merely indicate*
> *where the smiles have been.*
> —Mark Twain

HILL:

Then it is not age that is the determining factor in our attitude toward defeat. It is the habits through which we discipline our mind or perhaps the absence of controlled habits?

CARNEGIE:

Now you have it precisely. But no mental attitude or thought habit can alter the fact that wisdom is acquired through the maturity of years and practical experience. Young people seldom have the balance of judgment and reason that comes from age and experience. That is why I have two types of people in my mastermind group:

- Planners: Those with mature experience, whose judgment is dependable.
- Action squad: Those who carry out the plans created by the more experienced people. In some instances, of course, the plans are the product of the minds of both groups, but the decision of the more experienced prevails when there is a difference of opinion.

HILL:

Then you do not believe in consigning people to the scrap heap when they begin to acquire age?

CARNEGIE:

That depends entirely upon the people themselves. Some have to be "scrapped" because of their own mental attitude and their habits. My policy always has been to place people in supervisory positions, as far as conditions would permit, when they reach the age when they are less capable than younger people of performing physical labor. In this way, their experience is preserved for the benefit of those who have not yet attained equivalent experience.

HILL:

I take it that your policy regarding the employment of the elderly is not based upon purely philanthropic motives?

CARNEGIE:

Modern industry cannot be operated on philanthropic motives alone! Those who try to run their business by employing only those who need employment or for friendly motive soon find themselves in economic difficulties. Modern business is keenly competitive. To succeed, a business must be managed through reason, not emotion. People should be charitable, but they need not wreck their business in order to engage in charitable acts.

HILL:

Then you consider it an act of sound business judgment to find ways and means of preserving the benefits of the experience of aged people?

CARNEGIE:

Exactly! No business of great proportions could operate successfully without the guiding influence of experience. The acquisition of experience is costly, and it requires time. Modern business can neither wait for the necessary elapse of time required for people to gain experience nor stand the loss that ensues from inexperience. Therefore, a successful business requires the guiding hand of experience in the supervision of the inexperienced. Only in this way can a business avert and absorb the mistakes of the beginners.

HILL:

You believe, then, that sound counsel may be as helpful as energetic physical action in the management of industry?

CARNEGIE:

Both are necessary. Sound counsel averts mistakes and costly failures. That old saying that "an ounce of prevention is worth a pound of cure" is more than an axiom. It is sound business philosophy. And it applies as well to individuals as to the management of industry. If people took the time to inform themselves properly before they acted, they would suffer fewer defeats. Snap judgment, impatience, and indifference toward facts are at the bottom of many defeats.

Every well-managed industry should have a fact-finding source consisting of experienced people. We have those people in our research department. They offer no personal opinions and express no emotional feelings. Their business is solely to organize the facts essential to the manufacture and the sale of steel. Without their aid, we could not operate profitably.

We have another group that assembles facts into working plans. Here may be found plenty of emotion, creative vision, enthusiasm, imagination, and all the other qualities needed to give life and action to facts. This group lays out the work of our plants.

We have still another group, known as the operating staff. They translate the plans of the planning staff into action. Every move they make has been carefully planned for them. This saves them time and effort and precludes costly errors.

Through coordination among these three groups, we manage to operate the steel industry on a profitable basis, thereby ensuring steady employment for all of us. The mistakes we avoid are directly proportional to the extent to which we harmoniously coordinate our efforts. If every individual does their part and does it well, our mistakes are few. They consist mainly of accidents that could not be anticipated.

HILL:

Then it is possible to so plan a business that it is bound to operate at a profit?

CARNEGIE:

Oh yes, it is possible, but the record of business generally shows that the average business is not scientifically managed in the manner I have described. Human emotion plays too strong a part in most businesses. There is a lack of planning, a lack of coordination of effort between those who operate the business.

Perhaps it is not a bad idea for me to remind you that the failure rate among individuals may be traced largely to the same cause. A carefully planned individual life is the only sort that has better than an average chance of success. That is why I am so deeply concerned with giving the people of America a dependable philosophy of individual achievement. I wish individuals to be able to run their private lives as economically as successful industries are managed, and it can be done!

HILL:

You mean that individual defeats can be cut down through a proper understanding of the major causes of defeat and of the principles of successful achievement?

CARNEGIE:

Yes, and I also mean that defeat itself can be converted into an asset of priceless value to an individual through the right sort of mental attitude toward defeat. There are unavoidable defeats, but there is no form of defeat that may not be made to yield priceless benefits in connection with the development of self-discipline.

You see, it is only through self-discipline that one is enabled to take full possession of one's own mind. Defeat is, or may be, a powerful builder of self-discipline. It can be made to serve as food for the development of willpower, through which all self-discipline is administered.

HILL:

I get your viewpoint. Defeat may become either fuel for the fire of willpower or water with which to put out the fire, according to one's mental attitude toward it.

CARNEGIE:

Your illustration states the matter clearly. It might have been more impressive if you had said that defeat becomes fuel for the fire of willpower or water with which to put out the fire, according to the habits of mental attitude with which it is accepted. Habit is the important thing. You might say that self-discipline is the act of developing and controlling habits of thought and of action.

HILL:

I see what you mean. Self-discipline is the tool of willpower, because it is only through exercise of willpower that habits are voluntarily formed and controlled?

CARNEGIE:

That's the principle I had in mind. I wish to make sure you understand that self-discipline is a method, a means to an end, in the formation and the control of habits of thought and action, that it is subject entirely to willpower. It could be stated in a few words by saying that self-discipline is willpower in action.

HILL:

Is it not true, Mr. Carnegie, that temporary defeat growing out of illness or physical affliction sometimes has the effect of causing a person to acquire greater spiritual power?

CARNEGIE:

I have known that to happen. I have always believed that Thomas A. Edison's tremendous capacity for overcoming defeat arose from the spiritual power he gained from self-discipline in connection with the loss of hearing. It is a well-known fact that the loss or impairment of any of the physical senses tends to strengthen one or more of the others. This is nature's way of compensating one for unavoidable loss.

When we strengthen our will to master any physical ailment, we thereby add permanent strength to our will. Thus, nature has provided us with a means by which we may compensate ourselves for physical handicaps. But willpower may be strengthened through any form of action based on its use. Action is the important thing—not that which inspires the action.

HILL:

If I understand your theory correctly, you believe that everyone should engage in some form of mental and physical action as a means of mental development.

CARNEGIE:

Yes, that is true, and my belief is based on my observations of those who have grown through struggle and of those who, because of their economic independence, have been relieved from the necessity to struggle. Necessity forces initiative.

It is dangerous to be entirely relieved from all necessity of using our mind, for the mind, like the physical body, remains strong and alert only through use.

Whatever I have tried to do in life, I have tried with all my
heart to do it well; whatever I have devoted myself to,
I have devoted myself completely.
—Charles Dickens

HILL:

You feel that people are by nature inclined to take the line of least resistance and that this leads to the habit of procrastination if counter habits are not developed?

CARNEGIE:

Yes, all human endeavor is based on motive! Sometimes the motive is negative, sometimes it is positive, but no exertion is made without motive. Now, it is much more beneficial to an individual to initiate their own motives voluntarily, because they will do best that which they like to do.

HILL:

You believe, then, that those motivated by their desire for personal expression in response to their pride of achievement will do a better job than those motivated only by the need to earn a living?

CARNEGIE:

Unquestionably they will. For this very reason, every person should be willing to make great sacrifices, if necessary, to follow the line of endeavor they enjoy best.

EDITOR'S NOTE:

Steve Jobs, co-founder and former CEO of Apple, was one of the innovators of modern information technology. In the 1970s and 1980s, he was instrumental in developing personal computers and in the evolution of the information technology industry. In 1985, the corporate structure of Apple forced him out, and he was forced to pursue other interests.

But as Carnegie stated, "Nothing can stop the person who accepts defeat as a challenge to exert greater effort." Rather than dwell on his misfortune, Jobs learned from his defeat. He embarked on a new venture, the aptly named NeXT, which became so valuable that in 1997 it was purchased by Apple for $429 million, plus more than 1 million shares of Apple stock. A few months later, Jobs was appointed Apple CEO once more.

His tenure from that point until his sad passing in 2011 revolutionized the world in countless ways. Of his acclaimed creative output, Jobs said, "The only way to do great work is to love what you do. If you haven't found it yet, keep looking. Don't settle."

HILL:

What about "native ability"? Aren't some people suited by nature for only certain types of work?

CARNEGIE:

To an extent this is true, but there has been a great deal of false reasoning on this subject. Now it has been my experience that most people are good at what they wish to do. A person's own mental attitude toward their work is far more important than their inherited qualities, and mental attitude is something they can control.

HILL:

There is an old saying: "Salespeople are born, not made." Do you subscribe to that viewpoint, Mr. Carnegie?

CARNEGIE:

Without doubt there are people who possess certain personality traits that aid them in selling, such as flexibility, enthusiasm, keen imagination, personal initiative, self-reliance, and persistence. But every one of these is an acquired trait. I have known people who were so timid that they shunned the responsibility of meeting strangers on every occasion possible. Yet because of an impelling motive, they became able salespeople.

No, I would reverse that old axiom by saying, "Salespeople are made, not born." Anyone can become an effective salesperson if they take the time to learn all about the product or service they wish to sell and acquire an obsessional desire to sell it. The same principle holds good in connection with most other types of work.

HILL:

Well, would you go so far as to say that all people are born equal?

CARNEGIE:

Certainly not! The man who set that idea afloat intended to say that in America all people are born with equal *rights*. He had no intention of saying that all people are born physically and mentally equal, because obviously that is not true.

For the same reason, it is obvious that not all people are able to do one sort of work as well as others might do it. There are people, for example, whose physical and mental inheritance is such that they cannot master mathematics, or the languages, or other subjects. These people are, of necessity, limited in the types of work in which they can excel no matter what their motive or what sort of work they may prefer.

I went to school with a young man who was twice my age, but he never got beyond the fifth grade in school because he did not have the mental capacity to go further. That type of person never could excel in any sort of work calling for an alert mind.

When I said that it had been my experience that most people are good at that which they wish to do, I referred, of course, to people with normal mental capacities. There are natural dullards, and no applied stimuli can ever make them anything else. They are, by nature, limited in their achievements.

HILL:

Then there is one form of defeat about which a person can do nothing, and it cannot be converted into an asset. It is the defeat one suffers through poor breeding. Is this correct?

CARNEGIE:

I would agree with a part of your statement but not with all of it. Those with limited mental capacity or physical affliction may always bridge these deficiencies through the mastermind principle, by borrowing the education, experience, and native ability of others. Of course, not all who are thus handicapped have the willpower or the initiative or the vision to make use of the mastermind, but the possibility of its use is nevertheless available to all. You see, nature has provided a means of compensating every human being for the things of which they have been deprived.

> *It is best to take inventory of one's self before defeat,*
> *so as to avoid it; but it is absolutely essential to do so after defeat,*
> *so as to avoid a repetition.*
> —Andrew Carnegie

HILL:

Generally speaking, you believe, then, that defeat is detrimental only when we accept it as permanent and use it as an excuse for not making another start?

CARNEGIE:

I cannot think of any circumstance of defeat at the moment that could not be converted into an asset through the right sort of mental attitude toward it.

Thomas A. Edison had one of the most convincing excuses for failure that one could imagine, if he had chosen to use it. He had practically no schooling. He was practically stone-deaf. He had no money and no influential friends. Therefore, when he first began experimenting with the incandescent electric lamp and met with his first dozen or so failures, if he had given up the whole idea and quit, he would have been doing the usual thing.

Now, the fact that he did not quit but kept on with his work through several thousand temporary defeats—some would have called them failures—indicates the major difference between Edison and thousands of other would-be inventors whose names are never known outside the little communities in which they live. It also represents the major difference between success and failure in all walks of life—just this lone idea of keeping on in the face of temporary defeat. They call it persistence or resourcefulness, but it has its source in willpower.

HILL:

Is it not difficult to keep on working when our reason tells us that our efforts are in vain?

CARNEGIE:

Most people have a very convenient tool in their faculty of reason, but they use it as a *conspirator* instead of as an aid to achievement. They train their reason through the habit of accepting defeat as permanent. They give up and quit by killing off their willpower. I have yet to see the person whose outside enemies do them even a fraction of the injury they do to themselves through their mental habits.

Not all the enemies in the world can equal that which we set up in our own minds by failing, for any cause, to use our willpower for the attainment of our desires. That is one enemy that can defeat any person no matter how intelligent the individual may be or how much ability they possess.

HILL:

Mr. Carnegie, it looks to me as if you have so definitely traced the causes of success and failure to individual effort that no room is left for excuse making for those who fail.

CARNEGIE:

Well, that would be putting most people out on a limb, but I would modify your statement slightly by saying that there is very little room left for excusable failure in a country like ours except in cases of those who were born physically or mentally deficient. Practically all other excuses should be ruled out.

HILL:

I have heard it said that the average person never uses more than 50 percent of their inherent ability. Would you agree with that?

CARNEGIE:

Yes, with the exception that your estimated percentage is high. I would say that the average person never uses more than a small fraction of their inherent ability. Even the exceptions to this rule—those who promote themselves into leadership and become what the world calls a "success"— probably never use as much as 50 percent of their inherent ability, with a few rare exceptions.

HILL:

What about the person who says, "I would do this or that if I had time"? How does it happen that successful people seem to have all the time that is necessary to carry on stupendous individual endeavors while unsuccessful people bemoan a lack of time?

CARNEGIE:

Now you are touching upon one of my pet themes. It has been my experience that successful people have not one second more time than unsuccessful people, but the difference is this: successful people have learned how to budget and use their time efficiently, whereas unsuccessful people waste their time explaining and executing their failures.

Unless people organize their efforts and work according to a definite time schedule, they are almost sure to find themselves in a position in which it appears that they do not have enough time. The appearance is deceiving— that is, it is deceiving to people who use this excuse but not to others.

When I hear people say, "I haven't had time," I know then and there that I am listening to someone who does not apply themselves through the principle of organized endeavor. I never permit myself to get in a position where I could not divert my efforts, any minute of the day, from that which I am doing to whatever needs to be done. Study successful people anywhere and you will be astounded at the amount of available time they have for any use they choose.

The mastermind principle is the means by which very successful people "stretch" their time. Through this principle, they relegate details to other people, thereby keeping themselves free for major endeavors. Show me any person who really hasn't time to do what is necessary to promote their own interests and I will show you a person who does not make the best use of their time.

No one is really free unless they have themselves so well organized that they have enough time available to enable them to make use of their personal initiative in any direction they select. Through lack of organization, anyone can become a prisoner in their own mind.

> *Success is giving 100 percent of your effort,*
> *body, mind, and soul to the struggle.*
> —John Wooden

HILL:

You have given me an entirely new slant on this question of time, and I fear you have upset one of my own major excuses, Mr. Carnegie. I was just wondering how I was going to find time to interview the five hundred or more people whose cooperation I shall need in organizing the achievement philosophy, but your analysis of the subject of time has put me on the spot.

CARNEGIE:

Yes, I rather suspect it has. Well, if a writer could sit down and dash off a practical philosophy of individual achievement without conducting research, such a philosophy would have been written long ago. You have one very great compensating advantage in regard to the extensive time that will be required to gather the information that will be necessary for this philosophy. It consists in the fact that you will have few, if any, competitors.

I suspect that the major reason the world has never been given a philosophy of individual achievement suited for the needs of the person of the streets is that the organization of such a philosophy will require no less than twenty years of continuous effort and the analysis of thousands of people, both those who have succeeded and those who have failed, in addition to the fact that this sort of research does not pay while one is engaged in it.

HILL:

I see your point, and I fully appreciate your views, although they connote both the foundation of hope and a sound reason for discouragement.

CARNEGIE:

I see plenty of reason for hope but none whatsoever for discouragement, because you have embarked upon a life work in which you are not apt to have any real competition, given the great amount of perseverance that the job will require. On the other hand, the promise that lies ahead of you is in exact proportion to the hazard you are assuming in beginning such a task. You are risking everything, but you are promised everything any human being could desire in return for your assuming the risk.

In your case, temporary defeat will become doubly beneficial to you because it will be a part of your responsibility to learn all about defeat and how to convert it into an asset. That is the major burden of the philosophy on which you are working. And I think I should warn you that your own reactions to defeat will determine, more than everything else, the soundness and practicability of the philosophy of individual achievement. You cannot teach others how to make use of defeat until you learn how to do it yourself. Keep this thought in mind and it will sustain you when defeat overtakes you, as it most certainly will.

HILL:

And I get the impression from what you have said that one of the first things I must learn is to accept defeat gracefully!

CARNEGIE:

That's the first thing everyone should learn in connection with defeat. But that doesn't mean we should accept defeat meekly. It should be accepted in a militant spirit of determination not to permit it to affect our will to win but never in a spirit of fear or resentment.

HILL:

What should be our attitude toward enemies who bring about our defeat? Should it be defiant? Should we strike back at such enemies?

CARNEGIE:

Now I wish to tell you something about so-called enemies that may be of great benefit to you if you will pay attention to what I say. Enemies— meaning those who oppose and sometimes defeat us—can be of help in many different ways. First, they can keep us from going to sleep on our jobs. Second, they cause us to discipline ourselves more closely, lest we be guilty of some act for which we might be justly criticized.

HILL:

But Mr. Carnegie, some enemies are vicious and destructive and must be handled in a far more drastic manner than merely resenting their efforts to damage us. Passive resistance may be sufficient in dealing with those who merely oppose us in a sportsmanlike manner, but what of the person who is determined to destroy? The character assassins! The "whispering campaign" artist who starts falsehoods afloat! Is one merely to smile and forget it when opposed by this sort of person?

CARNEGIE:

No, there is something that can be done to defeat this type of enemy, but you may be surprised to learn what it is. It has nothing whatsoever to do with the enemies. But it does have something to do with one's self.

The time most people spend in striking back at enemies could be employed a thousand times more beneficially if we used it to improve ourselves so that nothing that enemies might say against us would have any effect. I don't think you fully understand the force of passive resistance, because that sort of resistance adds to our strength of character, to our faculty of will, and to the full weight of all efforts we might devote to striking back at enemies.

Briefly stated, what I am recommending is this: deal with enemies by not dealing with them at all! Deal with them by using them as an incentive to improve yourself—to place yourself beyond their power to damage you. Ignore them completely except to the extent that they incite you to take fuller possession of your own mind.

In this manner you can throw a blanket of spiritual protection around yourself that no enemy can penetrate! Remember what I say about this, because the time will come when you can test its soundness from your own experience.

> *Hanging onto resentment is letting someone you despise*
> *live rent-free in your head.*
> —Ann Landers

HILL:

That's hard to accept, Mr. Carnegie. I was brought up in a section of the country where the first thing a boy learns is the art of self-defense through physical force. It seems to me that one would become soft and subject to defeat by anyone who wishes to trample on his rights if he neglects to defend himself through physical force.

CARNEGIE:

Yes, I know what you mean, and I also know many of the people who were reared in the section of the country where you came from. In fact, I have one of your neighbors on the operating staff of one of our most important plants. When he first went to work for us many years ago, he was so imbued with the idea of self-defense through physical force that he never went out of his house without a pistol in his pocket.

But he doesn't carry the pistol anymore! His possession of the pistol almost cost him his freedom several years ago, and it would have if I had not come to his rescue. He was about to use it to defend his position with an enemy when mental attitude would have served him much better. I induced him to give the pistol to me with the understanding that I would teach him a better way to settle arguments if he would never carry it again. That was the beginning of a turn in his career that made him, finally, one of our most important people.

You see, this man was trying to accomplish by physical force that which could be accomplished so much more easily by mental force. He learned to take possession of his own mind, and that victory over himself brought him victory over many other things. He now seldom has an enemy, but when he does have to deal with one, he uses his mind instead of physical force, with the result that he has so improved his mind through use that it now enables him to earn an income of $12,000 a year [$300,000 a year in today's dollars] instead of the $3 per day he earned at the time of the pistol episode.

Don't you think he made a valuable discovery when he learned that he could do with his mind that which he could not do with a pistol?

HILL:

Yes, of course! But are there not many circumstances in life that can be handled only with physical force?

CARNEGIE:

Perhaps there are some in the lives of those who have not learned of a greater force that is available to them, but of that I could not speak from personal experience because I have never resorted to physical force to settle any misunderstanding with anyone.

HILL:

Well, you are telling me something entirely new. Now, let me know about this "blanket of spiritual protection" that you say we may use to protect ourselves. What is it, and how is it used?

CARNEGIE:

You asked me one question too many when you asked what it is. But I can tell you *how* to use it. You use it by taking full possession of your own mind through self-discipline. You'll find that when you do this, you can settle with words and by your mental attitude misunderstandings you formerly were inclined to settle by physical force.

HILL:

Oh, I see what you mean! When we gain such control over our own mind that we can take a passive attitude toward our enemies, they become aware of our superior mental power and begin to respect it?

CARNEGIE:

Now you are getting the idea! Many times during my career I have been accosted by angry men who had some real or imaginary grievance they intended to settle through physical force, but I have yet to accept a challenge from any man who wished to settle an argument with me in that manner.

If I am to fight a duel, I prefer to choose my own weapons, and I have always done so. In the old days, men settled personal differences with dueling pistols, but I would stand no chance at all in that sort of combat, since I know nothing about pistols. But I do know something about the power of the mind. Therefore, I have always managed, when challenged by another, to shift the argument to a ground of my own choice, where I could use a weapon of defense with which I am familiar.

Generally, the man who knows only physical force is a poor match for the man who understands mindpower, and he is licked the moment he enters combat with another on that basis.

HILL:

But Mr. Carnegie, spiritual power would be no match for physical power if one were held up by a highwayman who stuck a pistol in his ribs and asked him to hand over his money, would it?

CARNEGIE:

Your question brings to mind something that happened at one of our mills many years ago. One afternoon, as the workers stood in line to receive their pay envelopes, a man stepped up to the window, shoved a large pistol through, aimed it at the paymaster, and demanded that he hand over the pay envelopes. The paymaster did not comply but sat still and looked squarely at the gunman.

One of the guards saw what was happening, and without making any attempt to draw his pistol, he walked slowly toward the gunman. Not a word was spoken by either man, but the gunman turned around and pointed his gun squarely at the guard. The guard did not hesitate but walked firmly up to the gunman until he was almost within arm's reach of him. Then, to the surprise of everyone, the gunman dropped his gun, said, "Please don't shoot. I give up," and stuck his hands high in the air.

You see, he was afraid of being shot. Not with a pistol, because none was in sight, but with something he somehow associated with a pistol. Only he recognized it as being more powerful than a pistol. It was the courage of the guard who so plainly showed that he did not fear pistols. I tell you there is a "blanket of protection" around anyone who relies on their mindpower, and no one can say under what conditions it may or may not serve as the master of physical power.

HILL:
Did you ever find out why the guard acted so carelessly, Mr. Carnegie?

CARNEGIE:
Carelessly? Why, I don't think he acted carelessly. On the contrary, he used sound judgment, because common sense told him that he would have no chance at all if he engaged in combat with an armed robber who had a gun aimed at him unless he dealt with the robber via a power that the armed man was less familiar with.

You see, the psychological act of an unarmed man walking straight into the barrel of a pistol without hesitating, without speaking a word, without making any attempt to draw his own pistol, was enough to disconcert the robber and cause him to lose his nerve.

HILL:

Then it was the robber's loss of nerve and not the "blanket of spiritual protection" that saved the guard?

CARNEGIE:

As to that point, neither you nor I could determine the facts definitely because spiritual power works silently. It is an intangible power. How it works or why it works, no one knows. In this case, we only know that a man without a gun mastered a man with a gun pointed straight at him. We can only guess as to what took place in the minds of the two men. Perhaps neither of them could give us the real answer.

The guard told me after the affair was over that he felt no fear until he reached down and picked up the pistol the robber had dropped. Then, he said, it occurred to him that he had done a very foolish thing. "But," he said, "something inside me told me that if I pulled my pistol someone would be killed," and that was as near as I ever came to learning why the guard chose to approach the robber with courage instead of armed force.

HILL:

You think, then, that people may develop spiritual power by gaining control over themselves?

CARNEGIE:

Not only spiritual power but mental and physical power as well. Those who gain control over themselves are no longer the victims of fear. They are no longer the victims of their own emotions, but instead they convert their emotional power to whatever end they desire. Defeat no longer bothers them because they convert it into victory through renewed effort and increased willpower.

> *Feel the fear and do it anyway.*
> —Susan Jeffers

HILL:

After people come into possession of this sort of power, is there a danger of losing it through some form of defeat over which they have no control?

CARNEGIE:

It is not likely that people who have taken charge of their own mind and learned how to use it will meet with any form of defeat over which they have no control. But if they should meet with such defeat, they will at least control their reactions to it without losing any of their courage. You see, people who have been released from their self-limitations come into a relationship with their spiritual being that gives them immunity against most of the causes of defeat.

HILL:

Do you mean that great sorrow arising from causes beyond their control could not break the spirit of people who have gained mastery over themselves?

CARNEGIE:

Yes. The people who have mastered themselves know how to shut the door against all forms of grief. That is one of the first things they learn.

HILL:

This is a strange power to which you have introduced me, Mr. Carnegie. Therefore, I hope you will excuse me if my questions seem elementary.

CARNEGIE:

The power through which people gain mastery over themselves is strange to most people. If it were not, there would not be so many people in the world who meekly accept defeat without putting up a fight. And there would be no such reality as poverty in a country such as ours, where there is an abundance of everything people need or can use.

HILL:

You believe, then, that every normal person has at their command sufficient mind power to solve all their problems and procure all their needs. Is that your idea?

CARNEGIE:

That's exactly my idea, and I have demonstrated its practical soundness. Now my problem is to find a way to awaken the American people to a full realization of the existence of a power they now possess but do not use. That is the entire burden of the achievement philosophy. No one who appropriates this philosophy and makes practical use of it is apt to ever need anything they cannot procure with a minimum amount of effort. Remember, however, that the philosophy does not promise something for nothing, because there is no such thing.

HILL:

You believe, then, that Emerson's essay "Compensation" was much more than a mere work of literary attainment?

CARNEGIE:

Yes, much more! Emerson described a great universal law that is directly related to our subject. Through the operation of that law, everything has its equivalent value in something else. If this were not true, there would be no way to convert defeat into an asset.

But despite the Law of Compensation, defeat cannot become an asset without effort on the individual's part. The benefit consists in the use we make of defeat through our reactions to it. The effort we put into the reaction is the price we pay for the benefits it may yield. Thus, clearly, defeat does not promise something for nothing.

HILL:

You mean, of course, that if we fail to act when overtaken by defeat, the possible benefits of the experience are lost?

CARNEGIE:

That is precisely what I mean, and most people lose the benefits of defeat in this very manner. They simply accept defeat with a negative attitude, often allowing it to undermine their willpower instead of adding to it. One cannot afford to temporize with the experience of defeat, because if it is not converted into some form of constructive action, it becomes a destructive force, and every such experience removes one just another step away from the control of one's own mind.

HILL:

Then it is correct to say that defeat is always an asset or a liability, a blessing or a curse, according to the way one reacts to it?

CARNEGIE:

Yes, there are no "blanks" in connection with the experience of defeat. It always helps or hinders, but its effect is never neutral.

HILL:

In other words, we always go either ahead or backward after defeat?

CARNEGIE:

Precisely! Fortunately, the choice as to which it shall be rests with the individual. There is some unknown law of nature that adds to a person's character every thought reaction and every physical act in which they indulge, no matter what the cause. If the majority of our thoughts and acts are negative, you can see what will happen to our character.

HILL:

Do you mean that we never release a thought without adding its equivalent to our own character?

CARNEGIE:

Yes, that is what I mean! You can see, therefore, why controlled thought habits must be established if we're to build our character to order. If we do not build it to order, it will be built for us, through this law of which I spoke. The building blocks will consist of the stray influences that reach our mind.

HILL:

Then our character is never the same today as it was yesterday, if every thought we release is added to it?

CARNEGIE:

You might well say that our character is never the same for even two consecutive minutes. Every thought we release makes it stronger or weaker, according to the nature of those thoughts.

HILL:

Time, then, is humankind's asset or liability according to the way we use it?

CARNEGIE:

That's correct. Every human being who has reached the age of understanding literally stores up assets or liabilities, every second of their life, through the thought habits they acquire. If we control our thoughts by expressing the more important of them in appropriate, constructive action, time becomes our friend. If we neglect to take charge of our mind in this manner, time becomes our enemy.

From these conclusions, there is no escape.

HILL:

Your theory leads me to wonder if it doesn't partly explain why people seldom begin to attain success in the broader sense until they pass the age of forty, as you have stated.

CARNEGIE:

That is a logical conclusion. Before we succeed in any undertaking, we must become "success conscious." Now, what do I mean by this? I mean that we become success conscious by clearing our mind of all thoughts of failure and feeding it constantly with thoughts of success. In this manner, we sell ourselves the idea of success and learn to believe in our ability to achieve success; then our belief leads us naturally to opportunities to succeed.

Every thought becomes a part of our character. Therefore, in due time, we remove all self-imposed limitations, and then we find ourselves on the highway to achievement, with nothing in our way.

HILL:

But we may sell ourselves the idea of poverty or failure in the same manner?

CARNEGIE:

Our mind acts on the dominating thoughts we project onto it and proceeds, by every natural and logical means available, to carry out those thoughts to their conclusion. It will lead us to an opportunity to fail just as quickly and as definitely as it will to an opportunity to succeed.

The subconscious section of our mind picks up our dominating thoughts after they become thought habits and proceeds to carry them out regardless of their nature. Individuals have no control over the action of the subconscious mind, but we do have the privilege of controlling our dominating thoughts, and in this manner we can avail ourselves of the *benefits* of our subconscious mind.

> **As you think, so shall you become.**
> —Bruce Lee

HILL:

Some people question the existence of a subconscious mind. Is there any solid proof of its existence?

CARNEGIE:

Some people question the existence of Infinite Intelligence. After we limit our mind—through fear, doubt, and indecision—until these thoughts become a fixed part of our character, it is then only natural that we question many things that we might use to our advantage if we had the capacity to believe.

There is just as much evidence of the existence of a subconscious section of the mind as there is of the existence of electricity! Now, I am not going to try to find out what electricity is or what the source of its power may be, but I am going to keep on using electricity wherever it will serve me—and I can say the same of my subconscious mind.

I do not know what portion of the brain it is located in or what causes it to work as it does, but I do know that it works in precisely the manner I have described and that I shall continue using it as a means of translating my plans and desires into their material equivalent, just as I have been doing in the past.

There is only one way for people to convince themselves of the existence of a subconscious mind, and that is by experimentation, through the application of the instructions I have mentioned throughout this philosophy.

The power available through the subconscious section of the mind is an intangible power. It is not subject to isolation; nor can anyone explain its source. But the fact remains that it is a source of great power that is available to *any* human being. Those who, by their skepticism or indifference, neglect to make use of this power will never achieve success in the broader sense.

HILL:

I appreciate what you have said concerning the penalty for unbelief, but, Mr. Carnegie, we are preparing this philosophy to aid unbelievers. We wish to help people who have never been adequately informed as to the possibilities of their own minds, and I have asked questions from as many different angles as possible not because of my unbelief but to make sure that we don't overlook any opportunity to lead others into an understanding of how to avail themselves of their thought power.

It is very difficult for people to believe in something they do not understand. Therefore, I have purposely drawn you into many restatements of your views on the subconscious mind with the hope that in each statement you would disclose some idea or inspire some thought that would aid the students of this philosophy in acquiring your strong belief in this stupendous source of power.

CARNEGIE:

Of course. I understand the reason for your repetition of questions, and it is sound. And I agree that it is difficult for people to believe in what they do not understand. That is why I suggest that every student of this philosophy follow the suggestions I have offered, thereby acquiring belief in the power of the subconscious mind in the same way that I acquired mine—through personal experience! Belief acquired through personal experience is more likely to become permanent.

HILL:

If I understand you correctly, both belief and unbelief are tendencies that develop naturally from one's thought habits?

CARNEGIE:

That's correct. It is difficult for cynics to believe anything that lacks the most convincing proof, and they usually demand tangible proof. Of course, cynics never become empire builders, or industrial leaders, or outstanding successes in any calling, because cynicism is only another name for a closed mind. Cynics lock the door to their mind and throw away the key.

Cynicism, of course, is not a natural-born trait. It is acquired through the accumulation of negative thoughts, each of which is added to the character until at last one's capacity to believe is undermined.

HILL:

How can a cynic be freed from their self-imposed limitations?

CARNEGIE:

Usually through some catastrophe that tears down the wall of negative thought the cynic has built around themselves. A spell of sickness or the loss of something that is prized highly sometimes has the effect of bringing the cynic into a better understanding of the power of intangible things.

I once knew a cynic who hemmed himself in by unbelief until he became an atheist. He believed in no one except his wife. She was stricken by illness and died, and he came very near to succumbing to the same malady. He lingered on the borderline between life and death for almost a year but finally recovered. Through the shock of losing his wife and of being so ill, he was "born again." He became convinced that his wife was taken from him to shake him loose from his unbelief in the Creator.

After he recovered, he entered the ministry, and today he is one of the more influential men in that field. His capacity for unbelief has been translated into an equal capacity for belief.

HILL:

Then his misfortune was a blessing in disguise!

CARNEGIE:

Yes, if it could be called a misfortune. Personally, I would say that his experience was a blessing without disguise because it is obvious to everyone who knew this man, and to the man himself, that he found himself—his positive "other self"—through his experience of grief and sorrow.

HILL:

You believe, then, that sorrow may have beneficial effects?

CARNEGIE:

Yes; some people never seem to discover the intangible power of their own minds except by some personal experience that digs deeply into their emotions and breaks up their established thought habits.

> *You never know how strong you are*
> *until being strong is the only choice you have.*
> —Bob Marley

HILL:

You spoke of a natural law through which our thought habits are made permanent. Could it be that nature also provides a means by which the effects of this law, where they are negative, can be broken up?

CARNEGIE:

Without doubt, such a provision has been made. It would be necessary in order to provide everyone with the benefits of the Law of Compensation. Perhaps the Law of Compensation itself provides a means of release from self-acquired limitations. But be that as it may, there is no doubt that great sorrow growing out of failure and defeat and disappointments often has the effect of restoring to people their sense of faith, thereby giving them a new start and revealing to them the blessings that are available through belief.

If it is true that the salvation of people's souls depends upon their belief, then it must be equally true that the Creator has provided human beings with the means by which they can correct the damage they do themselves through unbelief. Perhaps they may have to be forced to avail themselves of those means through some catastrophe that tears down the wall of unbelief they have built around themselves.

EDITOR'S NOTE:

The Law of Compensation states that in life we are compensated for our contributions, both positive and negative. The reason many people neglect this great natural law is that they mistakenly associate its merits with short-term efficacy; if they recognize it and don't receive the immediate result they are after, they abandon it. However, they forget that the longer the term is, the more we regress to the mean—this is true of any universal law. Over time, we will receive what we deserve, which often may not be what we want.

Perhaps you've heard the saying "The house always wins," which is used justifiably to dissuade people from wasting money by gambling. Dazzling lights, extravagant fountains, and lavish fixtures are paid for by the accumulated losses of gamblers, and these elements then are used to lure others to the table. Gamblers try to cheat the Law of Compensation, often unconsciously, but the only sure bet is that casinos are experts at making the odds; they know that you might score a temporary win on a fluke, but the longer they keep you there, the greater the likelihood that the house will take your money.

This also can be seen with credit card spending, in which the power of compound interest works against those who don't manage their money properly. If the money is not readily available in a savings account, many people resort to what appears to be readily available money in a credit account. When the bank statement arrives, they receive their "compensation" in the form of exorbitant interest payments.

However, savvy investors use the same power to achieve financial freedom. Each month, they contribute a fixed portion of their salary, which increases in line with their skills and compensation, to build a diverse portfolio of quality assets that appreciate in value. This results in a perpetually growing portfolio that will provide a great reward for their self-discipline.

It's the same law but with totally different outcomes. Albert Einstein once said: "Compound interest is the eighth wonder of the world. He who understands it, earns it. He who doesn't, pays it." That statement echoes the Law of Compensation. You can try to fool it in the short term, but over time it always wins—in all areas of your life. Every thought that we release or action that we indulge in becomes part of our character and, depending on its nature, either strengthens or weakens us.

HILL:

Of course! Your theory is obviously sound. And it gives me an entirely new slant on failure and sorrow and the experiences that break people's hearts. Sometimes these are the only means by which people can become acquainted with their "other selves." It is encouraging to know that the Creator has provided humankind with a means by which they may redeem themselves from the follies of their own ignorance!

CARNEGIE:

Now you are getting the idea I wished to convey. No one should ever become cynical when overtaken by failure, illness, or catastrophe, because it may be that in the hour of their greatest trial they will find their greatest strength. That has been the experience of many whom the world has called "great." Perhaps it has been the experience of *all* such people.

Defeat and physical pain are two great benefits. They warn us that something needs correction, and if we respond to the warning inquiringly, with the right sort of mental attitude, we usually find what it is that needs our attention.

HILL:

This lesson has been a great revelation to me, the idea that failure, defeat, and sorrow may divert one away from habits that can lead to economic distress, but of far greater importance, that such experiences may reveal the way to the salvation of the soul.

CARNEGIE:

In conclusion, I would like to warn you about the importance of putting into action the knowledge you have gained from this lesson. Do not be contented with merely knowing! Instead, put this knowledge into active use through your thought habits. It can become yours permanently only on the condition that you make the fullest use of it.

ANALYSIS:
LEARNING FROM DEFEAT
By Napoleon Hill

Perhaps no other principle of the success philosophy provides as much hope for personal achievement as this one. Here we have convincing evidence that "every adversity carries with it the seed of an equivalent benefit."

The statement is definite! It contains no "ifs," "buts," or "maybes."

Moreover, it comes from someone who has proved beyond all reasonable doubt that no human experience is lost; that defeat can become a great benefit; and that failure is seldom more than a form of temporary defeat that can be converted into an equivalent success.

With the outlook of the world what it is today, this insight comes at a time when there is plenty of opportunity for its application. Millions of people have met with economic defeat during the past decade—they are in need of a practical means for staging a comeback. Millions more have met with defeat through the loss of their liberty because of World War II. Across the planet, there is a need for a better understanding of the modus operandi by which people may convert defeat into a practical means of recouping their losses.

Failure and pain are two methods by which nature speaks
to every living thing when something goes wrong
that should have attention.
—Andrew Carnegie

I have no intention of trying to improve on Mr. Carnegie's analysis of the philosophy of learning from defeat, but I shall offer what I believe to be sound testimony to support his thesis on this subject.

Nowhere in this entire philosophy have I found a more encouraging promise than that which is presented in this lesson. It is here that we have the assurance of one of the most practical people the world has ever known, who explains that the experience of defeat, which we have been accepting as a stumbling block, may actually be converted into a stepping-stone for us to climb toward our chosen goal.

To use a simple metaphor, we might say that this philosophy of learning from defeat enables us to say to life: "If you hand me a sour lemon through any sort of unpleasant experience, I will convert it into lemonade instead of allowing it to sour me."

It is encouraging to look upon failure as a common language in which nature speaks to all people and brings them into the spirit of humility so that they may acquire wisdom and understanding. When they accept failure and defeat in this attitude, these events once seen as negatives become assets of priceless value, because they lead almost invariably to the discovery of hidden powers that everyone possesses.

A little while ago, I had the privilege of talking with a man who lost a large fortune during the Great Depression that began in 1929. He was generous enough to enumerate the benefits he had gained from his financial loss.

Here is his story, in his own words:

Through the loss of my material fortune, I found an intangible fortune of such huge proportions that it cannot be estimated in terms of material things alone. The Great Depression was, at one and the same time, the cause of my greatest defeat and my noblest victory, for it introduced me to a philosophy of life that will take the sting out of all future defeats.

The Depression deprived me of my money, but it taught me that absolute individual independence is a theory only; that everyone is dependent on others in one way or another, throughout life. It taught me that:

- Worrying over things one cannot control is futile.

- Fear is a state of mind that generally has no cause that cannot be cured.

- The Biblical quotation "Whatsoever a man soweth, that shall he also reap" is more than a poetical sentence; it is sound philosophy.

- Anything that forces or inspires one to use one's initiative with definiteness of purpose is beneficial.

- Money, real estate, government bonds, and material things in general can become worthless through fear and a negative mental attitude toward the public at large.

- The dominating thoughts of one's mind have a definite way of clothing themselves in their physical equivalent, whether those thoughts are positive or negative.

- There is no such reality as something for nothing either in the realm of natural law or in the affairs of people.

- There is a Law of Compensation that pays all human beings in a common coin sooner or later.

- There is something infinitely worse than being forced to work, and it is being forced NOT TO WORK!

- The physical and legal possession of property ensures neither its permanency nor its value.

- A business that is conducted under the Golden Rule principle will survive a depression more easily than one that is not.

- Famines follow feasts as surely as night follows day, and feasts follow famines.

- A suit of clothes can be worn for more than one season, and the automobile does not need to be traded in every year.

- Fear can be spread, like an epidemic of disease, by mass thought and mass talk.

- It is more blessed and more profitable to render useful service than to demand something for nothing through subsidies.

- Temporary defeat need not be accepted as permanent failure.

- Both success and failure originate in the mind as the result of one's dominating thoughts.

- Riches in material things without riches of the spirit may be more of a curse than a blessing.

- A person's greatest blessing may consist in their greatest sorrow.

- There is truth in these great paradoxes: the blessings of adversity, the companionship of solitude, and the voice of silence.

- Riches of the purse without humility of the heart may be dangerous.

- There is one person on whom one can depend, without disappointment, in the time of adversity, and that is one's self.

- The sun rises and sets, water flows downhill, the seasons of the year come and go with regularity, the stars retain their accustomed places in the heavens nightly, and nature moves in orderly fashion during a business depression the same as at other times. Nothing changes because of a depression except the minds of people!

- People respond to the voice of defeat when they will listen to no other.

- All people become closely akin, in spirit and in deed, when they are overtaken by a common catastrophe.

- The possession of great wealth attracts many who profess friendship they do not genuinely feel, and the loss of one's money discloses the true identity of all who proclaim themselves friends.

Stated in one sentence, the Great Depression revealed to me my "other self"—the positive self that I had been neglecting; the self that accepts no such reality as permanent defeat or losses that cannot be recouped by accepting defeat as a challenge to engage in greater effort.

EDITOR'S NOTE:

What an incredible story! What I love most about the words of Carnegie and Hill and now those of Hill's acquaintance as expressed in this story is how they can cut to the root of today's problems despite having been written more than three-quarters of a century ago.

This man's roller-coaster journey contains themes that we can see echoed many decades after it was written. Its lessons are most evident in the economic crisis that struck in 2007 after subprime debt caused both the housing market and the stock market to collapse, leading to unprecedented worldwide volatility.

However, it wasn't all doom and gloom. Some savvy investors recognized that the market is driven by two things: fear and greed. These are the elements that turn paper losses to actual losses, creating ruin for some and unprecedented opportunity for others. Those others snapped up leading companies, in many cases household names that had enormous growth prospects despite having experienced short-term (and very public) turmoil.

Legendary investor Warren Buffett has been doing this for decades. In each downturn, recession, or financial crisis, Buffett chooses not to throw up his hands in despair or cower under his desk. Rather, he views the situation as an opportunity to consolidate his wealth; he buys deeply undervalued companies and sets up operational efficiencies and synergies that lead to enormous returns over time. Speaking of this strategy, he once said, "Be fearful when others are greedy and greedy when others are fearful."

You can bet that Buffett has been on the receiving end of some significant losses, but the experience gained from those losses is what enables him to make the major moves that deliver his most significant returns. Although we may experience significant loss in the short term, our experience, if properly channeled, leaves us capable of earning far more than we lost.

In contrast, those who focus on the fear driven by doomsday news stories published by outlets that directly benefit from the hysteria they create find that their actions and subsequent financial positions remain inverse to those of experienced investors such as Buffett.

There can be no such thing as permanent defeat for people who accept adversity in the spirit described by this man. His material losses were substantial. They amounted to more money than the average person ever possesses during an entire lifetime. Yet through his loss of money, this man found something infinitely greater than all the money in the world. He discovered that he has a mind that is capable of earning more money than he lost. I suspect he made other discoveries of greater importance to him than this, among them the fact that people who are rich in money *only* are poor in the things that make happiness.

This man benefited from loss of money because he accepted it as a test of his spirit. Through the test, he found that there is a hidden power in every mind that is capable of dealing with every human emergency. Now he is on better terms with himself, his business associates, and the public whom he serves through his profession.

However, the man's business partner took a different view of the loss of his material fortune. He looked upon the loss as irretrievable, gave up without a fight, and ended the matter by jumping off a high building. Further investigation of his situation revealed that he had been in the habit of yielding to defeat in connection with the daily experiences of his life. Therefore, when he was overtaken by a major emergency that called for great strength of character, he was caught short.

As Mr. Carnegie has so well stated, it is our daily thought habits that provide us with a strong "blanket of protection" or leave us susceptible to the negative life forces that bring defeat.

So what are these negative thought habits that lead to failure? They are the habit of:

- Accepting poverty as something one cannot avoid

- Neglecting to recognize that external matter and external circumstances have no influence over internal thought except as one permits such influence

- Wishing for a thing or meekly hoping to get it without firmly resolving to acquire it through definiteness of purpose

- Tolerating fear and the feeling of inferiority

- Procrastinating, arising from lack of a definite major purpose

- Expecting defeat before beginning a task

- Failing to carry through plans after they have been started

- Allowing the emotions to have full sway over willpower
- Associating with people who freely accept defeat as unavoidable
- Reading negative news stories and accepting them as indicative of one's personal condition
- Not having any controlled habits at all
- Allowing other people to do one's thinking
- Expecting nothing from life but the bare necessities of existence
- Desiring something for nothing
- Accepting temporary defeat as permanent failure
- Taking the path of least resistance wherever and whenever personal initiative is required
- Worrying over the effects of circumstances instead of searching for the cause and removing it
- Thinking of the plans that will not work and the things one cannot have instead of looking for plans that will work and centering the mind on things one may acquire
- Looking on the dark side of every situation: of seeing the hole in the donut but not the donut
- Speaking only of failure, defeat, and the negative side of life in ordinary daily conversations
- Being poverty conscious instead of success conscious
- Complaining of lack of opportunity instead of embracing the opportunities at hand or, better yet, creating opportunities
- Looking everywhere for the causes of failure except in a mirror
- Envying those who succeed instead of learning from their example
- Making snap judgments; guessing instead of getting the facts
- Losing one's temper instead of harnessing it and putting it to work

Now, these are some of the daily habits of people who, by the force of their own habits, have condemned themselves to failure. These are the habits that prepare the mind to accept defeat as permanent. These are the habits that put the subconscious mind to work in reverse gear, bringing failure instead of success. These are the habits that undermine willpower and leave people open to the influence of all forms of defeat.

It is said that "when you are truly ready for something, it will make its appearance." The habits we have mentioned prove that statement's accuracy, because they prepare one to be ready for failure and that is precisely what appears.

> **Don't cry because it's over;**
> **smile because it happened.**
> —Author unknown

When you hear of people that "everything they touch turns to gold," meaning that they succeed at everything they undertake, you may be sure that they prepared themselves for this sort of good fortune by conditioning their minds with a success consciousness.

Andrew Carnegie did not create the great United States Steel Corporation out of self-limitations; nor did he create it through any of the thought habits we have mentioned. He created it by taking possession of his own mind early in life, deciding what he wanted, and becoming determined to get it. Although things often went wrong, he harnessed his reactions to his defeats and put them to work on his behalf in the manner he has recommended in this chapter.

Henry Ford did not become the head of the great Ford industrial empire by mere chance; nor did he attain his position through his superior education, or influential backing, or money. He attained it by conditioning his mind, through self-discipline, such that it caused him to expect and demand of himself that he would build his empire. The idea was his own entirely. He created it thought by thought, although he met with defeat in one form or another at almost every step of the way.

Every time we stay positive in the face of defeat, refusing to react in a negative manner, we acquire greater mental power. Eventually, this habit becomes the foundation of our strength.

We can think and talk about anything until it is sure to make its appearance, for it is true, as Mr. Carnegie has stated, that "all thought has a tendency to clothe itself in its physical equivalent." Here, then, is the very crux of this lesson on learning from defeat: the experience of defeat becomes an asset or a liability according to one's beliefs about it.

George Washington did not win the American Revolution because of superior arms, or better trained soldiers, or a superior number of soldiers. He was outnumbered on all these points. But there was one area in which he excelled: he refused to accept the possibility of defeat. Washington believed he would win, and he transferred that belief to his soldiers, who accepted it. It was that belief, and nothing else, that won the American Revolution. Importantly, that same attitude toward personal defeat enables one to convert defeat into an *asset*.

When members of any group are bound together in a common cause and express their combined power through the mastermind principle, they can be defeated by nothing except a stronger group applying the same principle. Even when a mastermind alliance consists of but two people, they have available through this alliance a form of power sufficient in every way to save them from most of the average causes of defeat. But the alliance must be founded on that resolute will to win that accepts no failure as permanent defeat.

I was once told of a unique system for converting defeat into a practical, usable asset. The system is so simple that anyone may adopt it and use it by following these steps:

- Keep a diary in which you write down a complete history of every defeat you have experienced, no matter how inconsequential.

- Record the facts just as they occurred even though your account may show that you were defeated through your own neglect.

- Every month, revisit your diary. Under the record of each defeat, write out a statement of the benefit derived or of the benefit you expect to derive from it.

The man who first informed me of this system has been following it for several years. Since adopting it, he has never experienced a defeat that did not in time yield him a benefit equal to or greater than the loss temporarily sustained by the defeat. He explained that on one occasion the defeat was of such a nature that, had he not met with it, his business would have been ruined and he would have sustained a great loss financially.

Now, here is a man immune to defeat. He has learned how to respond in a positive manner, and he acknowledges that his system works so well that his defeats have become fewer with age. That is due, of course, to the fact that he has become success conscious, and because of this consciousness he anticipates the causes of many possible defeats and averts them before they happen.

His system has another great advantage—it provides tangible evidence that "adversity carries with it the seed of an equivalent benefit." This man does not have to take anyone's word for this; he has proved it through his own experience. That is proof that even a cynic couldn't resist.

This same man has worked out another system for making himself success conscious, which I strongly recommend. To use this system, take these steps:

- Get a large piece of cardboard, and write (or print) out a list of all the major causes of failure that were listed on page 156–157.

- Next to each of these, add 31 squares, representing the 31 days of the month.

- Then, each day, calibrate your performance by giving yourself a rating on each of the causes of failure. To do this, simply place an (X) or a (✓), symbolizing either your neglect or your mastery of each item.

The man then compares this chart with the previously mentioned daily diary. At the end of each month, the two systems show him exactly which of the causes of defeat he has not fully mastered. Of course, the object of the plan is to make himself success conscious by setting up in his mind an attitude of watchfulness in connection with the causes of defeat.

His system has become so interesting that every member of his family supervises him very carefully to make sure that he rates himself accurately, and he admitted that on one occasion one of his small children chastised him sharply for neglecting to record correctly an experience of defeat! Not only is this man conditioning his own mind to become success conscious, he is benefiting every member of his family with his system.

What we all need is a practical system for taking inventory of ourselves. If the inventory is taken honestly, it will disclose our major weaknesses and reveal our hidden powers that have been neglected. Such a system should become a sort of daily self-confession.

EDITOR'S NOTE:

An opportunity for candid self-reflection is essential on the route to success, and that is the exact reason we created *The Napoleon Hill Success Journal*. You will find that it gives you an opportunity to state your definite major purpose alongside your daily intent. This clarity about what results need to be achieved enables us to channel our efforts into the most important areas. After all, it's impossible to win the day if we don't even know what victory looks like.

Another important component is the ability to audit your time, energy, and results. This introspective review highlights how effective your actions are while offering a framework that will help you succeed in the coming week.

You don't need to spend hours on this. The *Journal* requires a few minutes of self-discipline, with bountiful rewards for those who are committed. It will unleash your imagination, restore your focus, unlock hyperproductivity, help create balance, and give you an awareness of what's most important in your life. Being dedicated to mastery will mean that each day you will become more effective, and that will lead to dramatic improvements in happiness and all the relationships in your life.

Countless CEOs, entrepreneurs, and athletes have spoken out about the benefits of introspection and intent. Now it's your turn!

One of the greatest life insurance salespeople in the US has an entirely different system to insure himself against defeat. This man was selling an average of $250,000 worth of insurance each year before he discovered this system and put it to work. He now belongs to the Million Dollar Club, an organization of life insurance salespeople who to remain in the club must sell a minimum of $1 million worth of insurance each year. This man has been a member for nine consecutive years, and he now sells more than ten times what he used to over the same period.

His system consists of selecting a definite major purpose, which he wrote out, pasted on the mirror (where he could see it every morning while he was shaving), and then read aloud so often that he committed it to memory. Now he repeats it three times daily, once after each meal. It is as follows:

A LIFE INSURER'S DEFINITE MAJOR PURPOSE:

1. My major purpose in life is to write a minimum of $1 million worth of life insurance annually.

2. To accomplish my aim, I will work with a list of 100 properly qualified prospective buyers of insurance that will be kept in my possession at all times, and I will keep this list filled by adding a new name every time a prospective buyer becomes a life insurance policy holder.

3. I will make a minimum of ten calls every working day even if I have to work late into the night to do so.

4. I will make every interview profitable, regardless of whether I make a sale, by inducing prospective buyers to introduce me to at least one new prospective buyer among their personal friends every time I interview them.

5. I will approach my prospective buyers not as the representative of my company but as their personal representative whose business it is to counsel and protect them and their beneficiaries.

6. When interviewing prospective buyers, I will think of a refusal to buy as being not a final but merely a deferred decision, and I will so inform prospective buyers, and I will remain with each prospective buyer as long as they indicate they have not made a decision, no matter if I remain there all night.

7. Every person to whom I sell insurance will be transferred to my "courtesy cooperation" list, and I will call on them regularly (at least once a month) so that I may serve their friends by selling them insurance through their influence.

8. I will remember, always, that "No" may mean "Yes," and I will negotiate with all my prospective buyers on that basis.

9. I will accept no such reality as defeat, because my system is such that it is bound to convert every interview into a sale—if not to the person whom I interview, then to one of their friends.

10. I believe in my system because it is sincerely designed to benefit all whom it affects, and believing in it, I will work it with all the power at my command.

(SIGNED) ————————————————————————

If you read this commitment carefully, you will observe that it allows for no such reality as defeat. The best evidence of its soundness is to be found in the fact that the man who operates it has increased his sales by more than 1,000 percent, yet he works no harder than ever before! But he works more intelligently, with greater determination, and under the principle of organized endeavor.

The most important part of his "organized endeavor" is his positive mental attitude. He *expects* to sell more insurance now than he previously sold, he has a *plan* for selling more, and he is working his plan in a *spirit* that makes no provision for defeat.

> *There is no defeat, in truth, save from within;*
> *Unless you're beaten there, you're sure to win.*
> —Henry Austin

More than six thousand life insurance salespeople have been trained to use this philosophy in their profession, and not one of them, as far as I know, has failed to increase their sales ability, although the case I mention is an exception as far as the increased sales ability is concerned.

The training of these salespeople began with a complete character analysis, during which an accurate inventory of their mental assets and liabilities was disclosed to them. They were checked point by point on the major causes of failure described in this lesson. At first, many of them protested vigorously when their weaknesses were disclosed to them, and their protests were sincere. They had been deceiving themselves, just as the majority of people deceive themselves, about traits of personality and character that were standing between them and greater achievements in sales.

I wish to emphasize the importance of using a frank and honest self-analysis based on a point-by-point checkup that uses the major causes of failure described in this chapter as the measuring stick. A careful self-analysis is needed so that you can learn for yourself in what ways you might have developed habits that are detrimental to you.

There is another fundamental error that leads to defeat, and it is an error that is common to many. Let me describe it by relating the experience of two brothers who lived in a mountainous section of the country.

One of the boys was eighteen years old, and the other was only twelve. Their father presented each of them with a new Winchester rifle. Excitedly, they went on a hunting trip, looking for some bears they had seen in the woods near their farm. In due time they came upon a bear, but they began to argue about who had seen it first and who would have the first shot at it. They finally compromised by agreeing that they had probably seen the bear at the same time, so it was only fair for them both to aim and fire at the same time.

They shot the bear, and it tumbled into the weeds. The boys ran to claim their kill, with the older boy arriving first. He looked down and saw the bear, which was still kicking around in the weeds. The younger boy became alarmed lest he be cheated of the honor of helping to kill the beast, so he yelled at his brother, "Say, bud! We killed a bear, didn't we?"

The older boy turned around with a look of disgust on his face and yelled back at his brother, "'We,' nothing! YOU SHOT PA'S CALF!"

Now that is a characteristic of human nature: nearly everyone is inclined to claim the honors when things go well, while most people naturally disclaim the responsibility when things go wrong.

That trait deprives one of all possibility of leadership whenever it is allowed to get a foothold. As Mr. Carnegie has appropriately stated, "An enemy discovered is an enemy that is almost mastered." Every person has hidden enemies in their own character traits, habits, and personality, but those traits cannot be mastered until they are recognized.

Mr. Carnegie has listed forty-five of these major enemies. The first on the list: the habit of drifting through life without a definite major purpose. This should be the *first* enemy to be uncovered in your analysis if you lack such a purpose. Unless you master this enemy, you may as well not bother about the others, because it is the key to the others. Analysis of more than twenty-five thousand people, representing a cross-section from all backgrounds, clearly showed that 98 percent of people fail because they lack a fixed, definite goal in life. That's an astounding fact! It is astounding because the lack of a definite major purpose is something that anyone can easily correct.

Formulating a definite major purpose takes first position in the principles of individual achievement because that purpose leads to the development of habits of definiteness in connection with one's *minor* purposes. It's wise to analyze yourself very carefully on this point, because the habit of drifting and lacking a definite major purpose carries with it a flock of related habits of indefiniteness in other important matters connected with your daily life. Both good and bad habits have relatives—they never exist singularly.

Study the list of the forty-five major causes of failure on page 104–106 and observe how working with a definite major purpose can wipe out many of them, including:

5. Lack of self-discipline

7. Lack of ambition to aim above mediocrity

10. Lack of persistence

11. The habit of maintaining a negative mental attitude

14. The habit of indecision

15. The habit of fear

21. Lack of concentrated effort

23. Failure to budget and use time properly

24. Lack of controlled enthusiasm

25. Intolerance

31. The habit of forming opinions not based on facts

32. Lack of vision and imagination

33. Failure to make a mastermind alliance

38. The habit of procrastination

41. Failure to act on personal initiative

42. Lack of self-reliance

44. Lack of an attractive personality

45. Failure to develop willpower

Of the forty-five major causes of failure, eighteen of them disappear as if by a stroke of magic when one adopts and begins to carry out a definite major purpose. Better still, these eighteen causes are the most significant on the entire list—significant because they are the most common causes of failure. And those "enemies" can be conquered through a single move!

Every time you stumble and fall, but rise again,
you learn wisdom. Wisdom comes from failure
much more than from success.
—Andrew Carnegie

Therefore, if you're creating a success-conscious chart like the one we discussed on page 160, I suggest you note these eighteen causes in red ink so that you may give them close attention as you begin to carry out your definite major purpose. Let them become danger signals, because that is precisely what they are. Do not wait for them to disappear automatically; instead, go to work on them by proactively developing habits of a nature *opposite* to each of them.

With mastery of these eighteen enemies, you will see that others on the list automatically disappear, because every formed habit encourages other related habits. The major cause of failure is the habit of drifting through life without a definite major purpose. Get this habit out of the way and you will have little difficulty in mastering the related habits we have mentioned.

Life consists of a great variety of human problems. No one is strong, smart, or wise enough to solve all their problems with one move. Therefore, these problems must be dealt with one at a time, and the sensible thing to do is to begin with the major problem and get it under control, because major problems control minor problems.

For example, if a man is faced by a gang of hoodlums, he does not undertake to fight the whole gang at once, but if he is wise, he picks the leader of the gang and deals with him first. If the leader can be defeated, the others lose their courage, and they fight poorly if they fight at all. Similarly, these eighteen causes of failure represent enemies that can be defeated by mastering the chief of them all—the habit of drifting without a definite major purpose.

As Mr. Carnegie has stated, the first and the last of the forty-five major causes of failure control all the others except one. Give your first attention, therefore, to these two by developing a strong willpower and placing it squarely behind a definite major purpose. Begin, right where you stand, to put this purpose into action.

Thinking and talking will not suffice. *Act.* Keep on acting until your goal has been achieved. Your strength will come from action. It will:

- Give you self-reliance

- Give you enthusiasm

- Give you a keener imagination

- Lead you to use your personal initiative

- Wipe out the limitations you have set up in your mind

- Give you persistence

- Give you a definiteness of decision in all matters

- Give you a strong willpower

With these qualities mastered, you will have no difficulty in converting defeat into a constructive force that will serve as a challenge to rise to greater effort.

In Memoriam

By Lord Alfred Tennyson

I held it truth, with him who sings
To one clear harp in divers tones,
That men may rise on stepping-stones
Of their dead selves to higher things.

I recommend that you begin your action habits by following the habit of Going the Extra Mile! You can begin this habit right where you are, without preparation or ceremony. Begin with the members of your own family. Carry on with those you work with.

Although the rules of your employment might limit your hours, they do not—and cannot—limit the quality of work you perform. Once get the self-satisfaction that comes from doing more, and better, work than is expected of you, and observe how this habit attracts the favorable attention of those whom you serve, and you will never discontinue the habit.

Action, therefore—the sort of action that will benefit you most—narrows itself down to four habits you should form and follow out with regularity:

1. The habit of definiteness of a major purpose

2. The habit of Going the Extra Mile

3. The habit of moving on your own willpower

4. The habit of accepting defeat as an incentive to greater effort

These four habits are on the "must" list of all who wish to avoid the consequences of defeat. Alone, they are insufficient to provide the full benefit, but they are sufficient to provide a good start. Once this start has been made, the going will get easier.

Throughout this chapter, two nouns are used more frequently than any others: "action" and "habit." All success is based on action habits! Defeat is converted into an asset through action habits. As Mr. Carnegie has so impressively stated, knowledge itself is without practical value. Knowledge becomes valuable only when it is expressed in appropriate action. A person can be a walking encyclopedia and still starve to death. On the other hand, a person who has but limited knowledge may, through the habitual *expression* of that knowledge, acquire every material thing they need.

EDITOR'S NOTE:

One of my favorite Hill quotes is "Action is the real measure of intelligence," reinforced through consistency. Unfortunately, many people who hear the title *Think and Grow Rich*, the best-selling self-help book of all time, mistakenly believe that it focuses almost exclusively on using thoughts to provide extensive results. Yet in every chapter and on almost every page, Hill emphasizes the importance of *purposeful action*, which Carnegie has reiterated throughout this book. Thoughts alone are insufficient to catapult one into the realms of greatness.

As we've read, we're either rewarded or punished, depending on our action habits, so let's explore how that might work in a practical sense, using content creators as an example. Today smartphones have given very many people an opportunity to share their voice with the world and monetize their passion; this means that anyone with a smartphone can become a content creator if he or she chooses to. Despite initial excitement about their new hobby, the majority of aspiring content creators either:

- Fail to publish content in the first place because they don't believe they're good enough, or

- Spend a great deal of energy comparing their progress to what others, who have been on the journey for much longer, have achieved. This is typically done by using a variety of vanity metrics such as number of YouTube subscribers, Instagram followers, and Facebook likes.

As these people enter their thirties and forties, although they might have had the grandest aspirations or started many endeavors, they have very few, if any, tangible results to show for their efforts.

In contrast, those who live with a growth mindset—and apply the lessons Hill and Carnegie espouse—recognize that all their favorite entrepreneurs started at the bottom. To enjoy the same influence and rewards their idols enjoy, they need to replicate their purposeful action in their own way over time. As Zig Ziglar said, "You don't have to be great to start, but you have to start to be great."

Most people engage in plenty of physical action, but the major weakness of their activity is that it is not *planned* action. It is not directed toward the attainment of definite ends. It uses up physical energy without attaining desirable results.

The time that is wasted by the average person through the lack of planned action would be sufficient to provide more material success than one person needs if that time were properly organized and directed to a definite end.

Potential Benefits of Failure and Defeat

People who neglect to analyze the circumstances of their life—and to think those experiences through, from cause to effect—are apt to overlook the potential benefits of failure and defeat. As a result, they miss their opportunity to profit by the fact that "every adversity carries with it the seed of an equivalent benefit."

To assist, let us consider some of the potential benefits of those experiences known as failure and defeat.

- Defeat may break up some negative habit one has formed, thereby releasing one's energies for the formation of other and more desirable habits. Physical illness, for example, is nature's way of breaking up established habits of the body and freeing it to form better habits that are more conducive to sound health. In the process of readjusting their physical health, many people have discovered the power of their own minds. Therefore, illness was a blessing.

- Defeat may have the effect of supplanting arrogance and vanity with humility of the heart, thereby paving the way for the formation of better human relationships.

- Defeat may cause one to acquire the habit of taking inventory of oneself (something everyone should do without defeat, but most don't) for the purpose of uncovering the weakness that brought about the defeat.

- Defeat may lead to the development of stronger willpower, provided one accepts it as a challenge to rise to greater effort and not as a signal to quit. This perhaps is the greatest potential benefit of all forms of defeat, because the "seed of an equivalent benefit" lies entirely in one's mental attitude or reaction toward the defeat. One cannot always control the outward effects of defeat, for example, when it involves the loss of material things or damages other people as well as one's self, but one may control one's reaction to the experience.

- Defeat may break up undesirable relationships with other people, thereby paving the way for the formation of more beneficial relationships. In fact, after years of detrimental and habitual clinging, the relationship can often be shaken loose only by some form of defeat.

- Defeat may lead one into the deeper wells of sorrow through such experiences as the loss of a loved one, the breaking up of a love alliance, or the destruction of a deep friendship. These are experiences that force us to seek consolation in our own soul, and in seeking, we sometimes find the door that leads to a huge reserve of hidden power that would never have been discovered without defeat.

The sort of defeat mentioned at the end of our list often serves the purpose of diverting our attention and activities from the material to the spiritual values of life. Thus, it may well be assumed that the Creator gave humankind the capacity for deep sorrow for a definite purpose.

It has been said often that nothing but deep sorrow will make a great artist, the reason for this being, of course, that sorrow brings humility of the heart and causes one to search within for the creative force needed to heal the wounds of one's sorrow. When one finds this force, one may discover that it can be transmuted into many forms of creative effort other than that of healing wounds of the heart. This force may lead one to great heights of individual creative effort in a spirit of humility, which alone can make one truly great!

Success without humility of the heart is apt to prove temporary and unsatisfying. This is evidenced in most instances in which people suddenly become successful without experiencing hardship, struggle, and defeat. Success obtained the short and easy way is apt to be temporary.

> **Nothing in life is to be feared. It is only to be understood.**
> —Marie Curie

Those who can go through defeat that crushes their finer emotions without allowing their feelings to be smothered by the experience can become a *master* in their chosen field if they convert their sorrow and disappointment into an urge to creative action. In this manner, the world has discovered its great musicians, poets, artists, empire builders, technology innovators, and literary geniuses. History is replete with evidence that the most admired in all these fields attained greatness through some tragedy that introduced them to hidden spiritual forces.

However, we do not need to turn to the past to prove that defeat may become an asset of great value. Examine the records of those who attain success in whatever calling you wish and you will be convinced that they have formed the habit of accepting defeat as an impetus to take greater, and better-planned, action. And if you analyze all the facts carefully, wherever you find successful people, you may discover that their success is in exact proportion to the extent to which they have mastered their reactions toward defeat.

The person who fails and still fights on usually uncovers a source of creative vision that enables them to convert failure into enduring success. In his poem "Opportunity," Walter Malone expresses this thought precisely:

OPPORTUNITY

By Walter Malone

They do me wrong who say I come no more,
When once I knock and fail to find you in;
For every day I stand outside your door,
And bid you wake, and rise to fight and win.
Wail not for precious chances passed away!
Weep not for golden ages on the wane!
Each night I burn the records of the day—
At sunrise, every soul is born again!

. . . . .

Laugh like a boy at splendors that have sped,
To vanished joys be blind and deaf and dumb;
My judgments seal the dead past with its dead,
But never bind a moment yet to come.

This poem inspires hope, courage, and the will to try again after being overcome by defeat. Moreover, it harmonizes perfectly with the experiences of those who have risen to fame, power, and fortune on the wings of defeat. Malone had a clear vision of this potential power, which he expressed in the line "At sunrise every soul is born again."

Andrew Carnegie captured the idea inimitably when he said, "Every adversity carries with it the seed of an equal or greater benefit." This statement clearly indicates that there is something one must do in order to benefit by defeat: one must discover the nature of the "seed of an equivalent benefit" and cause it to germinate and grow through some form of organized endeavor.

Mr. Carnegie did not say that adversity carries with it the full-blown flower of an equivalent benefit, but only the *seed*. Nature has arranged the principle of defeat so that the individual who benefits by defeat must make some sort of contribution of individual effort both in uncovering and in germinating the seed of potential benefit that defeat carries with it. Here, as elsewhere throughout nature, there is no such reality as getting something for nothing.

If you recognize the full meaning of the thoughts passed on through this chapter (and this can be done only by meditation and thought), this chapter alone might well be regarded as the turning point at which you become acquainted with your "other self," that self which recognizes the truth that defeat is nothing but an experience that should serve as an inspiration to take greater and more determined action.

PART 3

THE GOLDEN RULE APPLIED: WHAT YOU DO TO ANOTHER, YOU DO TO YOURSELF

There is no asset comparable in value with sound character, and this is something that an individual must build for oneself, through thoughts and deeds. Character is of definite, practical value.

—Andrew Carnegie

THE GOLDEN RULE APPLIED

This chapter begins in the private study of Mr. Carnegie, with Mr. Carnegie leading.

CARNEGIE:

We come now to the principle of the Golden Rule applied—the principle that nearly everyone professes to believe but few people practice, due, I suspect, to the fact that so few people understand the deep underlying psychology of this principle. Too many people interpret the Golden Rule as if its meaning were not to do unto others as if they were the others but to do others and do them plenty before others do them.

Of course, this false interpretation of this great rule of human conduct can bring nothing but negative results!

The real benefits of the Golden Rule applied do not come from those in whose favor it is applied, but they accrue to the one applying the rule in the form of a strengthened conscience, peace of mind, and the other attributes of sound character—the factors that attract the more desirable things of life, including enduring friendships, fortune, and happiness.

To get the most from the Golden Rule, one must combine it with the principle of Going the Extra Mile, wherein lies the applied portion of the Golden Rule. The Golden Rule supplies the right mental attitude, while Going the Extra Mile supplies the action feature of this great rule. Combining the two gives one the power of attraction that induces friendly cooperation from others as well as providing opportunities for personal accumulation.

HILL:

I assume from what you have said that there are few benefits to be acquired through a mere belief in the Golden Rule?

CARNEGIE:

Very few! Passive belief in this rule will accomplish nothing. It is the *application* of the rule that brings benefits, and they are so numerous and varied that they touch the life through almost every human relationship. This rule:

- Opens the mind for the guidance of Infinite Intelligence through faith
- Develops self-reliance by building a better relationship with one's conscience
- Builds a sound character sufficient to sustain one in times of emergency
- Develops a more attractive personality
- Attracts the friendly cooperation of others in all human relationships
- Discourages unfriendly opposition from others
- Gives one peace of mind and freedom from self-established limitations
- Makes one immune to the more damaging forms of fear, since the person with a clear conscience seldom fears anything or anyone
- Enables one to go to prayer with clean hands and a clear heart
- Attracts favorable opportunities for self-promotion in one's profession
- Eliminates the desire to get something for nothing
- Makes the rendering of useful service a joy that can be had in no other way
- Provides one with an influential reputation for honesty and fair dealing, which is the basis of all confidence
- Serves as a discouragement to the slanderer and a reprimand to the thief
- Makes one a power for good, by example, wherever one comes into contact with others
- Discourages all the baser instincts of greed and envy and revenge and gives wings to the higher instincts of love and fellowship

- Enables one to recognize the joys of accepting the truth that everyone is, and by right should be, one's "brother's keeper"

- Establishes a deeper personal spirituality

These are no mere opinions of mine. They are self-evident truths, the soundness of which is known to every person who lives by the Golden Rule as a matter of daily habit.

HILL:

It is apparent from your analysis that the Golden Rule is the very foundation of all the better qualities of humanity, that the application of this rule provides one with a powerful immunity against all destructive forces.

CARNEGIE:

Your illustration is good. It does provide immunity against many of the ills that beset humanity, but immunity is negative; it provides also the positive attracting power by which we may acquire whatever we demand of life, from peace of mind and spiritual understanding on down to the material needs of life.

HILL:

Some people claim that they would like to live by the Golden Rule but find it impossible to do so for fear that those who do not live by this rule would take advantage of them. What has been your experience on this point?

CARNEGIE:

When people say they cannot live by the Golden Rule without suffering damage from others, they clearly show their lack of understanding of this principle—a common misapprehension. If you carefully study the benefits I have enumerated, you will observe that they are benefits of which no one can be deprived.

I think this common misunderstanding of the working principle of the Golden Rule grows out of the belief that the benefits of applying the rule must come from those who receive the benefits, whereas they may come from entirely different sources. Also, the misunderstanding arises from the false belief that the benefits consist only of material gains!

The greatest of all benefits attained through application of the Golden Rule are those that accrue to those who apply it, in the form of harmony within their own minds that leads to the development of sound character. There is no asset comparable in value with sound character, and this is something that individuals must build for themselves through their thoughts and deeds. Character is of definite, practical value.

> *The content of your character is your choice.*
> *Day by day, what you choose, what you think, and what you do,*
> *is who you become.*
> —Heraclitus

HILL:

But is it not true, Mr. Carnegie, that some people do take advantage of those who live by the Golden Rule, viewing this habit as a weakness to be exploited instead of as a virtue to be rewarded?

CARNEGIE:

Yes, some people do this, but the percentage who regard the rule in this manner is so incomparably small that it becomes insignificant. Thus, by the law of averages, you can see that it pays to overlook the damage that one may cause. Moreover, the Law of Compensation enters into the transaction, and by some strange plan of nature, even the damage suffered from the shortsighted one is offset by the ninety-nine who do respond in kind. Emerson gave a very clear account of this in his essay "*Compensation.*"

HILL:

But there are so few who are acquainted with Emerson's essay or with the Law of Compensation. And many of those who *are* acquainted with it look upon it as a mere preachment by a moralist, one that has no real value in the practical affairs of modern life. Will you, therefore, give your views as to the practicability of the Law of Compensation in the modern business sense, such as you have experienced?

CARNEGIE:

My entire experience, in business and all other relationships, has forced me to accept the soundness of the Law of Compensation. It is an eternal verity from which no one can escape regardless of how smart they may be or how hard they may try to avoid it.

There is always some compelling circumstance that raises or lowers us substantially to where we belong in life, according to our thoughts and deeds! We may escape the influence of this law for a time, but viewed over a period of an average lifetime, the law forces all of us to gravitate to the exact position where we belong. Our own thoughts and deeds establish the space we may occupy and the influence we may wield in our relationships with others. We may temporarily dodge our responsibilities to others, but we cannot permanently dodge the consequences of dodging our responsibilities.

EDITOR'S NOTE:

This is one of the most important tenets of success: we are free to make whatever choices we like, but we are not free from the *consequences* of those choices. This applies to any goal we might have. For example:

- A finance goal: Some high-earning (or financially irresponsible) friends suggest that you join them on a European vacation. Not wanting to miss out but recognizing that you do not have enough money in your savings account, you book the flights on your credit card and then add in all your travel expenses. Because of the exorbitant interest rate, a single vacation diminishes both your ongoing pay and your credit score.

In time, you discover that it greatly hinders your chances of buying a car, owning your own home, and taking your family on a vacation.

- A fitness goal: A fast-food restaurant opens up a short stroll from your office. Although you had told friends you wanted to complete a half marathon before the end of the year, the lure of the high-calorie meals and sugary drinks becomes too much, and you indulge enthusiastically almost every day of the working week. Zapped by carbohydrates, you feel too sluggish to exercise, and eventually the goal becomes a distant memory. Many years later, you realize that the biggest impact of your decision to make the fast-food eatery your primary source of nutrition has been on your well-being and your wallet as you desperately try to restore your health and cover the rising medical costs.

- A business goal: One day in the office you notice some associates engaging in office gossip. Because the people they are talking about aren't present, you feel comfortable joining the bantering and view it as an opportunity to fit in with your colleagues. Not long afterward, you discover that the people who had been gossiping have started blaming you for unflattering rumors that are spreading through the office like wildfire, making it to the ears of your manager. Your big goal for the year had been to get the promotion you'd been working toward for as long as you could remember, but your manager explains that it will be difficult for you to regain trust in the workplace and even to retain your job.

Our lives depend on what we choose from the thousands of forks in the road we're faced with each day, so choose wisely.

HILL:
Then is it not expedient to apply the Golden Rule, since its application will obviously bring immediate returns, whereas refusing to apply it will mean temporary disadvantage?

CARNEGIE:

To get the fullest benefit of this rule, one must apply it as a matter of habit—in all human relationships. There are no exceptions! Many people make the mistake of choosing the circumstances under which they apply the rule.

HILL:

That is a pretty conclusive statement; it gives one no leeway in which to temporize with the Golden Rule. We must either go the whole way or suffer from the results of our neglect?

CARNEGIE:

That is correct! And let me warn you that we're all confronted with circumstances that tempt us to neglect to apply the Golden Rule as a means of temporary expediency. However, it is fatal to yield to the temptation. Others may not know of the yielding, but our own conscience knows. If the conscience is overridden, it becomes weak and fails to serve the purpose of guidance for which it was intended.

We should never try to deliberately deceive others, and what is more important, we cannot afford, under any circumstances, to try to deceive our own conscience, since doing so can only weaken the source of our guidance. Those who try to deceive themselves are as unwise as the person who would slip poison into their own food.

> *Relationships are all there is.*
> *Everything in the universe only exists because*
> *it is in relationship to everything else.*
> *Nothing exists in isolation.*
> —Margaret Wheatley

HILL:

Obviously you believe, Mr. Carnegie, that one can apply the Golden Rule in all human relationships and still prosper in this age of materialism?

CARNEGIE:

I would not state it just that way. I would make the statement stronger by saying that those who live by the Golden Rule—mind you, live by it as a matter of principle—will be bound to prosper within the limits of their own individual capacity, whatever that may be. The results of applying the rule will accrue automatically and from sources that are often the least expected.

HILL:

That is a pretty definite statement, Mr. Carnegie. Your own achievements prove that the Golden Rule can be applied in a material age such as this with profit. I am assuming, of course, that you have always lived by the Golden Rule, but I should like to have an expression from you about this.

CARNEGIE:

It is a poor teacher indeed who teaches one thing and practices the opposite. My first understanding of the Golden Rule was acquired from my mother at an early age, before I came to America. My real knowledge of its soundness came from my experience in applying it to the best of my ability and understanding.

HILL:

Have you ever suffered temporary loss by applying the Golden Rule?

CARNEGIE:

Oh yes, many times! But I am glad you said "temporary" loss, because I cannot truthfully say that, on the whole, I have ever lost anything from living by the Golden Rule. Such losses as I have sustained from an occasional circumstance under which the rule was applied without a direct response have been repaid many times from other circumstances in which the response was abundant.

Let me give you an example of what I mean.

When I first entered the steel manufacturing business, the price of steel was around $130 per ton. That price seemed much too high, so I began looking for ways and means of lowering it. At first, I lowered the price below the then cost of production, although my competitors complained that I was dealing unfairly with them by the practice. Very soon, the increased business that came as a result of the lowered price enabled me to make still further reductions. I soon discovered that lowered prices meant bigger production, and bigger production meant lower unit costs and made lowered prices possible.

I kept up this policy until we finally got steel down to around $20 a ton. Meanwhile, the lowered price of steel led to the use of steel in many new forms, and after a while my competitors discovered that instead of damaging them, I had actually *benefited* them by forcing them to lower their prices. Thus, the public benefited, the workers in the steel plants benefited, and the manufacturers of steel benefited from a business policy that at first had meant a definite loss to the manufacturers of steel.

Today, steel is being used to manufacture a great variety of articles that could not have been manufactured from it at the old prices, and on the whole I have never lost anything by forcing the price down. My temporary losses were more than offset by my permanent gains, and I think this demonstrates how the Golden Rule works. It may, and often does, cause temporary losses, but over time the gains are greater than the losses.

HILL:

You mean that the Golden Rule philosophy harmonizes with sound business economy. Is that the idea?

CARNEGIE:

That's precisely the idea, and if you wish to see how it works out, keep your eye on Henry Ford and watch what happens to his business. He has adopted a policy of giving the public a dependable automobile at the lowest price at which automobiles have been sold. He is putting fine materials and workmanship into his product, and the public will reward him with its patronage no matter how many competitors he may have. Mr. Ford will prosper beyond the expectations of most of those who are now criticizing him.

This is a prophecy, but you watch it and see for yourself that it is a sound prophecy. Mr. Ford is likely to dominate the automobile industry, and he will be sure to do so unless some other far-sighted manufacturer comes into the field and follows his example.

EDITOR'S NOTE:

Clearly, this was a prophecy that proved accurate! Henry Ford built a company with such strong fundamentals that in 2020, more than seven decades after his passing, the Ford Motor Company employs more than two hundred thousand people, manufactures more than 6 million vehicles each year, and remains one of the largest automotive companies in the world. Since its inception, Ford has manufactured more than 350 million vehicles.

Henry Ford once said, "My best friend is the one who brings out the best in me." In the context of what Carnegie has just outlined, perhaps the automotive titan was talking not just about his personal mastermind but also about the external motivation of competitors.

HILL:

Would it not be impractical for certain professions to live by the Golden Rule, for example, lawyers, whose profession requires them to prosecute cases in which it would be difficult to apply this rule?

CARNEGIE:

I could preach you a sermon on this subject, because I have had a great deal of experience with many types of lawyers. However, I will confine myself to the mention of only one lawyer, the professional policy of whom—along with its results—should provide an answer to your question.

This lawyer will not accept a case unless he is convinced that he is being retained on the right side. That is, he will not accept a case that is without merit, and I hardly need to tell you that he turns away far more prospective clients than he serves. But I must also tell you that he is busy all the time, and his income, judging from all I know about him, is approximately ten times that of the average type of lawyer. I pay this lawyer a substantial sum annually for his counsel, quite aside from any other service he renders me. A great many of my friends do the same. We employ him because we have confidence in him, and our confidence is based mainly on our knowledge that he will not mislead a client in order to earn a fee, nor will he accept a case that is unjust or unfair to anyone.

HILL:

I see your point. Lawyers can live by the Golden Rule and prosper provided they are willing to forgo the handling of cases that have no merit. But what about the client who comes with the other sort of case—the type that is unjust? It seems that this sort of case is more prevalent than the other type.

CARNEGIE:

In every profession, business, and occupation, there are ways to make money through unfair practices and there are individuals who are willing to earn money unfairly, but all of them are surrounded by hazards that sooner or later dry up the source of income or bring with it evils, if not losses, that are out of proportion to the gain.

It is true that there are many legal cases that have no merit; some of them are out-and-out attempts to get something for nothing through fraud and deceit. A lawyer who chooses to can of course accept this sort of case, but I stand on my original statement that such cases bring with them evils out of proportion to the gain to the lawyer.

Money obtained unjustly through the tricks of the legal profession may *appear* to be as good as any other sort of money, but there is a strange influence that accompanies such money that some people do not wish to be burdened with. Somehow, it has a way of becoming quickly dissipated without serving its greatest worth, just like money that is stolen by highwaymen and thieves. Have you ever heard of a successful highwayman or thief? I have known of many of them getting away with large sums of money. Most of them are now residing in prison or dead.

All natural law is moral! The whole universe frowns upon immoral transactions of whatsoever nature they may be. And the person has not yet been born who can successfully run counter to the trend of natural law for more than a brief period.

> *The most important thing is to try and inspire people so that*
> *they can be great in whatever they want to do.*
> —Kobe Byrant

It is my belief that the secret of the great power of the Golden Rule consists in the fact that it is in harmony with moral laws. It represents the positive side of human relationships; therefore, it has moral law behind it.

HILL:

Let us consider young people just beginning their career. In what ways may they profit by the Golden Rule?

CARNEGIE:

Well, the first essential for success in any calling of merit is sound character. Applying the Golden Rule develops sound character and a good reputation. You perhaps want a more concrete example of how young people may profit materially by application of the Golden Rule, so let us combine the principles of the Golden Rule and of Going the Extra Mile and see what result we get.

Let us go one step further and add the principle of definiteness of a major purpose. We now have a combination that, if persistently and sincerely applied, will be sufficient to give any young person more than an average start in life.

HILL:

Of course, this combination would serve adults as well as youths, would it not?

CARNEGIE:

Yes. When we know what we want, make up our mind to acquire it, form the habit of Going the Extra Mile to get it, and use the Golden Rule to relate to others, the world cannot ignore us. We will attract favorable attention no matter how humble our beginning may be.

HILL:

Wouldn't these three principles be a pretty good combination for those going through high school or college in preparation for a career? Wouldn't they give one a definite advantage over those who failed to apply these principles?

CARNEGIE:

Yes, they would. It is one of the weaknesses of most people that during their school days they study for "credits" and to pass examinations without knowing what they are going to do with their schooling after they acquire it. It is my notion that most purposeless action is wasted no matter when or where it is performed. The "go-getters"—as the world calls alert, dynamic, and successful people—move with a definite purpose in ractically all that they do. They move by a definite motive, a definite plan, and they generally reach their destination because they know where they are going and are determined not to be stopped until they get there.

HILL:

Do you believe that those who use the Golden Rule to relate to others and who make it a habit to Go the Extra Mile will face less opposition from others?

CARNEGIE:

Generally, they will have practically no opposition from others. On the contrary, they will have the willing and friendly *cooperation* of others. That has been the history of those who live by these two rules.

HILL:

Then we may say that these two principles not only serve as a moral guide but also clear one's path of the usual forms of opposition?

CARNEGIE:

That's the story in one sentence. Now I must call your attention to another benefit one may enjoy by living by these two principles. It consists of the fact that those who live by these principles as a matter of daily habit will profit, in contrast with others who neglect to apply the principles. Need I call attention to the fact that most people pay no attention to either of these principles?

We are rapidly becoming a nation of greedy, selfish people, most of us struggling to acquire material possessions while having a total disregard for the rights of others. This trend is so definite that a blind man can see it without looking! If this popular trend continues for another two or three decades, the United States will be known throughout the world as a grasping, greedy nation.

If the trend continues indefinitely, it will lead to the destruction of our present form of government, because greed is a contagious and self-perpetuating evil that knows no bounds within the range of human rights. It will destroy the spirit of Americanism that made this nation rich and free. It will replace every statesman we have with greedy politicians who seek personal aggrandizement instead of an opportunity to serve the people.

I tell you, and I wish to emphasize what I say, that the Golden Rule spirit is the only human-made power that can hold this nation together in its present form. Therefore, those who live by this rule will be doing more than merely benefiting themselves; they will be making a distinct contribution to the nation as a whole, a contribution of value in proportion to the individual's influence in their community.

This nation has little to fear from forces outside itself. It has much to fear in the forces now being created by the habits of the people. Our motto in the past has been "All for one and one for all!" That motto is represented in our form of government, in the friendly alliance between the state and federal governments.

But I can see, from the present trend of individual habits, that this motto is rapidly being transformed into another: "Everyone for themselves, and may the devil take the hindmost."

HILL:

You believe, then, that everyone should begin preaching the Golden Rule as a common foundation for all human relationships, whether they are social or business relationships. Is that the idea?

CARNEGIE:

No, emphatically no. That is not the idea at all. Everyone should stop preaching the Golden Rule and begin *practicing* it!

Some people believe that preaching about the rules of sound relationship fulfills their obligation to society, but that is not enough. Preachments that lack action supporting that which they advocate become monotonous. A single individual practicing the Golden Rule will do more good to popularize this rule in their community than all the preaching a dozen people might do.

The same might be said of business: let one company adopt the Golden Rule as the basis of its relationships and prove the soundness of the rule by its own prosperity, and immediately other firms will fall in line and emulate the example. If both the employers and the employees related themselves to one another on the Golden Rule basis, we would hear no more about labor troubles because there would be no basis for trouble. Nor would there be any room for professional agitators, whose business it is to exploit workers and employers alike by stirring up animosity between them.

HILL:

Which side should be the first to initiate the Golden Rule policy—the employers or the employees?

CARNEGIE:

Whichever side is smarter! The group that takes the initiative in applying this rule in its dealings will have a tremendous advantage over the other. It will be in a better position to command the sympathy and the support of the public because as surely as tomorrow's sun will rise, the public will recognize and adequately reward any individual or group who lives by the Golden Rule. And when I say "live by it," I do not mean the mere preachment of the rule but the application of it in all relationships.

HILL:

Would you mind enumerating some of the major advantages an employer may gain by adopting the Golden Rule as the basis of their business policy?

CARNEGIE:

First, the employer would benefit from a better relationship with their employees. This would eliminate labor disputes and increase production. The increased production would make increased wages possible.

It would engage the attention of the public to such an extent that the new policy would command free media publicity of great value, leading to a greater consumption of the employer's product.

It would cut down the expense of labor turnover because it would place a premium on every job. This is quite an item with many employers, given that the training of skilled workers takes time and money.

It would take drudgery out of labor for both the employer and the employees.

It would reduce waste, by minimizing the costly errors of employees.

HILL:

With all those possible benefits awaiting the employer who adopts the Golden Rule as the basis of their business relationships, why have so few employers taken advantage of the opportunity to profit by it?

CARNEGIE:

Because of one of the oldest of human faults—lack of vision! People change their habits slowly and often grudgingly—especially when the change calls for the introduction of new ideas.

EDITOR'S NOTE:

In the increasingly competitive world of business, companies look for every advantage to get ahead as they seek to appease financial analysts with their quarterly earnings reports. Unfortunately, this shortsighted focus typically results in extreme cost-cutting measures such as firing staff, reducing the size or quality of the product (and hoping that no one notices), paying the minimum wage, and investing in automation to make the human touch obsolete.

However, some companies are bucking the trend, such as Costco. The American retailer now operates in more than a dozen countries, and its success is due in large part to its holistic strategy and long-term vision. Costco pays above-market wages to its staff while offering enormous savings to its customers. This counterintuitive strategy is effective because the retailer works with its vendors to create more affordable products in huge volumes, creating strong brand advocates among its three most important stakeholders: staff, customers, and vendors.

Currently, Costco's 245,000 workers are paid *double* the national retail average, and 88 percent receive company-sponsored health insurance. Despite being opposed by more frugal shareholders, this formula has proved to be a winning one for Costco, with its stock increasing 387 percent since 2000.

True vision incorporates the Golden Rule applied rather than simple cost-cutting measures.

HILL:

And you believe that the introduction of the Golden Rule as the basis of business relationships would be a new idea?

CARNEGIE:

It would be an old idea given a new use. One of the difficulties we have had in connection with the adoption of the Golden Rule as the basis of business relationships is that most people have associated this rule with preachments concerning dogma and creed, overlooking entirely the possibilities of this rule as an economic force. The Golden Rule is broader than any dogma, deeper than any religion, yet it has in it something of the finer spiritual qualities of humankind.

HILL:
You believe, then, that the Golden Rule should be taken out of the pulpit and into the field of every profession?

CARNEGIE:
Well, the pulpit has done only fairly well with it, considering that it has been preached for nearly two thousand years! I would say leave it in the pulpit for whatever good it may do there but give it a broader application in the practical affairs of daily life.

HILL:
What do you believe would happen, Mr. Carnegie, if a labor leader came out with the announcement that henceforth all members of their union would be required to render service on the Golden Rule basis and then carried out that promise both in spirit and in fact?

CARNEGIE:
What would happen? I'll tell you what would happen. The leader would soon gain control of organized labor. The members of the union would be in demand. The employers would be the leader's friend, and so would the public. That's precisely what would happen, but mind you, the announcement would have to be backed with deeds. No mere gesture would do the leader any good.

It makes no difference what the person's calling may be or whether the person is an employer or an employee or from the upper or the lower economic class. There are no patent rights on the Golden Rule—it is the property of anyone who wishes to adopt it. If someone procured a patent right on this rule, you would see others infringing on the patent in a hurry.

The very moment one starts to prohibit the use of anything, others begin to search for ways and means of defying the prohibitor.

> **Waste no more time arguing about what a good person should be.**
> **Be one.**
> —Marcus Aurelius

HILL:

You believe, then, that if the Golden Rule were something that came with a stiff fee, it would quickly come into popular use?

CARNEGIE:

That's the way the human mind works! It usually undervalues everything that is free.

HILL:

If you were asked to name the greatest single benefit of living by the Golden Rule, what would be your answer, Mr. Carnegie?

CARNEGIE:

The answer to that question is obvious. The greatest benefit available through practice of the Golden Rule is the changed mental attitude it gives one. Those who live by this great universal law have no place in their minds for selfishness and greed. They GIVE before trying to GET. As a result, they attract friends, because they are friends themselves.

HILL:

The Golden Rule spirit leads to a better understanding of the impersonal, selfless life. Is that the idea?

CARNEGIE:

Yes. Not only does it lead to a better understanding of the impersonal life, but it inspires one to desire to live that life.

HILL:

And you believe that personal success is more easily attained by those who forget themselves and live for the benefit of others?

CARNEGIE:

Every great achievement is the result of the application of the Golden Rule. Study the lives of those who have been acclaimed as great and you will learn that they lived the impersonal life as a matter of choice:

- Michelangelo became one of the greatest artists of all time because of his passionate desire to inspire others with his paintings.
- Ludwig van Beethoven made himself immortal because of his desire to inspire others with his music.
- Thomas A. Edison did not work for money alone but gave his entire life to scientific research because he was inspired by an impersonal desire to uncover the hidden secrets of nature for the benefit of humanity.

And I can truthfully say that throughout my own business career, I was more concerned with finding and developing people who were willing to serve others than I was with acquiring personal riches. The riches were the natural result of the service rendered.

HILL:

What would you say has been the crowning achievement of your career?

CARNEGIE:

Perhaps that is a question that could best be answered by someone else, but my answer would be that my greatest achievement has been the number of workers whom I have helped to live a fuller life by rendering more useful service.

HILL:

I observe that you make no mention of the fortunes you have helped these workers to accumulate. Is that not also a part of your achievement worthy of mention?

CARNEGIE:

I do not consider the accumulation of personal riches, of itself, an achievement! The achievement consists in the service one renders, not in the pay one receives!

HILL:

Yes, of course! I see the distinction clearly. But is it not true, Mr. Carnegie, that the world recognizes a person's achievements more by the money they accumulate than by the service they render?

CARNEGIE:

Yes, that is a common mistake of most people. And it is a mistake that leads too many young people to devote more thought to GETTING than to GIVING! It is rapidly becoming the outstanding error of the American people. It is not in harmony with the Golden Rule spirit, in which people find themselves by first losing themselves in useful, unselfish service to others.

HILL:

Mr. Carnegie, what, in your opinion, can change this trend of American habit?

CARNEGIE:

Nothing, perhaps, except some overwhelming catastrophe that will reduce all the people substantially to a common level, where they will be forced to acquire humility of heart. It may come in the form of war, or it may grow out of a collapse of our entire economic system.

World history provides convincing evidence that when people lose sight of the impersonal life and become steeped in greed and selfish desire for personal power and riches, they are overcome by disaster in one form or another. The rise and fall of the Roman Empire is a good example of what I mean.

HILL:

And you believe that this same rule applies to individuals who live only for themselves?

CARNEGIE:

Yes, without a doubt! In my own business experience, I have observed that those who endeavored to promote themselves at the expense of their fellow workers were the first to fall by the wayside. A few of them managed to lift themselves into positions of authority, but authority only served to inspire them with greater selfishness, and they soon fell by the sheer weight of their own weaknesses.

I do not recall a single worker who promoted themselves to a permanent position of affluence, either in my own organization or elsewhere, without willingly carrying others with them. And I observed that those who aided the greatest number of others were the ones who gained most for themselves.

There is one infallible rule for the attainment of individual success, and it is the habit of helping others to attain it! I have never known of the rule failing to work. And it applies to all forms of human relationships. Those who GET most from life are those who GIVE most or help others GET. Selfishness is not one of the success rules, but it stands near the head of the list of the causes of failure.

HILL:

Therefore, unselfishness is one of the "musts" of all who achieve permanent success in whatever occupation they may be engaged?

CARNEGIE:

That is correct, and I wish to call your attention to the direct relationship between unselfishness and the Golden Rule. No one can live by the Golden Rule until they learn to lose themselves in unselfish service to others.

HILL:

What particular quality does the spirit of unselfishness develop that gives it such universal power for self-promotion?

CARNEGIE:

I would say that it develops humility of heart and gives one a better understanding of that intangible quality known as the "power from within." We sometimes speak of this power as faith, but by whatever name it may be called, it is the source of all genius. One who develops an impersonal life lives more in the lives of others and through them draws nearer to the Creator.

HILL:

If I understand you correctly, you mean that unselfishness leads to the development of an open mind that enables one to recognize and adapt oneself to the guidance of Infinite Intelligence.

CARNEGIE:

That is precisely what I mean. Selfishness influences us to be guided by our own vanity. Then we overlook the source of that power from within that has no relationship to our own faculty of reason but is greater than all the faculties of our mind.

HILL:

And you believe that this power from within may be recognized and applied as a guiding spirit in the solution of the practical problems of one's daily life?

CARNEGIE:

Yes, that is my belief. And may I add that those who prepare their minds for guidance through this power have no such thing as an unsolvable problem, because it has the answer to all problems, both great and small, material and spiritual. It is the power that enables one to convert adversities into benefits regardless of the nature and scope of the adversities.

If you hate somebody, it's like a boomerang that misses its
target and comes back and hits you in the head.
—Louis Zamperini

HILL:

How may one go about "preparing one's mind" for this sort of guidance?

CARNEGIE:

The starting point of all individual achievement is definiteness of purpose—knowing exactly what one wants from life. People may give action and life to their major purpose by backing it with an obsessional desire for its realization. Purpose, backed by sustained desire, leads to the development of practical plans through the exercise of the imagination, for the attainment of that purpose.

It also transfers to the subconscious section of the mind a clear, definite picture of what is wanted, and here, by some method unknown to humankind, the mind makes contact with that power from within. Thus, briefly, you have a description of how one may prepare one's mind for guidance from within.

HILL:

You make no mention of the Golden Rule. What part, if any, does it assume in the process of "preparing the mind" for guidance from within?

CARNEGIE:

A very definite part! It would seem that this secret power from within frowns upon selfishness, greed, envy, hatred, intolerance, and all other traits of the mind associated in any manner with the injury of others. Those who charge their mind with a definite purpose that is free from all desire to profit at the expense of another—as one does when one relates to others on the Golden Rule basis—thereby free themselves from all opposition from others and in fact gain their friendly cooperation. Thus, they have cleared the way for the realization of that which they want.

Thoughts are things, and powerful things at that! And thoughts of unfriendly opposition in the minds of others may outweigh one's desire for what one seeks from life. The opposition reaches and influences one's mind, causing it to hesitate through fear and doubt. If there is no such opposition, there can be no fear or doubt. You see, therefore, that the Golden Rule spirit is a great builder of self-confidence, and self-confidence leads to faith, and faith leads to guidance from within. It is very simple once you get the idea clearly.

HILL:

Oh yes! I see your idea very clearly. The Golden Rule spirit places people in harmony with their own conscience, and it frees them from the opposition of fear and doubt that would otherwise slow them down in the pursuit of that which they seek.

CARNEGIE:

That's the idea, perfectly stated. We cannot have the full benefit of guidance through faith if we are not at peace with our own conscience. Without this guidance, we may not avail ourselves of the power from within.

It is a well-known fact that the subconscious mind carries out one's mental attitude—not merely one's desires but the belief *behind* the desire. If that belief is colored by fear, doubt, indecision, envy, greed, or any other form of selfishness, these states of mind are recognized and acted upon by the subconscious mind, and of course the results are negative!

ANALYSIS:
THE GOLDEN RULE APPLIED
By Napoleon Hill

There is a master key that opens the door to abundance of *everything* that human beings need. But the key fits two doors: one is the door to FAITH, and the other is the door to FEAR.

The power behind the master key is so limitless that it can surmount all human problems, making royalty of the humblest if it is approached through the door of faith. This master key gives the privilege of complete control—a privilege that is irrevocable and may be lost only through neglect of use.

The master key is called the POWER OF THOUGHT!

Through the proper conditioning, the mind can be prepared to recognize, appropriate, and use this power from within—power that moves by inspired guidance.

> *Be silent and listen to the voice that speaks only through the power of thought.*
> —Andrew Carnegie

It was this power from within, applied through inspired guidance, that enabled Michelangelo to overcome poverty, cruel opposition, and physical weakness and led him at long last to world recognition as one of the greatest artists in history. That same power revealed to Thomas A. Edison the secrets of nature and enabled him to become one of the world's greatest inventors; it lifted Beethoven to the status of a genius in the composition of music despite his loss of hearing; it revealed to Marie Curie the secret of radium; it made Charles P. Steinmetz a recognized authority in the field of electricity; and it uncovered for Marconi the principle of wireless telegraphy that led finally to the discovery of radio.

These and all the others whom the world has recognized as geniuses attained their greatness by "conditioning" their minds to receive guidance through that power from within, that power which has free access to all of nature's secrets and does not recognize failure as an element of reality.

The "conditioning" begins with recognition of the power that is available to those who live the impersonal life, devoting their lives to the service of humankind in a spirit of unselfish desire to do good—to give before getting!

The first step by which one may live the impersonal life is known as the Golden Rule. It has been recognized and applied by every person who has attained true greatness. It has been recognized by every great religious leader and every true philosopher.

Confucius discovered it and made it the basis of a philosophy that made him beloved. The Man of Galilee discovered it and, during the Sermon on the Mount, clothed it in the most understandable terms ever expressed: "Therefore all things whatsoever ye would that men should do to you, do ye even so to them."

Many sermons have been preached on the Golden Rule, but few of them have interpreted the full depths of its meaning, the gist of which is this:

Lose yourself in unselfish service to others. You will thereby discover the master key to the power from within that guides you unerringly to the attainment of your noblest aims and purposes.

There is no mystery to this formula! Anyone may apply it without opposition, because it benefits all whom it affects.

It is a well-established fact that the space we occupy in the world is determined precisely by the quality and the quantity of service we render and by the mental attitude with which we render it. These determining factors are within the control of everyone.

It is an equally well-established fact that those who have occupied the greatest amount of space (through their influence and public recognition) have conquered fear, envy, hatred, intolerance, greed vanity, egotism, and the desire to get something for nothing.

This, too, is a part of the necessary "conditioning" of the mind to recognize and appropriate that power from within that guides one triumphantly through the resistances of life.

Let us now analyze those who have applied the Golden Rule by living the impersonal life so that we may observe the spirit and the way in which they related themselves to others.

I shall begin with Andrew Carnegie, because he has revealed to us through these chapters intimate details of the inner workings of his mind. At the outset of his career, he adopted the spirit of humility of heart, and this he maintained throughout his life.

In his upward climb from poverty to riches, he made it a part of his responsibility to inspire others to share his success, a mandate that extended to the humblest workers in his company. While he accumulated a great fortune, he also made more millionaires than any other industrialist known to the American people—and most of these began with very little education and with nothing to give except sturdy hands and willing hearts.

After Mr. Carnegie had accumulated a fortune, he began to devise ways and means of giving it all away, thereby proving his understanding of the impersonal life.

However, he was not content merely to *give* away his money. He recognized that his greatest asset was the knowledge through which he had acquired his wealth. This knowledge revealed to him the scope and possibilities of the abundant internal power that he had drawn from so eagerly throughout his colorful career.

Andrew Carnegie thought not only of his own welfare but also of the welfare of generations yet unborn. His legacy is captured in the philosophy of American achievement, which consists of the known principles of individual achievement as they have been applied in the development of the American way of life in a great variety of callings.

They are able who think they are able.
—Virgil

He knew the value of the impersonal life because he had disciplined himself through living by it! The space he occupied, therefore, is as great as the world, and though he has become a citizen of the universe, his spirit goes marching on, inspiring people to acquire an understanding of the impersonal life through higher education and the reading of books.

In 1929, Thomas A. Edison celebrated a triumph over adversity unparalleled in world history—one that, by contrast, makes the pageants of Roman triumph seem like an ordinary circus. The Roman triumph was a restricted area of only a minor fraction of the planet. The world that acclaimed Edison, however, embraced both hemispheres and all countries of earth.

No such recognition of individual genius had ever been witnessed before. This was the first Golden Jubilee where the world celebrated a triumph of peace; where no victims in chains followed the procession of the victor; where malice, envy, and hatred were dethroned and replaced by manifestations of universal gratitude. The benefits conferred upon humanity were nothing short of miraculous, and they were bestowed by a man whose genius figuratively made the sun shine at night through the conversion of stored energy into a miniature reproduction of incandescent mass.

Alfred O. Tate, Edison's former secretary, said:

On the 21st day of October, in this Jubilee year, the spreading rays of Golden Light which flooded the country were focused on Dearborn, Michigan, where Henry Ford had organized a celebration in honor of Edison, distinguished not only by its magnificence but also by the ingenuity which produced some of the salient events in the history of his career that literally made them live again.

About 11am of this historic day I stood on the platform of a small railroad station in the grounds of the Ford enclosure, waiting to "see the train come in." The station was a replica of one of those on the line of the railroad on which in early youth Edison had been employed as a newsboy, and where in a corner of the baggage car he edited and printed a newspaper of his own, retailing the gossip of the line.

When the train stopped, the first passenger to alight was the President of the United States, Herbert Hoover, followed by Mr. and Mrs. Ford and Mrs. Edison and their guests. Then came a white-haired man with a quizzical smile on his face. He was the newsboy, who, while this train was making its short journey, had been engaged in selling replicas of his original newspaper to the distinguished passengers in the coach—Thomas Alva Edison.

At 7pm of this day, in the pillared chambers of a building, a replica of Independence Hall in Philadelphia, the most notable gathering of men distinguished in all walks of American life ever assembled under one roof had been convened as the banquet guests of Henry Ford to honor Edison.

The laudatory address honoring Edison was delivered by the President of the United States. When Edison arose to reply, he was overcome with emotion which sympathetically was communicated to his whole audience. It was the first time he had ever attempted to speak in his own behalf on an occasion of this nature. He never again made a similar appearance.

Here was humility of the heart in its highest form! And here was evidence that those who lose themselves in service to others will be discovered and adequately rewarded.

Edison seldom spoke of his achievements. His motto was: "Deeds, not words."

He was so completely lost in his work that he had neither the time nor the inclination to think of himself. He admitted that never in his entire life did he give serious thought to what he might GET for his labor. His greatest concern was in connection with what he might GIVE!

It was inevitable, therefore, that he should discover the internal power that was the real source of his genius. He conditioned his mind to recognize and appropriate that power. Whether he did this consciously or unconsciously is of little importance. But it is important that we recognize that he lived the impersonal life, through which he prepared his mind to recognize and appropriate that internal power for the benefit of humankind.

The world has been talking about the Golden Rule for nearly two thousand years, and thousands of sermons have been preached about it, but only a few have discovered that its power consists in its *application*, not merely in the belief in its soundness.

The purpose of this chapter is to describe what happens when the Golden Rule is applied in relationships with others. Therefore, I call attention to two related principles:

1. Harmonious attraction

2. Retaliation

There is something in our nature that often causes us to retaliate in kind when we are injured by another through word or deed. We also respond in kind when we are favored by word or deed. This part of humanity's nature existed long before the philosophers discovered the secret power of the Golden Rule, and it was doubtlessly their interpretation of this part of humanity that led to the pronunciation of the Golden Rule.

Emerson discovered that the Golden Rule is more than a mere moral precept. He realized that its roots exist in the realm of natural law that governs not only human beings but also every atom of matter and every unit of energy throughout the cosmos.

Emerson wrote:

Polarity, or action and reaction, we meet in every part of nature; in darkness and light; in heat and cold; in the ebb and flow of waters; in male and female; in the inspiration and expiration of plants and animals; in the systole and diastole of the heart; in the undulations of fluids, and of sound; in the centrifugal and centripetal gravity; in electricity, galvanism, and chemical affinity. . . .

The same dualism underlies the nature and condition of man. Every excess causes a defect; every defect an excess. Every sweet hath its sour; every evil its good. Every faculty which is a receiver of pleasure has an equal penalty put on its abuse. It is to answer for its moderation with its life. For every grain of wit there is a grain of folly. For everything you have missed you have gained something else; and for everything you gain, you lose something. . . .

The waves of the sea do not more speedily seek a level from their loftiest tossing than the varieties of condition tend to equalize themselves. There is always some leveling circumstance that puts down the overbearing, the strong, the rich, the fortunate, substantially on the same ground with all others.

Of course, the rule Emerson describes works precisely the same when someone injures their neighbor, either by acts or words, because the injury sets in motion a cause that is bound to result in a related effect. If the neighbor does not retaliate in kind at the first opportunity, some of their friends will, or the "retaliation" may come from some entirely unknown person, but come it will, in time.

But overlooking the effects of retaliation entirely, there is another inescapable effect that we experience when we injure another: a proportionate weakening of our own character. The transaction offends our own conscience, lowers our self-reliance, undermines our self-respect, and weakens our willpower.

> **Success goes to those who can negotiate their way through**
> **life with a minimum amount of friction in their relationships.**
> —Napoleon Hill

Thus, the whole system of natural law that controls the universe has been designed to force every living thing to accept the results of its own acts. And every thought, as well as every act in which one indulges, becomes a fixed part of one's character!

Here, then, is the most forceful of all arguments in favor of the Golden Rule as the basis of all human relationships: *That which you do to another, you do to yourself.* The inexorable laws of nature give you no choice in the matter except that of deciding whether you will aid or hinder yourself by your thoughts and deeds in your relationships with others.

Apply the principle and observe where it leads.

When Andrew Carnegie opened the doors of opportunity to the humblest workers in his plants—and gave to those who were prepared to accept it the full benefit of his experience, his capital, and his established reputation as a sound industrialist—he was doing more than merely aiding others to accumulate riches. He was adding immeasurable value to his own wealth, value represented by sound traits of character as well as by material possessions.

He could have acquired his fortune and kept it at his disposal, but a strange quality attaches to ill-gotten gain that causes it to become dissipated. This phenomenon is sometimes referred to as "Easy come, easy go!"

Mr. Carnegie gave himself financial security by helping others to benefit. There is no escape from this conclusion, and the facts are so well-known that they cannot be questioned.

Let this be an answer to those who, through ignorance or intolerance, complain that Mr. Carnegie got his riches at the expense of the laboring workers on his payroll. He got it with their cooperation, to be sure, but it is safe to say that for every dollar he acquired from the labor of his associate workers, they received a hundred dollars or more! And let it be remembered that he held the door of opportunity open to the humblest person in his employ and to every employee who had the ambition to rise above the mediocrity of manual labor, that he gave every worker who cared to accept it the same opportunity to accumulate the riches that he possessed.

And let it be remembered, too, that Mr. Carnegie so arranged his fortune that it *still* goes marching on, aiding others to prepare themselves to get from life whatever they wish, in proportion to that which they have to give in return for it.

Even you who are reading this page can profit from this philosophy, a circumstance arising from the thoughtfulness of a great philanthropist who took the necessary steps to provide you with easy access to the knowledge that built his fortune.

Here is unselfishness that could have been expressed only by someone who had learned the value of living the impersonal life and of sharing his wealth and opportunity with all who would accept them.

This analysis is made not to extoll the virtues of Andrew Carnegie but to describe to you—someone who is seeking your place in the world—

the method by which you may do so: by GIVING in order that you may GET!

The valuable effects of this service, rendered in a spirit of unselfishness, become eternal because they multiply on and on. The money that Andrew Carnegie accumulated and gave away is but an infinitesimal part of the riches his mind produced. To this should be added the hundreds of millions of dollars that have been paid out to workers and will be paid to workers by the great steel industry he founded and the additional millions he has saved those who use steel products by the frugality of his brain that helped to reduce the price of steel from $130 a ton to $20 a ton.

Thus, we see that character perpetuates itself and goes marching on, for good or for evil, long after the physical being has passed. This, too, is in response to the eternal laws of nature, particularly the Law of Compensation, which Emerson so adequately described.

Therefore, when you hear someone say that they believe in the Golden Rule and that they would like to practice it but cannot do so because those with whom they must deal do not live by it, you know that they do not understand the basic premise. They have overlooked the fact that the benefits of the Golden Rule accrue to those who live by it, separate and apart from the acts and deeds of others. These benefits accrue in the form of strengthened character, greater self-reliance, personal initiative, peace of mind, creative vision, enthusiasm, self-discipline, the ability to profit from defeat, definiteness of purpose, and a better understanding of the internal power that is revealed to those who have conditioned their minds to recognize and embrace it.

It was this last stated benefit that Emerson had in mind when he said, "Do the thing and you shall have the power!" Emerson knew that every thought we release and every act in which we indulge becomes an inseparable part of our own character, to aid or curse us, according to its nature.

He knew, too, that sound character does more than create a favorable reputation. It provides one with the surplus of faith that is needed in times of emergency, when willpower and the reasoning faculty are inadequate for human needs.

Pause here and meditate over this thought!

It is the very crux of the Golden Rule, and its interpretation is the essence of this chapter. Lose yourself in useful service and your problems will disappear as if dispelled by some stroke of magic. The history of humankind supports this statement, and to overlook it would be a tragic loss to those who are struggling to master the problems of the complex age in which we live.

Throughout this book, Andrew Carnegie has stressed the importance of maintaining a positive mental attitude. He has shown, through numerous examples, that the outward circumstances of our life correspond in the finest detail to our mental attitude. He has also given indisputable evidence that harmonious relationships with others are the seed from which all personal success germinates.

We cannot be in harmony with those whom we selfishly exploit. We cannot succeed through any sort of relationship that injures others. Success comes to those who carry others along with them, sharing both their opportunities and their knowledge in the true spirit of the Golden Rule. Here, then, is the explanation of the strange fact that our problems can best be solved by helping others to solve theirs. The whole world is closely akin. That which affects one, affects proportionately the *whole* of humankind. When work is plentiful and wages are abundant, the whole neighborhood profits. When work is scarce and people are idle, the whole neighborhood feels the effects of the scarcity.

This effect is known to many but understood by few. The few who understand it are blessed with success in everything they touch—they march on with their work, surviving despite business depressions, wars, and other widespread emergencies that affect everyone around them.

If you want more concrete evidence that it pays to live the selfless life, start where you stand and give a helping hand to those around you who are less fortunate than yourself—not necessarily by giving them money but by giving them encouragement and providing them with an opportunity to serve. Every burden you lift from the shoulders of another will remove an equivalent burden from your own shoulders, or, if you have no burdens, helping others will bring you benefit in some other form appropriate to your desires and needs.

You cannot appropriate the benefits of the Golden Rule by merely believing in it. You must put your belief into action, as Mr. Carnegie has repeatedly stated.

One of the major desires of all people is the desire for happiness! We seek material riches because we believe they can be transmuted into some form of happiness, because, obviously, the mere possession of money cannot give happiness.

We build and maintain friendships because of the happiness they provide. And love, the highest and noblest expression of the human emotions, is universally sought by all people because it gives happiness.

> *Unhappiness is not knowing what we want*
> *and killing ourselves to get it.*
> —Don Herold

We might say, therefore, that the major purpose of life is to find happiness and keep it, yet the great majority of people never enjoy more than a few fleeting moments of this divine gift at a given time, and some go through life without ever experiencing it.

Expressing the Golden Rule in all human relationships is the only satisfying guarantee of happiness.

John Rathbone Oliver, writing in the *Trinity Church Bulletin* of Columbia, South Carolina, expressed a true description of the approach to happiness in these words:

Many people who write to me complain because they are not happy. They often say, "I want the happiness that is my birthright." As a matter of fact, no one has the right to happiness in this world. We may feel that we have a claim to happiness, but in legal terminology there is a great deal of difference between a claim and a right. Claims are often not established and there are many false claims made. A right, however, means an absolute and just possession of a thing because of some inherent characteristic of the person who possesses it.

To say that we have a right to happiness and then to own that we are unhappy is as much as to say that we are being unjustly treated and are not getting our due desserts. This is an absolutely unchristian attitude of mind. No one has a right to happiness in this world, and the people who demand happiness as a right hardly ever get it.

Happiness is a byproduct. It comes sometimes unmasked and unexpectedly. More usually it comes from a willingness to accept the duties and difficulties of everyday life and to do one's work in the world with as little mental friction as possible.

The trouble is that we are not grateful enough for past happiness. We say "I was so happy some years ago when I was loving such and such a person or doing such and such a thing. But now I have lost my happiness and therefore I am depressed and discouraged." We ought to be thankful for past periods of happiness. Usually, however, we feel our loss all the more because we have once possessed something that brought us joy.

When we are temporarily happy, we expect that the happiness is to go on indefinitely. We ought to learn the lesson of the "departing angel." In the Acts of the Holy Apostles you may read how God sent an angel to deliver St. Peter from prison. At the angel's touch the chains fell from St. Peter's hand and the doors of the prison opened from their own accord. Then St. Peter and his guide passed out into the night. They went through one street together, and then the angel departed from him. St. Peter expected perhaps that the angel who had already done so much for him would take him all the way home. But God took the angel away so that St. Peter might learn how to get home by himself.

In life, the same thing frequently happens: the person or the thing on which our happiness was based is suddenly taken away. A beloved child dies or a loving wife is separated from her husband. A husband's love grows cold or a friend forgets his friendship. The angel who has brought us out of our prison of loneliness is taken away and we are tempted to sit down and wait. Like Job, we are told to curse God and die. But that is not the right way to meet the loss of the departing angel. The loss may be not a source of unhappiness and tragedy, but a source of new strength and of new ways of usefulness in the world.

We lay out the plan of our life for ourselves and are bitterly rebellious when something smashes that plan to atoms. We have started in a certain direction and we feel that we are contented and are achieving something. Then something happens, our road is blocked, and we can no longer go on in the same direction. It seems sometimes as if God stretched out His hand and stopped us dead in our tracks. Then comes the temptation to give up. We say, "If I cannot go on in my way, I will not go at all." We do not realize that there are other directions in which we can go, and that God turns us back because He has something more important for us to do in some other direction and in other circumstances.

If people could realize these things a little more clearly, there would be fewer complaints about lost happiness. Real happiness is never lost. If it has been a true happiness, the memory of it and the power of it will abide with us forever.

Yes, Mr. Oliver is correct! True happiness enriches the soul of all who experience it, and it is generally found by those who help others find it. Moreover, happiness may be found through the Golden Rule, which inspires us to enthusiastically live the selfless life because this sort of zeal is, of itself, one of the highest and noblest forms of happiness.

> *If you were your employer and he or she were you,*
> *would you be satisfied with the quality and the quantity*
> *of work you are performing and the mental attitude*
> *with which you perform it?*
> —Napoleon Hill

Here, then, is an appropriate place to explode a popular fallacy concerning the working principle of the Golden Rule. Those who do not understand the law behind this great rule of human conduct often make the mistake of assuming that it is nothing but a fine theory that cannot be made to work in a material world in an age of selfishness and greed. They erroneously argue that they cannot afford to live by the Golden Rule because their neighbors refuse to do so, so adhering to the rule places them at a great disadvantage.

"I would gladly operate my business under the Golden Rule," said a prominent businessman, "but if I did so, I would become bankrupt because those with whom I do business would take advantage of me."

Examined at face value, his statement would appear sound. But the Golden Rule philosophy is deeper than surface transactions. It is a part of the natural law that governs the universe, and to understand its effects we must go deeper than face value.

The proverbial exception (or what may appear to be an exception) can exist in the person who receives the benefits of the Golden Rule applied but refuses to reciprocate in kind, thereby leaving the benefactor at a disadvantage. Yet minority exceptions to any rule of human conduct are unimportant.

The important question is this:

Doesn't all human experience prove that by and large, the vast majority respond in kind in all their dealings with others?

Therefore, what difference does it make if one person out of every one hundred with whom one has business dealings receives the benefits of the Golden Rule relationship but refuses to recognize those benefits through appropriate reciprocation? The other ninety-nine will reciprocate. Thus, the law of averages will give the benefactor their just compensation for their deeds, not to mention the benefits they confer upon themselves by adding the sum of their deeds to their own character and thereby projecting their influence through improved reputation.

The great retail store of Marshall Field & Company in Chicago has a standing rule that makes it possible for any customer to bring back merchandise that is not satisfactory and, without giving any reasons, exchange it for exactly what was paid for it. Has the rule proved profitable? Do some of the customers take advantage of the rule and impose upon the store? Let us hear what a department manager has to say:

"Sometimes," said the manager of the glove department, "people come in, buy an expensive pair of gloves, wear them one evening, and then deliberately rip the seams apart, bring them back, and demand their money back."

"What do you do in such cases?" he was asked.

"We not only give back the money, but we apologize for the time the customer has lost in bringing the merchandise back."

"But how can the store afford to indulge such obvious dishonesty?"

"The store," he explained, "cannot afford not to indulge it. Perhaps not more than one out of every five hundred customers will impose upon us in this manner, and even this one exception often pays us handsomely because the person spreads the news far and wide that our store keeps its words and adjusts claims without an argument."

In the city of Chicago, there is a chain hat store that sells hats at the popular price of two dollars. The store policy is to sell hats with the understanding that any hat that proves to be unsatisfactory can be returned at any time during the life of the hat and exchanged for a new hat. One customer purchased a hat, and every six months or so thereafter, for more than three years, he returned his old hat with a one-word explanation—"unsatisfactory"—and each time he was given a new hat.

When asked why he did not throw the cheater out of the store the next time he came in, the owner of the store replied: "Throw him out? Why, if I had a hundred customers like this man I could retire from business in a few years. He is a walking advertisement for the store, and never does a week pass that we do not receive one or more new customers who tell us they came to buy our hats because they heard the 'cheater' say we kept our word. This man gives us more advertising, and much better advertising, for the price of a two-dollar hat every six months than we could purchase in newspaper space for hundreds of dollars."

EDITOR'S NOTE:

The American coffee chain Starbucks offers a simple assurance to all of its customers: if you're not satisfied with your beverage, we will gladly remake it until we get it right. This all but guarantees that each customer has a positive experience, leading to repeat patronage—and expanded customer lifetime value—over many years.

You can bet that there have been many times when some unscrupulous customer has consumed half of his or her drink and then requested a complete remake under the guise of an "unsatisfactory" product in order to indulge in more than what was paid for, in essence taking advantage of the store's customer satisfaction policy. But the unscrupulous outlier has seemingly had no material impact on the coffee chain, which now boasts more than thirty thousand locations worldwide and a market capitalization of more than $100 billion.

And yet there are people who say, "I would like to live by the Golden Rule, but I cannot afford it because the other person would not do likewise."

Never mind the "other person." The Golden Rule should begin at home, and if it is truly the Golden Rule applied rather than mere theory, it will bring adequate rewards regardless of what others may do.

> **Comparison is the thief of joy.**
> —attributed to Theodore Roosevelt

Two acquaintances of mine recently formed a business partnership involving a financial outlay by one of them of a considerable sum. Although the partnership involves the remainder of their lives in the association, the contract between them is entirely verbal; not even a scratch of a pen was used to record it. It so happens that both understand and, to the best of their ability, live by the Golden Rule in all their relationships with others. They know, therefore, that a verbal contract based on a meeting of the minds, under the Golden Rule philosophy, when entered into by those who live by this rule, is worth more than all the legal contracts ever drawn up by lawyers.

Let us see how this contract is working out in practice!

Six months after the deal was made, one of the partners—the one who did not invest any money—voluntarily had his life insured, with his partner as the beneficiary, for an amount well above the amount of money the partner had invested. Moreover, he made a will in which he named his partner as the sole beneficiary; it read, in part, as follows:

I do devise and bequeath to my dear friend and business associate, _____, all my rights and interests in the business in which we are the joint owners, and all other property, both real and personal, of which I may be possessed, and I nominate and appoint _____ as Executor and Trustee of this, my last will and testament, with the request that he be permitted to serve without bond.

I have been moved, by my own free will, to bequeath all my property to my business associate, as a measure of my appreciation of his sympathy, his understanding, and his willingness to enter into a business partnership with me and to invest large sums of money in the partnership solely on the strength of his confidence in me, and without any written evidence of our agreement, thus demonstrating his belief in and his practice of the Golden Rule as the proper basis of all human relationships.

The possible value of this man's estate, considering all the facts connected with it, might well extend beyond a million dollars, yet he obviously released it to his business associate with a deep feeling of gratitude, based solely upon how his partner dealt with him, in that the word-of-mouth agreement was considered sufficient to ensure fair dealing.

Knowing the two partners as I do, I am confident that the cleverest lawyer living could not have drawn up a legal contract that would have served their purpose and been more binding than their verbal agreement. The arrangement will necessarily work out satisfactorily because it is based upon the Golden Rule and it was entered into by two people who made this rule a part of their lifelong philosophy in dealing with others.

Now, I do not mean to suggest by this illustration that everyone should enter into business relationships on verbal agreements alone, because I am practical enough to know that there are people—too many of them—who neither respect nor make any attempt to live by the Golden Rule. The error is their loss, of course, but the facts are, unfortunately, that the world in general has not yet discovered the deep and profound benefits that are available to those who live by this rule instead of merely accepting it as a theory of human relationship.

SOME OF THE MAJOR BENEFITS OF THE GOLDEN RULE APPLIED

As we know, motive is of major importance in all human relationships. Let us, therefore, take inventory of the benefits one may receive by applying the Golden Rule and let us determine how many of the nine basic motives one acts upon in applying this rule:

1. The motive of love:

This, the greatest of all the emotions, is founded on the Golden Rule spirit that inspires us to put aside selfishness, greed, and envy and to relate ourselves to others as if we were in their place. The motive of love, expressed through the Golden Rule, enables us to comply freely with that age-old admonition to "love thy neighbor as thyself." It brings us to a full recognition of the oneness of humankind, in which anything that damages our neighbors damages us too.

Let us, therefore, apply the Golden Rule in *all* relationships as a practical means of demonstrating the spirit of humanity. This is the greatest of all motives for applying this profound rule.

2. The profit motive:

This is a sound and universal motive but one that too often is selfishly expressed. Financial gains attained by applying the Golden Rule are more enduring. They carry with them the goodwill of those from whom the gains are attained. This sort of gain establishes no ill will, organized opposition, animosity, or envy toward the one who gains it. In fact, it carries with it a form of willing cooperation from others that can be had in no other way. It is blessed gain in the strictest sense of the term.

3. The motive of self-preservation:

The desire for self-preservation is inborn in every human being. It can best be attained by those who, in their efforts to acquire it, aid others in their attainment of the same desire. The rule of "Live and let live," when applied, ensures an in-kind response from others. Thus, the Golden Rule applied becomes the surest method of attaining self-preservation through the friendly cooperation of others.

4. The motive of desire for freedom of body and mind:

There is a common bond that affects all people, and because it is universal, it influences every human relationship, placing life's advantages and disadvantages, the losses and the gains, substantially on the same level. Just dues are meted out to those who try to take more than their fair share of the gains or to dodge their share of the losses.

Those who gain freedom of body and mind the quickest are those who aid others in attaining similar freedom. This is evidenced in every human relationship, whether it be one of profit or of loss. Freedom must become the common property of one's neighbors and associates if it is to be enjoyed by one's self.

Emerson had this same thought in mind when he said, "Nature hates monopolies and exceptions. The waves of the sea do not more speedily seek a level from their loftiest tossing than the varieties of condition [of life] tend to equalize themselves. There is always some leveling circumstance that puts down the overbearing, the strong, the rich, the fortunate, substantially on the same ground with all others."

5. The motive of desire for power and fame:

Both power and fame, the desire for which is one of the nine basic motives of humankind, are circumstances that can be attained only through the friendly cooperation of others, through the Golden Rule applied. There is no escape from this conclusion—test the statement as you will!

Here again, one may profit by the slogan of the Rotary Club: "One Profits Most Who Serves Best." We cannot "serve best" without putting ourselves in the place of all those whom we serve in every form of relationship. We cannot acquire and hold power and fame without benefiting others in proportion to the benefits we ourselves enjoy. We begin now to understand why one should practice as well as preach the soundness of the Golden Rule! It is the practice that yields dividends, not merely the belief in the rule.

Thus we see that those who relate themselves to others by applying the Golden Rule in all their acts thereby gain cooperation through five of the nine basic motives. Moreover, they provide themselves with a high degree of immunity against the influences of the two negative motives—fear and revenge! We might say, therefore, that those who live by the Golden Rule thereby profit by seven of the nine basic motives and provide themselves with protection against the two negative motives.

Here is the true road to personal power! We may acquire this form of power with the full consent and harmonious cooperation of those from whom we acquire it. Therefore, it is permanent power.

This is the type of power that reflects itself in sound character. Therefore, it is power that is never used to damage another person.

Now let us emphasize one feature of the Golden Rule that is too often overlooked—namely, that its benefits can be attained only through its *use* and not merely by believing in its soundness or in preaching about its soundness to others. A passive attitude toward this great rule of human conduct will not avail anything. Here, as in the case of faith, a passive attitude is of no practical value. "Deeds, not words" must be one's motto!

The Golden Rule has been preached in one form or another for more than two thousand years, but the world at large has accepted it only as a preachment. Only rarely have people in each generation discovered the potential powers available through the application of this great law and profited from its application. If this were not true, the world would not now be engaged, as it is, in tearing the works of civilization asunder.

The benefits of this philosophy are so varied and stupendous in number that it would be impractical to undertake to enumerate them, but this one point I wish to emphasize: the benefits accrue to those who apply the philosophy, as a matter of habit, in all their relationships with others.

Do not always expect to receive direct benefits from those with whom you relate yourself on the Golden Rule basis, because if you do, you will be disappointed. There are some who will not respond in kind, but their failure will be their loss, not yours.

Here is an excellent example of what I mean. In a certain small town in the northern part of the United States lives a man who is recognized far and wide as the "leading citizen" of the town. He has held that position for the better part of the past twenty-five years or more.

Single-handed, he raised the money for one of the finest churches in the town. In return for this service he received—what? He received epithets and abuse from some members of the church and from some of the townspeople outside of the church, from people who disliked him because of his leadership, and perhaps for the reason that the architect whom they wished to see get the contract did not get it.

This man financed and built the most important subdivision of the town, thereby adding beauty and value to the surrounding real estate and to the town in general. He owns and operates one of the largest and most successful businesses in the town, at which he employs a large number of people who are provided with excellent salaries. His influence extends throughout the United States, and because of his reputation for "getting things done," he has attracted many new industries to his section. By and large, he has probably done more for his state than any other individual now living.

He has managed to keep his record so clean that he is friendly with all political parties and practically all local politicians, although he is allied with none of them. His influence at the national Capitol is such that he has gained for his state many advantages from the federal government. If ever a man lived by the Golden Rule in its most practical application in all human relationships, it is this man.

You might think, therefore, that he would be a hero in his own town, but perish the thought! He is not. On the contrary, the "ne'er-do-wells" have nothing but envy for him. On occasion they have been unjust toward him both in their words and in their deeds. Given these actions, he would be justified in retaliating, but the only way he "retaliates" is by going right on serving his neighbors whenever and wherever they will permit him to do so.

He never speaks of their ingratitude, nor does he show by act or deed that he resents it—because he lives by the Golden Rule.

Some will ask: "What good does this man get from living by the Golden Rule?"

In the first place, he is prospering materially and is doing so much more dramatically than the average citizen of his town. We suppose that would satisfy some people, but let us look further. This man is still comparatively young. He is growing rapidly—spiritually, mentally, and financially. He is prospering in the broader sense that comprises not only material benefits but also a sound reputation that constantly attracts unsolicited opportunities to project his influence and add to his material fortunes.

Not long ago, a delegation of industrialists voluntarily placed in his hands an opportunity to render a far-reaching service for his state on a basis that was highly remunerative to him personally. He accepted the responsibility but declined to profit by it. His office is a clearinghouse of influence that touches practically every interest in his state, and many leaders, both political and industrial, make a beaten path to his door.

His word is better than most people's bonds. Everyone knows that. His adherence to the Golden Rule has gained for him the confidence of most of the people, and despite the shortsightedness of a few, he prospers.

This man is not a part of the community where he lives. He is the community itself in the larger sense, not by his own acclaim but by the acclaim of those who recognize sound character and gravitate toward it. It would be no exaggeration to say that he is the most fortunate man in his community—fortunate not by luck or chance but because of his own philosophy of life.

What he is, he has become through his own efforts. He was not born to great estate. On the contrary, he began his business career heavily loaded with debts that he did not incur. Nothing was ever given to him that he did not earn well in advance! And that is another peculiarity of those who live by the Golden Rule—they have the habit of Going the Extra Mile.

This man has some enemies who would not say a kind word of him, but they would give a king's ransom, if they had it, to change places with him.

Be prepared, then, you who wish to live by the Golden Rule, to live with some who will not emulate you, but they will envy you. Take no heed of their envy—it is one of the low faults of humankind, a fault that damages none but those who indulge in it.

My best friend is the one who brings out the best in me.
—Henry Ford

I interviewed this man recently and asked him, frankly, to express his opinion about the results he had attained by applying the Golden Rule. At first, he was inclined to think in terms of the unpleasantness some of his neighbors had caused him by their refusal to reciprocate his favors. He went over these circumstances one by one and then examined himself very carefully for several minutes, looking off into space silently. Finally he turned around, looked me squarely in the face, and with deep emotion he said:

"The real benefits I have received from my way of dealing with people have not come from others; they have not come in terms of material gain; they consist in the feeling I have within my own soul, where I am at peace with myself."

And now give thought to that statement!

Here is a man who is at *peace* with himself. Do you realize what that sort of peace means? It means that this man has faith in himself—faith that enables him to back his judgment with a firmness of decision that is rarely seen in another. He does not need anyone to help him make up his mind about anything. He makes decisions quickly and firmly. He moves on his own initiative and with great enthusiasm, bolstered by the will to win that is helping him to win.

This man undeniably wields great power in his state. He comes by that power through his own attitude, and he gets that attitude because he is at peace with himself. Thus, he has profited by the Golden Rule in a manner that has nothing whatsoever to do with the refusal of others to live by that rule in their dealings with him. Here, then, is an important tenet of the Golden Rule applied: it gives one the courage to make definite decisions and to stand by them through any form of opposition.

Those who live by the Golden Rule as a matter of habit are always at peace with themselves. They have immunity against most forms of fear. They can afford to face their fellow citizens in a spirit of frankness because they have a clean conscience.

It's been said that people cannot take full possession of their own mental power unless they're on good terms with their own conscience. The

Golden Rule is the medium through which we may form a close affinity with our conscience, and it is the only dependable rule by which this can be accomplished.

DOES IT PAY TO APPLY THE GOLDEN RULE?

Let us examine the Golden Rule by analyzing the tangible benefits enjoyed by those who live by it. We will begin with the great Rockefeller fortune, much of which is now being used for the benefit of humankind through scientific research designed to advance civilization.

John D. Rockefeller, Jr., who is carrying on the noble work of his family in the spirit of the Golden Rule, announced the following creed:

I believe in the supreme worth of the individual and in his right to life, liberty and the pursuit of happiness.

I believe that every right implies a responsibility; every opportunity, an obligation; every possession, a duty.

I believe that the law was made for man and not man for the law; that government is the servant of the people and not their master.

I believe in the dignity of labor, whether with head or hand; that the world owes no one a living but that it owes every man an opportunity to make a living.

I believe that thrift is essential to a well-ordered living and that economy is a prime requisite of a sound financial structure, whether in government, business or personal affairs.

I believe that truth and justice are fundamental to an enduring social order.

I believe in the sacredness of a promise, that a person's word should be as good as his bond; that character—not wealth or power or position—is of supreme worth.

I believe that the rendering of useful service is the common duty of mankind and that only in the purifying fire of sacrifice is the dross of selfishness consumed and the greatness of the human soul set free.

I believe in an all-wise and all-loving God, named by whatever name, and that the individual's fulfillment, greatest happiness and widest usefulness are to be found in living in harmony with His will.

I believe that love is the greatest thing in the world; that it alone can overcome hate; that right can and will triumph over might.

Here we find the embodiment of the Golden Rule principle as the basis of the Rockefeller creed as perfectly as it could be stated. Mr. Rockefeller is under no economic strain. Therefore, he is in a position to make and live by his own creed without any thought of its monetary value. Presumably, he chose to adopt the Golden Rule as the foundation of his relationships with others because he believes the rule to be sound, and it yields him dividends in personal satisfaction. Such conduct has brought him peace of mind. It has built for him a public reputation that has no mark against it.

Has the Rockefeller fortune suffered because of this form of applied "idealism"? Has Mr. Rockefeller found it difficult to live by the Golden Rule and still maintain possession of his fortune?

The answer may be found by examining the record of the businesses in which the Rockefeller fortune is invested. I am not familiar with all of them, but I know that some of them have prospered and will doubtlessly continue to prosper.

Take Radio City, for example. When the Rockefeller money purchased the site on which the enterprise is built, the real estate was a motley, declining section of Manhattan. It is now a nationally prized entertainment venue, so attractive that huge crowds of people daily pay a sizable fee just to visit.

The rental fees are far greater than those that were received for the use of the ground before the Rockefellers took it over, and it has rapidly become the center of business activity of New York City.

Take the Standard Oil Company as another example. It was through the operation of this company that much of the Rockefeller fortune was accumulated. Has it prospered? Well, ask anyone on the street whether they would like to own stock in Standard Oil and you will get your answer.

Despite all the keen competition in the oil business, Standard Oil continues to rank high in this field. The company's products have such a fine reputation that no exaggerated claims have to be made in the company's advertising in order to create a market for them. Standard Oil has set the pace for all other oil companies in first-class merchandising. The manner in which the public has responded, by its continued patronage, is the best of evidence that the Golden Rule is profitable in business.

EDITOR'S NOTE:

In 1911, because the Standard Oil Company had become so successful, the Supreme Court of the United States forcibly split it into thirty-four companies. The merits of this decision are still debated more than a century after it was made, but the main entities that own the remnants of Standard Oil today are household names: BP, Exxon, Marathon, and Chevron.

It is estimated that if this forced breakup had not taken place, Standard Oil would now be worth more than $1 trillion.

The Rockefeller enterprises, all of them, are the envy of the business world. Because of the high ethical standards under which it is conducted, the business has not suffered. On the contrary, it has prospered and continues to prosper, although there may be some who believe that the Golden Rule is impractical in this modern age.

Search wherever you may, but you are not likely to find a group that adheres more strictly to the Golden Rule as a business policy than those who manage the Rockefeller interests. They have proved that the Golden Rule can be applied in modern business without causing economic disadvantages. They have proved that the Golden Rule can become a powerful benefit in modern business.

The Coca-Cola Company is another striking example of prosperity based on the Golden Rule applied in business. The business was founded under the humblest of circumstances more than two generations ago. Asa Candler started the business with one large kettle, a formula for making Coca-Cola syrup, and a wooden paddle to stir the syrup.

Step by step, the company has grown the business until it now belts the earth. The company has prospered so universally that it has made fortunes for many who were responsible for its development, including the bottlers and those who drive the trucks that deliver the drink to the dealers. Coca-Cola stock has long been a favorite among investors. The company is known to be among the best managed industries of America. Its officials and employees are of the highest type of American citizens, and we have heard it said that the esprit de corps among the employees is such that they look upon the business as one big family of contented people. Everyone is well paid, and everyone is happy.

When the Great Depression struck in 1929, Coca-Cola did not feel the sting of the blow as others did. No employees were laid off, no salaries were cut, and the business went through that trying experience without slowing down in the least.

Like the Rockefeller enterprises, the Coca-Cola Company bases its business on what amounts to the Golden Rule policy of fairness to all. The company has found that adhering to this policy is sound business philosophy.

EDITOR'S NOTE:

There may not be a more renowned investor globally than Warren Buffett. Known for his logic, thoroughness, and love of fundamentals, the "Oracle of Omaha" epitomizes the Golden Rule applied, in addition to all the other lessons espoused by Carnegie and Hill. Is it any wonder, then, that in 1988 he purchased more than 6 percent of Coca-Cola?

Buffett pounced on the company during the volatility that surrounded the 1987 stock market crash, buying approximately $1 billion worth of its stock at favorable prices. He recognized that the company's fundamentals remained sound even though many were selling their shares feverishly and that it enjoyed unparalleled brand awareness around the world in its category.

Today, Buffett and his associated companies own almost 10 percent of Coca-Cola. Its stock currently trades at around fifty-five dollars a share, meaning it is worth more than twenty-two times Buffett's original investment, plus dividends—a percentage change of more than 2,100 percent!

Perhaps the most striking example of the power of applying the Golden Rule in business can be found in the organization of McCormick & Company from Baltimore, manufacturers and importers of teas, spices, and drugs. The structure of the relationship among the employees and between employees and management is known as the "Multiple Management" plan. This plan was inaugurated by Charles P. McCormick, the president of the company, in 1932, and it is so far-reaching that it affects beneficially each of the two thousand or more employees as well as the management.

Here we find the mastermind principle in operation on a grand scale, with every employee of the company—from the president down—as either an actual or a potential member of the mastermind alliance under which the Multiple Management plan operates.

The Multiple Management plan provides a multitude of benefits and has, as far as I can determine, no objectionable features whatsoever. I shall mention a few of its advantages.

The plan:

- Provides every employee with a definite, strong motive for doing their best under all circumstances, thereby ensuring the individual's advancement in the business on merit and their mental and spiritual growth

- Inspires definiteness of purpose

- Develops self-reliance through self-expression

- Encourages friendly cooperation among all employees, eliminating the usual tendency of people to "pass the buck" and dodge individual responsibility

- Develops leadership by encouraging personal initiative

- Creates alertness of mind and a keen imagination

- Provides an outlet for individual ambition on a basis that is highly beneficial to the individual

- Gives everyone a feeling that they belong, so that no one is left without a means of gaining personal recognition

- Inspires loyalty among the employees and ensures loyalty from the employees to the company, thereby eradicating labor troubles

- Gives the company the fullest benefit of all talents, ingenuity, and creative vision of the employees, at the same time providing adequate compensation for these talents in proportion to their value

> *If you do not perform service above and beyond what you are paid, on what basis would you request more pay?*
> —Napoleon Hill

Let us now examine the working plan of Multiple Management as it has been described by Mr. Robert Littell, who wrote the story of this Golden Rule policy of human relationship for *Reader's Digest*:

Something that an ambitious and capable young friend of mine said the other day seemed to me a significant criticism of the way too many American businesses are run—all the more significant because it echoed complaints we've all of us heard time and again, or perhaps personally felt.

"I have something to give our company that it doesn't seem to want," said my friend. "The management is somewhere way up in the clouds and I have no contact with it. At first, I tried making suggestions, but soon learned to keep my mouth shut and do as I was told. In frequent speeches to us employees, the president—who hardly recognizes me when he sees me in the elevator—asks me to be 'loyal.' As if loyalty were a one-way street. The few raises I've got I've had to beg for, and they were granted grudgingly. But more than money I want recognition, freedom, and a sense of being involved in the company's affairs. The aloofness of the higher-ups makes a lot of us juniors fall into a 'don't care' attitude. I think it does the firm more harm than a sit-down strike."

Such a complaint could not be made by the employees of McCormick & Company of Baltimore. For McCormick & Company, through its Multiple Management plan, has found out how to draw upon hidden resources of energy, initiative and enthusiasm often neglected by centralized management, and has learned how to enlist the hearts as well as the heads of the men who work for it.

For 43 years, this spice, tea, and extract business was run by its founder, Willoughby M. McCormick, a genius. Upon his death in 1932, at the height of the Great Depression, he was succeeded by his nephew, Charles P. McCormick. Young McCormick, even after 17 years of apprenticeship, did not feel able to assume a one-man crown. He wanted to share responsibility with those who could be taught to take it. He felt that independence must be restored to an organization sunk in routine, and the creative imagination should be revived among those who had been saying "yes" to one man's mind so long that they were using only half of their own.

The company's board of directors were men aged 45 and over. Their habits of thought were colored by the past. Something more was needed. And so out of necessity was born the idea of Multiple Management. McCormick picked 17 younger people from various departments and said to them:

"You are the Junior Board of Directors. You will supplement the Senior Board, and feed it with ideas. Elect your own chairman and secretary. Discuss everything that concerns the business. The books are open to you—the minds of your superiors will be wide open to you, also. Make any recommendation you like—upon one condition: it must be unanimous."

A flood of energy and new ideas was released. People who had felt themselves to be merely glorified clerks tasted responsibility, and clamored for more. Even in the first year and a half, practically all of the Juniors' recommendations were adopted. With so many improvements, McCormick & Company hardly knew there was a depression. But more important than dollars and cents, the Junior Board was a brilliantly successful experiment in human engineering.

I saw the Junior Board in action: 17 young people around a long table, each one bursting with ideas for raising the business a notch higher. Some of the ideas were laughingly turned down, others were referred to a subcommittee for further study, all of them were picked clean of their meat by a gathering of equals. The atmosphere was free, there was plenty of kidding, but over it all was the shadow of that day, twice a year, when the Junior Board elects three new members—after dropping the three whom a ballot declares to have been the least efficient.

I saw the Factory Board in action, too. It was a logical outcome of the Junior Board's success. In most factories, foremen or supervisors live apart with their machines all day and shake their heads at the mental processes of the front office. But here they were with a chairman and a secretary, meeting once a week to suggest, to thrash out, to do their part in running the business; here again were discussion and consent, rather than orders and obedience.

Every Saturday, the three boards meet together. Titles and rank are forgotten—they mean almost nothing at McCormick anyway. The healthy give and take of these wide-ranging discussions has long since banished logrolling, departmental jealousies, and office politics. The arithmetic of Multiple Management is simple: 40 heads, if you can get at what's inside them, are better than one.

And Multiple Management doesn't stop with these boards. Formerly, the placing and promotion of new employees was rather hit or miss, and the turnover among them was high. But today every newcomer who shows signs of promise is at once sponsored by a member of the Junior Board, whose job is not so much to supervise their work as to give them general advice—if they have the sense to ask for it. After three months, each month under a different sponsor, the protégé is either dropped back into the ranks of plodders or singled out for training and advancement. To ambitious beginners, the encouragement is invaluable.

At this point, some businesspeople may inquire: "All very pretty and democratic, but does it pay?" Yes. It pays the company: overhead is 12% under 1929, labor turnover is down to 6% a year, to less than that for the younger employees. It pays the rank and file employees with bonuses at Christmas, larger every year for the last five years; and a minimum wage double that of the prosperity peak and way above the wage for similar work in Baltimore. The total payroll is 34% higher than it was in 1929, but production is 34% higher also.

The three boards, working together, have gradually evolved a personnel policy that puts McCormick & Company in the front rank of enlightened employers. The McCormick work week is 40 hours (nine years ago it was 56). This includes two 10-minute rest periods every day, during which employees drink a cup of McCormick tea, on the house.

There is no piecework, no speedup. Hands tending automatic machines change off periodically to relieve the monotony.

There are eight holidays with pay, and a week's vacation with pay every year for all those employed over six months. The seasonal peaks and valleys have been leveled off to a steady 48-week year.

And it is one of the few companies I know of where getting fired is almost as laborious a process as getting hired. To dismiss a worker, the signatures of four of that worker's superiors are necessary. Usually they would be called before the Factory Board, and allowed to plead their case. McCormick & Company charges itself with an error if it lets someone go before they have been helped to see that their going is just and necessary.

In the United States, Canada, and England, more than 160 companies have set up Multiple Management on the McCormick plan. It seems to be the best answer yet to the centralization, dry rot, and bureaucracy that infects business as well as government.

The Multiple Management plan is working for McCormick's employees because of the spirit of human understanding and friendly cooperation the individuals have put into it—a spirit that began with the management and was readily embraced by the employees.

And, obviously, this spirit of understanding and cooperation provides sound company management because it recognizes and rewards merit appropriately down to the humblest employee, and at the same time it eliminates the unwilling and the unfit from the organization. Here, then, is a clever plan that gives every individual the fullest opportunity to market their services for all they are worth. Although the organization consists of around two thousand employees, every employee's individuality is so well preserved that they have as good an opportunity to attract attention to themselves as they would have if the organization were small.

Thus, the McCormick Multiple Management plan has at long last eliminated one of the major curses of large industrial organizations: people losing their individual identity in the crowd. Previously, only the bold and the aggressive had an opportunity to promote themselves by attracting attention to their work.

Most people will work harder for recognition and a word of commendation where it is deserved than they will for money. No one wants to feel like a cog in a vast machine. One of the major curses of industry is the fact that it has been developed so that people have been left no choice but to feel that they are unimportant. Thus, both management and its employees have been deprived of the greatest asset of industry—namely, the spirit of friendly cooperation such as that in the McCormick organization.

And what does it take to preserve this spirit?

Charles P. McCormick has given the answer to this question in his Multiple Management plan. Reduce this plan to its components and you will discover that it is simply the Golden Rule applied to industry.

Through its application, the McCormick Company has put the soul back into its industry. Further, I would be greatly surprised if the company were overtaken by any economic problem that it could not solve, because when a group of people blend their minds in a spirit of harmony for the attainment of a definite end, they always find a way of attaining it.

Obviously the plan is profitable for the company, as its financial record has proved, but let us not forget that it is also profitable for every individual employee too, since that spirit also extends to relationships with others outside the organization. Therefore, the plan is of great public benefit because it encourages the application of the Golden Rule whenever an employee of the company encounters others in private and social relationships.

Surely, if this plan were in operation in every business in the country, the American way of life would be in no danger of annihilation through belief in subversive philosophies. In fact, the spirit of the Golden Rule offers the individual more personal benefits than does any other philosophy.

The Industrial Age has brought a multiplicity of human problems, and the entire system of human relationships is undergoing a rapid change. We have no way of foretelling what sort of system will evolve from this change, but we do know that first, it must be based on common decency, and second, it must provide the means for people to voluntarily work together in a spirit of friendly cooperation. It must be so fair to all that it will not permit the exploitation of any individual or group of individuals under any pretext whatsoever, and above all it must provide for the full and free expression of individual initiative, as the Multiple Management plan does.

Remember, no system can endure unless it is founded squarely on the Golden Rule philosophy of "live and let live." That philosophy has never failed wherever it has been applied with sincerity of purpose.

One of the difficulties out of which has arisen much of the misunderstanding between employees and employers is that industry has become so vast that the human element has been neglected. Both employers and employees must recognize the necessity of humanizing their relationships under some such plan as the Multiple Management plan if America is to remain the richest and freest country in the world.

People are not free when they:

- Stand in fear of each other
- Lack mutual confidence
- Cannot exercise their personal initiative in their occupations
- Must bargain with one another through "professionals" who profit most when controversies exist

- Must pay for the privilege of holding a job
- Are not permitted to sit down together as employers and employees to work out their mutual problems, as the McCormick employees do

The future of the US population will depend very largely on the system through which employees and employers in industry are helpfully related in the future.

THE GOLDEN RULE AS THE BASIS OF MANAGEMENT-EMPLOYEE RELATIONSHIPS

It has been estimated that nine out of every ten people in the United States get their living directly or indirectly from the activities of American industry. It is therefore important that those who carry on our vast industrial enterprises—both the management and its employees—adopt a common ground so that they may work in harmony if this nation is to remain prosperous and free.

Let us take inventory of those who have a direct interest in industrial relationships:

1. The people from every walk of life who have their savings invested in the shares of industrial corporations

2. The managers who have the responsibility of overseeing operations

3. The workers, skilled and unskilled, who carry on the manual labor

4. The general public that consumes the products but has no direct part in its activities

5. The legislators and public officials who pass laws regarding industrial relationships and business policies and whose governments are supported by industry taxes

6. The millions of professionals who work in the companies along the supply chain, such as farmers, shopkeepers, and other tradespeople who sell products and services to the industries and to their employees

Here are six separate groups that have a vested interest in a spirit of harmony that sustains our industrial system. Every individual in these six groups is affected by the fortunes of industry, and if industry is to survive, every individual should assume their share of the responsibility in maintaining harmony among these groups.

But there is vastly more at stake than the mere personal welfare of any member of these six groups! Democracy is on trial, and every member of these groups is on the defensive side no matter what their personal opinions or self-interests may be.

Our democracy is founded upon American industry, since it is the major source of our economic life. If American industry collapses through the selfishness and greed of those who have the responsibility of maintaining it, the entire American way of life will go with it. Let us have no illusions about this fact. Better yet, let us face it with a spirit of joint obligation and mutual responsibility in efforts to save the institution that has been responsible for our right to claim this as the "freest and richest nation of the world."

To protect and maintain the American way of life, we must live the impersonal life. This is the same premise that was put forth by the Man of Galilee nearly two thousand years ago and by other great philosophers who, down through the ages, have called our attention to the power from within that is available to those who do unto others as if they were the others.

> *Carry out a random act of kindness, with no expectation of reward,*
> *safe in the knowledge that one day someone*
> *might do the same for you.*
> —Princess Diana

If the American way of life is to survive, and industry to be maintained, this rule must be adopted and applied by every member of the six groups. The true relationship of the members must be viewed from a perspective that is focused on higher things than wages and the accumulation of personal wealth. It must be regarded in the context of its bearing on the purposes for which humankind was created.

Capital and labor are essential to each other—their interests are so bound that they cannot be separated. In a civilized nation, such as that of which we boast, they are mutually dependent. If there is any difference, capital is more dependent upon labor than labor upon capital, because life can be sustained without capital.

No one can live on their wealth. They cannot eat their gold and silver; they cannot clothe themselves with deeds to property or with stocks and bonds. Capital can do nothing without labor, and its only value consists in its power to purchase labor or its results. It is, itself, the product of labor.

But labor cannot exist without capital, and for thousands of years labor has been offered as a means of exchange for purchasing life's necessities. We become more dependent upon others as our wants multiply and civilization advances. Each person works their profession and does *better* work because they can devote their energies to areas to which they are especially suited. As a result, they contribute increasingly to the public good. While they are working for others, all others are working for them.

This is the Law of the Impersonal Life, a law that rules everywhere in the material world. All those who are engaged in useful employment are philanthropists, public benefactors. A few dollars in a multitude of pockets are powerless, but combined—into what we call "capital"—they move the world, giving our people an outlet for their talents coupled with economic freedom better than the world has ever known.

Despite the claims of the rabble-rousers and those who exploit labor for a price, the condition of labor is constantly improving. The common laborer in the US has conveniences and comforts that princes of royal birth could not and did not command a century or less ago. They are better clothed, have a greater variety of both necessities and luxuries, live in more comfortable dwellings, and have many other domestic conveniences that money could not purchase but a few decades ago.

We are bound by common ties irrespective of which group we belong to. The rich and the poor, the learned and the ignorant, and the strong and the weak are woven together under the American way of life in one social and civic web. Harm to one is harm to all, just as help to one is help to all.

But the benefits of capital are not limited to supplying present wants and needs. Capital opens new avenues to labor and reveals new sources of income through scientific research. It is also largely invested in supplying the means of intellectual and spiritual culture. Books are multiplied at constantly diminishing prices, and the best education is available to the humblest person. For a nominal fee, the newspapers bring the history of the world to one's door, while the radio provides the humblest home with both news of the day and classics of music without cost.

Capital cannot be invested in any useful product without blessing a multitude of people. It sets the machinery of life into motion, it multiplies employment, and it places the products of all nations at everyone's door at a price within one's means.

If capital renders all this service—and if it can be brought into use by labor and derives all its values from labor—why should there be only conflict between them?

There is no real basis for conflict between capital and labor—it arises from both parties seeing only half the truth. Mistaking that for the whole, they fall into mistakes ruinous to both, although the misunderstanding is too often the result of agitation by those who profit most when capital and labor disagree.

EDITOR'S NOTE:

In 2005, the Turkish immigrant Hamdi Ulukaya converted an old Kraft manufacturing plant in upstate New York into the primary manufacturing facility for his yogurt start-up, Chobani. Eleven years later, while mass layoffs continued to plague the economy and with more than five hundred thousand Americans losing their jobs in 2016 alone, one company bucked the trend. The yogurt company, given little hope of success, had surpassed $1 billion in annual sales and felt it was time to give something back to the people who had helped get it that far.

Chobani gifted 10 percent of the company to its two thousand employees, a welcome bonus considering its $3 billion valuation, with the longest-serving employees receiving the largest allocations. This was the latest piece of good-will for Chobani, which donates 10 percent of its profits to charity each year and boasts a staff of which one-third are refugees.

In the announcement, Ulukaya celebrated with his colleagues, saying, "We used to work together; now we are partners." The unexpected gift was aimed at not only rewarding the people who made it possible but also help-ing to address the growing pay gap between executives and workers while recognizing its workforce as equals working in a spirit of harmony toward a common purpose.

Shortly afterward, the Chobani CEO said, "I've built something I never thought would be such a success, but I cannot think of Chobani being built without all these people. Now they'll be working to build the company even more and building their future at the same time."

Passion inflames the mind and blinds understanding. When passion is aroused, people will sacrifice their own interests, against their better judgment, to injure others, and both will suffer loss. The conflict will be continued without doubt until both parties discover that they are mistaken, that their interests are mutual, and that those interests can be fully secured only through friendly cooperation and by giving to each the reward it deserves.

Strikes and lockouts will not settle fundamental problems for either cap-ital or labor, because the temporary gains made by either side are more than offset by the losses of both sides and of the community at large. Violence and threats won't work, and dynamite, whether in the form of explosives or the more destructive force of uncontrolled passion, will not heal or subdue any hostile feelings.

Legislation cannot, and should not, be expected to settle disputes bet-ween employers and employees. One side may get the benefit of such laws for a time, but whatever is gained by this method will be lost in the strained relationship growing out of it.

Peace of mind should be a portion of the pay that goes into every pay packet, and it should be shared equally by the buyer and the seller of labor:

- As workers, how can we live the impersonal life when our employment contract is determined by a law that fixes our wages, establishes our hours of labor, and prohibits us from rendering the sort of service that would get us promoted?

- As employers, how can we live the impersonal life when we are prohibited by law from working out our own economic problems with our employees and are forced to pay wages according to a fixed scale that has no relationship whatsoever to the quality and the quantity of service rendered?

Are the spiritual qualities or the economic welfare of employers and employees improved when both are compelled by law to regard each other as natural enemies? And what will happen to a nation where most of its citizens are kept at arm's length from each other by law in their business relationships?

What will happen to this temporary advantage when employers can no longer operate their business at a profit? Is it not obvious that labor's gain, through class legislation in its favor, is destined to become labor's downfall?

Every person, employer or employee, must be given the right to exercise personal initiative, skill, experience, and education and to render useful service to the full extent of their ability. Anything short of this violates the Golden Rule, and the violators can no more escape.

> *Don't be intimidated by what you don't know.*
> *That can be your greatest strength and ensure that*
> *you do things differently from everyone else.*
> —Sara Blakely

The laborer and the capitalist have a mutual and common interest that cannot be improved by legislation. Neither can prosper permanently without the prosperity of the other, and all the laws of the world could not change this. Let each take the Golden Rule as their guide. If 10 percent of people would practice the Golden Rule, it would have such a profound effect upon the world that 80 percent of our drafted laws would be superfluous.

It is a simple rule of conduct that covers every human relationship, profiting everyone and damaging no one. We have become known as a nation of "go-getters"! Would it not be wise if we would do an about-face and make ourselves known as a nation of "go-givers"?

Start by doing the following:

- Refrain from trying to change others, instead devoting your efforts to changing *yourself*!

- Rather than preach, express your convictions in *action*.

- Place less emphasis upon the "don'ts" and more importance on the "dos."

Only your example can change the habits of those around you. Start by improving your relationships with those nearest you. Take no heed of the faults of others but look well to the improvement of your own, because these are under your control and you can improve them at will. For example:

- If your personality is negative, you can change it.

- If your mental attitude is negative, you can change that, too.

- If the nature of your work makes it inconvenient or impossible for you to put into it more service and better service, you can at least put into it a pleasing mental attitude that will increase your friendships and gain for you a greater degree of appreciation for your services.

As your mental attitude changes, the circumstances of your life will change also, and you will discover one of the greatest secrets of the ages, the secret that has been the foundation of all great achievements, the secret that too many of the American people have lost.

The secret is this:

When we lose ourselves in unselfish service to others, we discover the path to that power from within that is the basis of all personal success.

To find ourselves, we must first lose ourselves. When you discover this secret, you will no longer be burdened by the unfriendly opposition of others. Discord and conflict will disappear from your life as if by the touch of magic, and you will experience the peace of mind that surpasses understanding.

You will recognize that the worries you have experienced in the past have been of your own making. You will know, too, that the solution of your problems is within your own control.

Further, another strange thing will happen. You will discover that you possess:

- Blessings you had overlooked because your mind had not been attuned to recognize them

- Blessings of liberty in a great democracy

- Blessings of freedom of personal initiative through which you may engage in the work of your choice

- Blessings of freedom of speech through which you may proffer your ideas without fear of reprisal

- The manifold blessings of opportunity to share in the riches of a nation that has provided its people with the highest standard of living known to civilization

You can read the biographies of those whom the world has acknowedged as great and see for yourself that they attained their greatness by living the selfless life born of the Golden Rule spirit, and you can emulate them. To make it easy for you to read the biographies of some whom the world has made immortal because of their spirit of unselfishness, I mention a few of them here.

Louis Pasteur, known for his research in physics, chemistry, and bacteriology, uncovered new methods for the prevention and the cure of physical ailments. He could have exploited these discoveries for significant personal gain, but he gave them to the world without price.

William Penn, whose insight into human psychology was so keen that he made peace with the Indians during the early residence in this nation of English colonists by dealing with them on the Golden Rule basis, thereby procuring their friendly cooperation.

Benjamin Franklin, whose Golden Rule spirit opened the doors of diplomatic relationship to him in France and other European countries. This cooperation during the American Revolution may well have contributed to the balance of power that brought final victory to Washington's armies at Yorktown.

Simón Bolívar, the "George Washington" of South America, who led the forces that ultimately achieved the independence of the nations now called Venezuela, Colombia, Ecuador, Panama, Peru, and Bolivia. Having expended his great personal fortune in the cause of the freedom to which he so generously devoted his life, Mr. Bolívar is perhaps the greatest example of public service of the Golden Rule principle in all of South America.

Florence Nightingale, whose unselfish service in nursing the sick and the wounded during the Crimean War remains imprinted upon the minds of all who know her history. Even though disease raged all around her and she was chronically ill, she continued faithfully at her post. After the war ended, Ms. Nightingale devoted her time to spreading health and nursing knowledge that now benefits the sick and the ailing throughout the world.

Fanny Crosby, who, despite going blind shortly after birth, devoted her life to writing songs that will live forever and to spreading kindness from the lecture platform. She composed more than eight thousand songs of hope and love that comfort people throughout the world. Denied the light of the sun, Mrs. Crosby shared the inner light of hope and faith with millions who have been moved by her Golden Rule spirit.

John Chapman, who won fame as the early American frontier's "Johnny Appleseed." He planted apple seeds before the pioneers arrived so that they might have fruit.

Jacob Riis, an immigrant from Denmark, who came to America and devoted the major portion of his life to improving the living conditions in the slums of New York. Although Theodore Roosevelt, both as governor of New York and as president of the United States, offered Mr. Riis appointment to high office, Mr. Riis refused with the explanation that he was already so busy helping his neighbors that he could not enter politics.

Knute Rockne, the great Notre Dame football coach, whose exemplary spirit of fairness and clean sportsmanship made the Notre Dame football team front-page news throughout the US and established an all-time-high standard for the Golden Rule relationship in athletics.

Will Rogers, the sage of screen and stage, whose homespun philosophy and dry wit made him an ambassador of goodwill throughout America. Although his earnings were significant, it can be truthfully said that his fun-making was carried out in the true Golden Rule spirit, because he never resorted to unfair or destructive ridicule to gain applause.

Sir Wilfred Grenfell, who unselfishly devoted forty-two years of his life to the welfare of those in what are now the Canadian provinces of Newfoundland and Labrador. Most of the citizens were native fishermen who had never seen a trained physician before he came to help them. Inspired by a generous love for the weak and helpless, Dr. Grenfell helped these northern fishermen, raising, through the cooperation of the people of Canada, England, and the United States, enough money to build and equip six hospitals, seven nursing stations, and four ships. In addition to providing medical care, Sir Wilfred promoted a properly balanced diet by helping people to plant vegetables that could be raised in the cold climate to help ward off scurvy.

Become familiar with the lives of these and others who have made unselfish contributions to civilization and you will be convinced that abundant opportunity exists for all those who live by the Golden Rule.

You will be convinced, too, that it is not the economic system of the Western world that needs changing but the mental attitude of those who have failed to recognize the blessings of this system, which provides an opportunity for every person who is willing to render any sort of beneficial services.

Fear doesn't prevent death. It prevents life.
—Naguib Mahfouz

McCormick employees do not have a complaint to register against the American way of life, because they have found a practical way to make it yield them material success through the rendering of useful service. Charles P. McCormick discovered that there was nothing wrong with the American industrial system except the maladjustment of the people who maintained it, and he busied himself with correcting the relationships of those who worked in his firm instead of finding fault with the system.

If McCormick & Company can adjust human relationships profitably and happily under the American industrial system, others can do the same, as indeed some of them are doing.

Mr. McCormick began the readjustment of relationships in his industry by providing every worker, from the highest to the humblest, with an adequate motive for putting their best effort and their best mental attitude into the business. As Andrew Carnegie has emphasized, everything one does is based on some sort of motive. As Mr. McCormick's firm has proved, when the motive is founded on the Golden Rule philosophy of give and take, live and let live, there is little if anything to cause maladjustments among human beings.

It is characteristic of the Golden Rule that those who live by it can neither cheat nor be cheated! The rule works for a just balance in all human relationships so that everyone receives in proportion to that which they give, both in quality and quantity. And let us not forget that one receives what one is justly entitled to without resorting to force, legislative coercion, or legal measures. Those who live by the Golden Rule find very little use for the services of a lawyer, and they rarely find it necessary to resort to the force of numbers to protect their rights or to acquire their just dues.

Some time after the Multiple Management system had been in operation in the McCormick plant in Baltimore, the representative of a labor union came to the plant and announced that he had been sent to organize some of the workers. Let's let Mr. Charles P. McCormick, president of the company, tell, in his own words, the story of what happened:

A labor union agent came to my office with the announcement that he had been delegated to organize certain workers in our plant. I told him to go ahead, if he thought he could get anywhere, but assured him that he would waste his time and effort. I then informed him as to how our factory is managed and what we are doing for our people. I assured him that if he would tell us how to do more for our workers, we would gladly adopt his suggestions, if it were possible under the limitations of the business. He asked a few questions, which I answered frankly. Then, after thinking over the proposition for a time, he remarked that he did not think it would pay to try to organize our plant, and he would so report to his superiors.

When employers and employees deal with each other on the Golden Rule basis, they have no need for outside interference in the settlement of their problems. McCormick & Company has the greatest of all unions, one that embraces, happily, both the management and the employees—a union that protects the rights of every individual more zealously than could any outside organization. The tenets of this union may be found in the Sermon on the Mount, describing as it does the greatest of all the rules of human relationship—DO UNTO OTHERS AS IF *YOU* WERE THE OTHERS!

EDITOR'S NOTE:

The American food giant McCormick & Company may have been founded in 1889, but its unique management style has ensured that it continues its meteoric rise. The food manufacturer now boasts more than twelve thousand employees serving customers in 150 countries, generating more than $5 billion in annual sales.

Has the culture changed since Charles P. McCormick established the Multiple Management plan in 1932? Absolutely not. In fact, McCormick & Company has built on its already strong foundation with thirteen local boards, three regional boards, and a global board, ensuring that the company continues to add value to customers, employees, and suppliers alike, working alongside employee ambassador groups that give all employees a forum to communicate and collaborate.

Its Power of People management style gives all those in the company an opportunity to solve some of its toughest challenges alongside its highest-ranking executives while sharing in the company's profits. In addition to offering real-world developmental opportunities, it ensures engagement between management and those on the front lines, retaining McCormick & Company's position at the helm of the food manufacturing business globally.

Since 1982, when it traded at just over $1 a share, McCormick & Company has grown to be worth more than $160 a share today, an increase of more than 15,000 percent! A win-win for everyone involved.

Some years ago, some people in Louisville, Kentucky, were astonished to see a man rush out of a store, propelling himself in a wheelchair, and lead a blind man across a busy corner. The man in the wheelchair was Lee W. Cook, who was born without the use of his legs. Investigation disclosed that Mr. Cook had not only made his own way through life but had also become the head of a successful business, from which he accumulated a fair-sized fortune.

In speaking of his philosophy of life, Mr. Cook said:

I never think of myself as being afflicted because I can see, by looking around, that there are so many people who are worse off than I. All my life I have made it my business to do some kind deed for someone who is helpless, wherever I find an opportunity. I do not recall having ever benefited directly from this sort of help, but the world has been kind to me, for I have prospered far beyond the expectations of one who is afflicted as I am. The kindness I have extended to others is a gratifying expression of my thankfulness for my own good fortune.

One of the strangest experiences I ever had was connected with a young man whom I sent through medical school. His people were too poor to pay his way, but the young man was determined to become a medical doctor, and I helped him. Many years passed and he dropped out of sight, having apparently forgotten his benefactor.

One night as I was leaving my store for the day I rolled my chair into the middle of the street, believing it to be clear, when suddenly an automobile turned the corner at rapid speed and was bearing down on me so fast that I could never have escaped without injury if someone had not rushed out and pulled me to the sidewalk. The man who saved me was the man I had sent through medical school. He was on his way to my store to tell me that he had settled in another city and was doing well in his practice. I took him home with me for the night, and we talked far into the night. I discovered that he had been paying off his debt to me by sending two young men through medical school. You see, therefore, when one plants the seed of human kindness it sprouts, grows, reproduces itself and spreads like the seeds of a wild weed. I now find that instead of helping one young man through school, I was in this case instrumental in helping three young men to acquire an education.

Sometimes I help people who are not worthy of help. But that is their misfortune, not mine. The benefits that accrue to me are of a nature that I cannot be cheated of them, for they become a part of my own character.

I remember, once, giving a dollar to an old man who limped into my store and told me he was hungry and out of a job. A dollar was all he asked for. As he left the store, I noticed that his "limp" was not nearly as pronounced as it was when he came in, so I decided to follow him and see what he did with the money. I didn't have far to go.

He made a straight line for the nearest saloon, walked up to the bar without the slightest sign of lameness, plunked the dollar down, and ordered the barkeeper to set up the full value of it in whiskey. I waited until he had emptied the first two glasses, then I rolled my chair in and gave him the surprise of his life.

Instead of calling him down for his deceitfulness, I motioned to him to come over in the corner and lean over while I gave him a message. Then I took out another dollar, handed it to him, and whispered very quietly, "This dollar is not given to you because of your truthfulness; it is given to you to shame you for telling a crippled man a lie. If you had told me the truth, I would have given you $10 as graciously as I have given you two."

The man backed away from me, glanced at the liquor he had left on the bar, then made a rush for the door, and I have never seen or heard of him since.

In telling this story, Mr. Cook laughed heartily, then explained that he had developed a keen sense of humor that had enabled him to make allowances for nearly all human weaknesses.

Probably I should have poked the old rascal on the nose, but that would have done less good than giving him the extra dollar. Besides, it is a part of my philosophy to convert into laughter many experiences which, if I took them seriously, would have led to tears. I am so eternally grateful for having been deprived of my legs instead of my eyes that I find it difficult to set myself up as a judge over anyone, no matter what his weaknesses may be.

It is little wonder that Mr. Cook prospered in business. He sent out good thoughts for everyone and engaged in beneficent deeds wherever he had an opportunity. The Law of Harmonious Attraction did the rest!

> *You can get another person to act toward you*
> *as you wish to act*
> *by first acting that way toward them.*
> —Napoleon Hill

Every Christmas evening for a great number of years, the people of Louisville were accustomed to seeing Mr. Cook in some part of the tenement section of the city with a mule hauling a wagon loaded with Christmas baskets of food. He gave out a hundred of these baskets every year, taking them in person to the neediest families, preferring those with small children. Each basket contained enough food for a good Christmas dinner. He never asked the names of any of those to whom he gave the baskets, and he never told them his name, but each basket contained a card on which was written this simple message:

With the compliments of one who loves his community.

No preachment, no bid for publicity, no attempt to humiliate the recipients of his hospitality. But the fame of this man spread far and near, and he prospered. Obviously, there was an unseen witness to his good deeds, and his compensation came as quietly and as mysteriously as he had moved in bestowing his benefactions.

"Eccentric sentimentality!" some may exclaim. Well, perhaps it was, but somehow we wonder what would happen if some of us who are not "eccentric" or "sentimental" emulated Mr. Cook's example and began to GIVE instead of devoting our best energies to trying to GET! Wouldn't this be a better world if every community had at least one such character as Mr. Cook, who made it their business to sow the seeds of kindness where such seeds are seldom if ever known?

The following is an interesting story of a lawyer who had been commissioned by a man with a miserly disposition to collect a debt from an elderly couple who had very few of this world's possessions:

"No," said the lawyer to his client, "I shall not press your claim against these old people. You can get someone else to press your case, or you can withdraw your claim, just as you please."

"Think there isn't any money in it?" the client inquired.

"There probably would be some little money in it, but it would come from the sale of the little house that this old man and his wife call home. But I don't wish to meddle with the matter anyhow."

"Oh, you got frightened out of it, eh?"

"Not at all. It was something deeper than fright that stopped me."

"I suppose the old rascal begged hard to be let off?"

"Well, yes, he did!"

"And you became weak-kneed and caved in?"

"Yes, if you wish to put it that way! I did."

"What in creation did you do that for?"

"Well, I believe I shed a few tears when I learned the real story."

"And the old fellow begged you hard, you say?"

"No, I didn't say so. He didn't speak a word to me."

"Well, may I respectfully inquire whom he did address in your hearing?"

"God Almighty!"

"Ah, the old scamp took to praying, did he?"

"Not for my benefit in the least. You see, I found the little house easily enough and knocked on the outer door, which stood ajar, but nobody heard me, so I stepped into the little hall and saw through the crack of the door a cozy sitting room, and there on the bed, with her silver head high on the pillows, was an old lady who looked for all the world like my mother did the last time I saw her on earth. Well, I was on the point of knocking again when she said, "Come, Father, now, begin. I'm ready." And down on his knees by her side went an old, white-haired man, still older than his wife, I should judge, and I couldn't have knocked then for the life of me."

The lawyer continued: "Well, he began. First, he reminded God they were still His submissive children, and no matter what He saw fit to bring upon them they shouldn't rebel at His will. Of course, it was going to be hard for them to go out homeless at their age, especially with poor Mother so sick and helpless, and oh how different it all might have been if only one of their boys had been spared. Then his voice kind of broke, and a white hand stole from under the coverlid and moved softly over his white hair. Then he went on to repeat that nothing could be so sharp again as the parting with those three sons—unless mother and he should be separated.

"But at last he fell to comforting himself with the fact that the dear Lord knew that it was through no fault of his own that Mother and he were threatened with the loss of their dear little home, which meant beggary and the almshouse—a place they prayed to be delivered from entering if it should be consistent with God's will. And then he quoted a multitude of promises concerning the safety of those who put their trust in the Lord. In fact, it was the most thrilling plea to which I ever listened. And at last, he prayed for God's blessing on those who were threatening justice."

More slowly than ever, the lawyer said: "And I—believe—I'd rather go to the poorhouse myself tonight than to stain my heart and hands with such a prosecution as that."

"Little afraid to defeat the old man's prayer, eh?"

"Bless your soul, man, you couldn't defeat it!" said the lawyer. "I tell you, he left it all subject to the will of God. He claimed that we were told to make known our desires to God, but of all the pleadings I ever heard, that beat all.

You see, I was taught that kind of thing myself in childhood. Anyway, why was I sent to hear that prayer? I am sure I don't know, but I hand the case over to you."

"I wish," said the client, twisting uneasily, "you hadn't told me about the old man's prayer."

"Why so?"

"Well, because I want the money the place would bring, but I was taught the Bible straight enough when I was a youngster, and I'd hate to run counter to what you tell about. I wish you hadn't heard a word about it, and another time I wouldn't listen to petitions not intended for my ears."

The lawyer smiled.

"My dear fellow," he said, "you're wrong again. It was intended for my ears and yours too, and God Almighty intended it. My mother used to sing about God's moving in a mysterious way, as I remember it."

"Well, my mother used to sing it, too," said the claimant as he twisted the claim papers in his fingers. "You can call in the morning, if you like, and tell them that the claim has been met."

"In a mysterious way," added the lawyer, smiling.

"Yes, in a mysterious way."

When the finer sentiments of feeling are eliminated from the human heart, human relationships become cold, mechanical, and mercenary.

There is no doubt that sentimental emotion is often expressed at the cost of monetary gain, but there is gain of another sort that some people value more than money or anything money can buy. It is the harmonious relationship we establish with our own conscience, the glow of satisfaction that comes from within when we know we have not damaged anyone intentionally, have not cheated anyone, and have gone out of our way to be helpful and are conscious of the fact that our word is accepted by all who know us as our bond!

Some may believe that this philosophy was organized primarily for the purpose of enabling people to accumulate material riches. Though it is true that those who master it and apply it have no difficulty in accumulating material riches in abundance, the major object that Mr. Carnegie had in mind in inspiring the organization of the philosophy was to help people live happily and negotiate their way through life harmoniously. He realized that there are riches available to people that are of far greater value than any that money represents. His own attitude toward money was revealed by the fact that he gave away most of his huge fortune before he died.

Mr. Carnegie considered that the greater portion of his fortune consisted of this philosophy, realizing, as he did, that it is a *complete* philosophy of life, sufficient for the attainment of all human needs. He gave the latter years of his life to aiding in the preparation of the material that went into the philosophy at a time when he was in a position to spend his time in any manner he chose. He chose to spend it to help generations then unborn.

Mr. Carnegie's life should offer an important clue to the rest of us in the choice of paths that lead to happiness. He had everything money could provide—had it in superabundance, yet he gave away most of his material fortune. This should suggest to the rest of us the thought that our time should be so divided that most of it goes into rendering useful service from which we may attain happiness rather than the accumulation of material things beyond our immediate needs.

I do not belong to that school of thought whose followers believe there is virtue in living in an attic and following a life of sacrifice; not at all! I believe in opulence within reason, but I do not believe in opulence at the expense of happiness.

When anyone finds that most of their time is required for the purpose of defending and holding their material possessions, you may be reasonably sure they are suffering from maladjustment to life in general and to themselves and their neighbors in particular. Beyond the point at which material possessions provide one with the freedom of mind to follow the occupation of their choice, material things become a millstone around their neck. I offer this suggestion not as a preachment but from practical experience. It is based on careful observations of many people who have imprisoned themselves by their fortunes until they have lost contact with everyone they know as far as the finer human relationships are concerned.

Happiness is when what you think, what you say,
and what you do are in harmony.
—Mahatma Gandhi

I have in mind, too, this strange experience through which the whole world is passing, an experience that seems to chastise the whole of humankind because of the common practice of worshiping material things. I cannot escape the feeling that in the future, the world will frown upon those who devote their entire lives to the accumulation of material fortunes at the expense of the good they might do by helping others who are less fortunate than themselves to acquire a more equitable portion of the necessities of life.

I believe I know what is wrong with our materialistic world. Andrew Carnegie knew what was wrong. He gave us the remedy by inspiring the organization of this philosophy because he realized that what is needed is a better distribution of the knowledge by which harmonious lives are lived and not the mere accumulation of material wealth.

IN REFLECTION

By James Whittaker

*The finest kind of security is the personal security
that is developed from within.*
—Andrew Carnegie

Congratulations on making it this far!

A lot is attempted but so little is completed; therefore, you should feel extremely proud of yourself for displaying enough self-discipline to read a book that, if properly understood and applied, will completely transform your life.

There's a strong probability that your mind is abuzz—mine certainly was on each occasion I have read this book. Through the fascinating conversation between Hill and Carnegie, and exemplified through the annotations, we've covered a whole suite of topics. These include financial independence, relationships, education, career advancement, and business management, among many others.

You've also been inspired by stories of individuals who stood up despite insurmountable odds and advanced toward achievement, freedom, and fulfilment. You've seen how several companies around the world are applying the exact principles and methods espoused in this book to create enormous value for their customers, employees, and stockholders.

These lessons were segmented into three comprehensive themes:

1. **Self-discipline:** Taking possession of one's own mind.
2. **Learning from defeat:** Every adversity carries with it the seed of an equivalent benefit.
3. **The Golden Rule applied:** What you do to another, you do to yourself.

Do you recall the very first quote mentioned in this book? Perhaps you noticed that it's the same one that's included at the top of this section:

The finest kind of security is the personal security that is developed from within.

This inspiring Carnegie quote reinforces the power we wield to create whatever circumstances we desire. The exact same amount of energy that we use to complain about how bad things are can be harnessed and redirected toward creating whatever it is that we want in life. The more accountable we are for our circumstances, the more empowered we are to change them.

When you develop the personal security from within, you will carry an aura of confidence, kindness, and helpfulness as you seek for ways to render service to more and more people. This, of course, stimulates the great lesson that the best way to get is to give, spurring you on to greater contribution. Eventually, you will notice that frequent opportunities begin finding their way to you, rather than you needing to constantly seek them.

Now that we're here, what's next? Well, it's time for you to make some mental dynamite of your own! You have officially been inducted as one of the great changemakers, a group that started with Carnegie, continued to Hill and the countless people he influenced (myself included), and now to you.

You have a responsibility to wield the torch and lead by example in all that you do—for your family, your community, and the world. In doing so, your example will inspire those around you, as we seek to recognize and unlock the potential of every individual on the planet. If we can do that, widespread harmony will finally be achievable, and the mission of Carnegie and Hill will be complete.

It doesn't matter what happened in your past, no matter how traumatic. You are much stronger than any adversity you will face—of that, I promise you. Be sure to remember that, as you are faced with moments of decision each day that, extrapolated, will determine your life, your impact, and your legacy.

Keep this book safe so you can revisit it as often as you need. And if I can ever be of assistance along your journey, just let me know.

Onward and upward always,
James Whittaker

AFTERWORD

By Sharon Lechter

Do you have a success conscious?

Mental Dynamite has allowed us to sit at the table with Andrew Carnegie and Napoleon Hill while they discuss the truth behind all personal achievement. As a lifelong student of both Carnegie and Hill, I was amazed at the additional insights I gained from *Mental Dynamite*. It truly is a roadmap to developing a success conscious.

Throughout Hill's body of work, Definiteness of Purpose is highlighted as the first step in all personal achievement. Without definiteness of purpose, you can easily fall victim to self-limiting beliefs like "I am not good enough," or "I don't deserve it," or "easy for him to say." These beliefs open the door for fear to take over and control our thoughts and therefore our actions. That fear can paralyze and prevent us from achieving the success we deserve.

In his book *Outwitting the Devil*, Hill explores the crippling effect of fear and introduces the concept of "drifting." In the book, the Devil defines drifting as:

I can best define the word "drift" by saying that people who think for themselves never drift, while those who do little or no thinking for themselves are drifters. A drifter is one who permits himself to be influenced and controlled by circumstances outside of his own mind. A drifter is one who accepts whatever life throws in his way without making a protest or putting up a fight. He doesn't know what he wants from life and spends all of his time getting just that.

Hill reiterates that having Definiteness of Purpose is the first step to overcoming drifting. It starts with taking control of our thoughts. Every thought we have becomes part of who we are. By clearing our mind of all thoughts of failure and self-limiting beliefs, we can convert our fear into faith. True faith evolves when we are at peace with our own thoughts and conscience.

Hill shares that this faith is the source of all genius as well as essential in developing a success conscious.

To help us in this quest, Carnegie and Hill share three important steps that are essential in realizing our greatest potential. They are

1. Developing self-discipline
2. Learning from defeat,
3. Practicing the Golden Rule

While appearing simple in definition, creating the habit of practicing all three takes tremendous attention, effort, and willpower. Carnegie and Hill share the importance of willpower and the role it plays in developing the self-discipline to take control of our lives:

Willpower is the instrument with which we may close the door against any experience or circumstance we wish to put behind us forever. With this same instrument, we may open the door to opportunity in any direction we choose. If the first door we try is difficult to open, we will try another and another, until at long last we will find one that will yield to this irresistible force.

I often challenge my audiences with the question: Is there a door in your life you need to close that so other doors of opportunity will open?

But Hill and Carnegie take it one step further:

The door should be closed tightly and locked securely so that there is no possibility of its being opened again.

Can you think of someone who is holding on to something that happened to them in the past? Unable to let it go? Could this be you? A failure is an occurrence, something that happened in the past. It is not a definition. Hill's and Carnegie's advice to close the door tightly and lock it securely is so very important to prevent those self-limiting beliefs from sneaking back in.

Close the door tightly and then re-engage your willpower to develop the self-discipline and learn from defeat or past mistakes. Mistakes are learning opportunities for growth. Your self-confidence will grow, and you will feel your fear transform into the strength of your faith. That faith will carry you through any obstacles you face along the way.

Right when we are taking control of our thoughts, Carnegie takes us outside ourselves and highlights the importance of our actions and, most specifically, the importance of practicing the Golden Rule as well as Going the Extra Mile.

… the first essential for success in any calling of merit is sound character. Applying the Golden Rule develops sound character and a good reputation.

To get the most from the Golden Rule, one must combine it with the principle of Going the Extra Mile, wherein lies the applied portion of the Golden Rule. The Golden Rule supplies the right mental attitude, while Going the Extra Mile supplies the action feature of this great rule. Combining the two gives one the power of attraction that induces friendly cooperation from others as well as providing opportunities for personal accumulation.

Your actions dramatically impact your success conscious. But then Hill and Carnegie bring it all together with one simple, but dramatic statement.

No one can live by the Golden Rule until they learn to lose themselves in unselfish service to others.

It is through unselfish service to others that our faith reveals the guidance we need to truly develop a success conscious. By having the willpower to master self-discipline, learn from defeat, and to practice the Golden Rule through unselfish service to others, we will realize the success of our greatest potential.

To your success conscious and to those you serve.

Sharon Lechter
Author of *Think and Grow Rich for Women*
Co-author of *Three Feet from Gold, Success and Something Greater,*
    Rich Dad Poor Dad
Annotator of *Outwitting the Devil*
www.sharonlechter.com

ABOUT THE AUTHORS

NAPOLEON HILL

Napoleon Hill was born in 1883 in a one-room cabin in the remote mountains of Wise County, Virginia. He was born into poverty, and his mother died when he was nine years old. One year later, his father remarried, and his stepmother became a source of inspiration for the young boy. With the influence of his stepmother, Hill began his writing career at age thirteen as a "mountain reporter" for small-town newspapers.

In 1908, Hill was assigned to interview Andrew Carnegie, and a three-hour interview became one that lasted three days. While Hill did the interviewing, Carnegie sold him on the idea of organizing the world's first philosophy of personal achievement based on the principles of success. Carnegie provided Hill with introductions to giants of the time, including Henry Ford, Thomas A. Edison, and John D. Rockefeller. Hill was to spend the next two decades interviewing, studying, and writing about these extraordinary individuals.

Twenty years later, Hill published the *Law of Success*. In 1937, Hill released *Think and Grow Rich*, which became the bestselling self-help book of all time and continues to sell millions of copies around the world.

Hill established The Napoleon Hill Foundation as a nonprofit educational institution whose mission is to perpetuate his philosophy of leadership, self-motivation, and individual achievement. Hill passed away in 1970 after a long and successful career writing, teaching, and lecturing about the principles of success. His work stands as a monument to individual achievement and is the cornerstone of modern motivation.

His books, audio recordings, video recordings, and other motivational products are made available to you as a service of the Foundation so that you may build your own library of personal achievement materials . . . and help you acquire not only financial wealth but the true riches of life too.

Learn more about Napoleon Hill:

http://naphill.org

JAMES WHITTAKER

BA, B.Bus(Mgt), AdvDipFS(FP), MBA

James Whittaker grew up in Australia, where he enjoyed a successful ten-year career in financial planning, running a company with more than $2 billion under management, before starting his own entrepreneurial journey. Today, James has launched companies and products across a range of industries including health, marketing, film, activewear, and publishing.

He is in demand internationally as a keynote speaker, and is a frequent guest in media, having appeared on more than 300 radio, podcast, and television shows, and in globally recognized publications such as *Entrepreneur*, *Money*, and *Success* magazine.

James is a two-time bestselling author, with his second book *Think and Grow Rich: The Legacy* released in 2018 as the official companion to the multimillion-dollar film based on Napoleon Hill's timeless classic. James is also a proud co-executive producer of the film.

In addition, he is the founder of The Day Won Mastermind, a program that helps professionals and entrepreneurs find their voice, build their tribe, and make an impact. In 2019, he with James Whittaker launched the *Win the Day* podcast to help people take ownership of their financial, physical, and mental health.

Through his tailored keynotes, bestselling books, and leadership programs, James has helped hundreds of individuals and companies reach new heights of accountability, happiness, and success. To complement his own experience, James shares lessons garnered from his interviews with more than 100 of the world's most accomplished business leaders, cultural icons, and athletes, to reveal what is possible for those who dream big, follow the right plan, and win the day.

Above all, he hopes to instill the important fundamental truth that each day, if we do not make the decision to win, we have automatically made the decision to lose.

Learn more about James Whittaker:

http://jameswhitt.com

ABOUT THE NAPOLEON HILL FOUNDATION

The Napoleon Hill Foundation is a nonprofit educational institution dedicated to making the world a better place. To learn more about Napoleon Hill, browse all Foundation products (including officially authorized books, audio recordings, and leadership programs), subscribe to the Thought for the Day email, and more, visit The Napoleon Hill Foundation online.

http://naphill.org

SHARE YOUR STORIES

There are no limitations to the mind
except those we acknowledge.
—Napoleon Hill

Journeys like yours help inspire the world!

Often, especially in our darkest moments or if we're stuck in a rut, we forget about the infinite possibilities that are available to us if we dream big, follow the right plan, and take action. Books such as this one help us rediscover who we truly are, giving us an alignment in all areas of our life that spur us on to great contribution, happiness, and success.

If you've enjoyed reading *Andrew Carnegie's Mental Dynamite*, or it has helped transform you in some way, we would love to hear from you! Visit the site below to share your comments and feedback with The Napoleon Hill Foundation.

After all, your story might be the very thing that saves a life.

Share your story:
http://naphill.org

ACKNOWLEDGMENTS

By James Whittaker

Any project of this magnitude, one that would do justice to the enormous legacy of Andrew Carnegie and Napoleon Hill, requires the contributions and support of many—a real-world example of the mastermind principle!

First, to Don Green and The Napoleon Hill Foundation for keeping these important lessons alive and making them available in almost every language and country on Earth. Your hard work continues to provide hope for those who need it most, revealing a much more prosperous future for all those who have the courage to think bigger than their circumstances. Thank you also for trusting me with this project—I am greatly honored to again be of service to the Foundation and look forward to promulgating these lessons for the rest of my life.

To Andrew Carnegie, who will forever be renowned as the archetypical philanthropist through his model of helping people to help themselves. Your vision to collate and disseminate a blueprint to success, one that could be applied by anyone—even those in the most meager or tragic of circumstances—continues to transform every industry on the planet. It also inspires others to contribute their time, resources, and expertise to raise the standards of living and create a brighter and more harmonious future than we could ever imagine. On behalf of humanity, I salute you.

To Napoleon Hill, whose innate curiosity was only bettered by his prodigious writing talents. Through books such as this one, *Think and Grow Rich, Law of Success*, and dozens more, you continue to show that there is hope for all of us, providing a clear blueprint to freedom, happiness, and success. I hope my contributions in this book are worthy of the exceptionally high standard you have set.

To Sharon Lechter for willingly assisting with this project and leading the financial literacy crusade. Aside from all the extraordinary work you do to make the world a better place, you are a great mentor to me and many others as an entrepreneur, speaker, and philanthropist.

To Sterling Publishing, who were excited about this project from day one and worked tirelessly to get it into the hands of as many people as possible. Thank you for trusting my creative vision and for leading the charge in the myriad essential behind-the-scenes tasks.

To my wife, Jennifer, for continually inspiring me through your hard work, love, and kindness. Your support and understanding during late nights, long travel, and urgent deadlines is very much appreciated. Thank you also to our beautiful daughter, Sophie, who, with a single smile, makes me feel like the luckiest man on the planet. To my parents, Noel and Geraldine, for creating a platform of unconditional love for your family and leading a life of steadfast integrity.

Finally, to all those who read this book and take consistent, purposeful action. Never underestimate how powerful your example is for those around you.

TESTIMONIALS

"Mental Dynamite takes us straight to the source in one of the most fascinating conversations ever. It is a riveting read and packed with actionable tips for people to transform their lives."

—Janine Shepherd

(Bestselling author, keynote speaker and resilience expert)

"Mental Dynamite reminds us why visionaries like Carnegie and Hill were so impactful. It is an extraordinary book released at a time when the world needs it most."

—Brandon T. Adams

(Emmy® Award–winning producer and host of *Success in Your City*)

"This book is a must read. James Whittaker goes straight to the fountainhead of success philosophy with Andrew Carnegie whose wisdom is even more relevant today. The impact of this book will be felt for generations to come."

—Satish Verma

(President/CEO of the Think and Grow Rich Institute)

"In every field of endeavor, there is a critical moment, intersection, or connection when the state-of-the-art takes a quantum leap. This happened in the field of personal development when Andrew Carnegie and Napoleon Hill got together. The world has never been the same, and you will not be the same once you experience Andrew Carnegie's *Mental Dynamite.* Read and grow rich."

—Jim Stovall

(President of the Narrative Television Network)

"Motivational, inspirational, and highly actionable. *Mental Dynamite* is THE blueprint for massive success in business and life."

—Dr. Steve Sudell

(Creator of The Neck Hammock™ and cofounder of Stretch Lab)

"Many of us dream of being a fly on the wall for some of the most important conversations in history. *Mental Dynamite* gives us the rarest of opportunities, as we witness how two of the greats discuss and deconstruct high performance. It's masterful. The nuances that are vital to getting traction in your life are extracted brilliantly by Napoleon Hill. In addition, James Whittaker brings it together beautifully, essentially turning a transcript into a powerful playbook for individual greatness. It truly proves that the outer chief is a reflection of the inner chief."

—GREG LAYTON
(Founder of Chief Maker)

"A lot has changed since the earliest conversations between Andrew Carnegie and Napoleon Hill in 1908. But even more hasn't changed. *Mental Dynamite* comes as a beacon from the past, reminding us of timeless wisdom that is used by the most influential predecessors of Carnegie and Hill in the present, and should be your guide to a successful future."

—JOSHUA ELLIS
(Editor-in-Chief of *Success* magazine)

"The lessons that Hill and Carnegie share in this book will help anyone turn perceived failure to triumph. It is a must read for anyone who wants to achieve at the highest level."

—DAVID MELTZER
(Cofounder of Sports 1 Marketing,
bestselling author, and award-winning business coach)